THE
INDIANA HOOSIERS FANS'
BUCKET LIST

THE
INDIANA HOOSIERS FANS'
BUCKET LIST

TERRY HUTCHENS
& BILL MURPHY

TRIUMPH
BOOKS

Library of Congress Cataloging-in-Publication Data

Names: Hutchens, Terry, 1958– author.
Title: The Indiana Hoosiers fans' bucket list / Terry Hutchens and Bill Murphy.
Description: Chicago, Illinois : Triumph Books LLC, [2017]
Identifiers: LCCN 2017006618 | ISBN 9781629372600
Subjects: LCSH: Indiana University, Bloomington—Basketball—History. | Indiana University, Bloomington—Miscellanea. | Indiana Hoosiers (Basketball team)—History. | Indiana Hoosiers (Basketball team)—Miscellanea.
Classification: LCC GV885.43.I53 H86 2017 | DDC 796.323/6309772—dc23 LC record available at https://lccn.loc.gov/2017006618

This book is available in quantity at special discounts for your group or organization. For further information, contact:

Triumph Books LLC
814 North Franklin Street
Chicago, Illinois 60610
(312) 337-0747
www.triumphbooks.com

Printed in U.S.A.
ISBN: 978-1-62937-260-0
Design by Andy Hansen
Page production by Alex Lubertozzi

Photos courtesy of Bill Murphy unless otherwise indicated

Contents

Acknowledgments   ix

Chapter 1: Game Day   2

Watch It at Assembly Hall   5

Watch the Game in Bloomington   12

Soak Up the Atmosphere in Cook Hall   14

Watch the Game Anywhere in the Country   18

Listen to Fish   20

See the Hoosiers Play on the Road   24

See the Hoosiers Play in Hawaii   25

Chapter 2: Players and Coaches   26

The Hall of Famers   28

The Best of the Rest   42

And Then There Were the Coaching Legends   79

Chapter 3: Venues and Games   110

Original Assembly Hall   111

Men's Gymnasium   112

The Original Indiana Fieldhouse   113

The New Fieldhouse (Gladstein Fieldhouse)   125

Assembly Hall (Simon Skjodt Assembly Hall)   134

The Greatest Games   144

Chapter 4: Traditions   160

Candy-Striped Warm-up Pants   161

The National Championship Banners   163

Martha the Mop Lady   170

The *William Tell* Overture   174

Big Heads Behind the Basket   177

No Names on the Backs of Jerseys   179

They Don't Retire Numbers at Indiana   182

No Mascot Either   183

Hoosier Hysteria ("Midnight Madness")   **188**
Senior Night   **192**

Chapter 5: The Cream and Crimson   **196**
Showing Off the Cream and Crimson   **197**
Get Involved with an IU Alumni Chapter   **202**
Indiana Man Caves   **204**
Must Reads for Indiana Basketball Fans   **218**

Chapter 6: The Ultimate Hoosiers Bucket List   **230**
Attend a Game at Assembly Hall   **231**
Buy Keith Smart or Christian Watford a Drink   **232**
See the Hoosiers Hang the Next Championship Banner   **234**
Complete the Hoosier Basketball Experience   **235**
Attend a Summer Tailgate Tour Stop   **236**
Have a One-on-One Conversation with Bob Knight   **237**
Hoist a Big Head   **239**
Sit with Your Dad and Watch Indiana Win a
    National Title   **239**
Attend Hoosier Hysteria   **241**
Camp Out at Assembly Hall   **242**
Be Out with the 1976 Undefeated Indiana National
    Champions on the Night When the Final Unbeaten Team
    from That Particular Season Drops Its First Game   **243**
Sit Right Behind the Bench at Assembly Hall   **244**
Watch Bob Knight Roam the Sidelines at Assembly Hall   **245**
Visit the Indiana Basketball Hall of Fame in New Castle   **247**
Get to See Don Schlundt Play in Person   **250**
Stay in the Steve Alford All-American Inn   **251**
Visit Hoosier Gym from the Movie Hoosiers   **252**
Run on the Assembly Hall Court with the Flags at the
    Under-Eight-Minute Timeout   **253**
Have Lunch with Angelo Pizzo   **254**
Attend a Game in the Original Assembly Hall   **255**

About the Authors   **257**

Acknowledgments

This book has been in the works for a long time. There were a lot of times along the way when I wasn't completely certain it would get done. Too many distractions, job changes, and life events all at one time. In the summer of 2016, however, my friend Bill Murphy entered the picture, and I finally started to believe we might get this done. Bill had written a couple of books on IU, and I have always considered him a great IU athletics historian. We have done several book signings together over the years and had always talked about someday writing a book together. We just couldn't seem to figure out what the perfect project would be to work on. And then this came about, and it seemed like the perfect fit.

So my first thank you in the book is to Bill Murphy for his willingness to help me finish this project. I had quoted Bill in a few of my previous Indiana basketball books and used him as a resource at times on my trivia books, but it was good to find a way to get his name on the cover along with mine. Perhaps there will be the opportunity for us to do another book in the future.

I would like to thank all of the folks at Triumph Books for approaching me with the idea for this book back in 2015. When I wrote my first book about the Indianapolis Colts (*Let 'Er Rip*) in 1995, I worked with Tom Bast when he was with Masters Press at the time. To have come full circle and do a second book with him more than 20 years later has been a great experience.

I want to thank all of the editors and page designers on this project for their help along the way. There is a lot of behind-the-scenes work that goes into publishing a book. As I've self-published four titles of my own now, I know exactly what is involved. It was fun to sit back, get the book written, and let someone else take on those responsibilities for a change.

Bill wanted to thank some of the man cave owners he interviewed along the way for that section of the book: Brady Evans, David Murrary, Chris Williams, and Brett White, among others, opened up their caves for Bill to see, study and enjoy. We both want to thank all of the former players, athletic department personnel, and media members whom we interviewed for this project. Bill also singled out Kate Mazelin and Ryan Murphy for their input on this manuscript. He also mentioned Indiana University for providing the inspiration for the many ideas that make up our bucket list.

Finally, we both want to thank our families for their support as we pursued another book project. This is my 11th book (12 if you count the *Indiana University Basketball Encyclopedia* revisions I did in 2013 and again in 2017), and I never could have envisioned I would have that many titles to my name. When I wrote the first one in 1995, I thought it was fun but I didn't see myself doing it again. I didn't write another one for 12 years until Coach Hep died and I wrote *Hep Remembered*. And then it just kind of took off. But knowing I've had the support of my wife of more than 30 years, Susan, my mom, Dena, in California, and my two grown sons, Bryan and Kevin, has made it all the more worthwhile.

Thanks to everyone who has supported us from the bottom of our hearts.

—Terry Hutchens

THE
INDIANA HOOSIERS FANS'
BUCKET LIST

Game
Day

If you're like a lot of Indiana University basketball fans, IU basketball becomes the center of your universe and you just revolve around it.

IU is playing on Saturday at 4:00 PM? Well, that can mean a number of things:

- If you have tickets for the game, you need to start planning what time you need to leave for Assembly Hall.

- If you're going to a friend's house to watch the game, you might have to figure out what snacks or drinks you're supposed to bring.

- If you're going to watch the game at a bar in Bloomington, or in any city across America where IU alumni groups gather to watch the Hoosiers, you may have to determine how early you're going to have to go in order to get the seat you want so that you can get in front of a certain television in that establishment.

- If you're just going to watch it in the privacy of your own living room, you may have to figure out everyone else's schedule in your family so that you can be 100 percent focused on watching the Hoosiers.

But there may be other factors that you have to weigh, too:

- Perhaps there's a certain sweatshirt or IU shirt that you've worn every time Indiana has won a big game in recent years, and you want to make sure you have that on.

- Maybe you're not sure if your candy-striped warm-up pants are clean, and you may need to wash them before tipoff.

- Maybe you have another game-day ritual that you do every game, and you're superstitious about that sort of thing.

- Perhaps you have to work and you can't see the IU game, but you're going to make sure that you set the DVR to record it so you can watch it later. You may even ask people around you to not tell you who won the game that day and just stay away from all forms of social media so that you can go home later and watch it as if it were live.

- Maybe you're one of those people who turns down the TV and turns up Don Fischer on game days. A lot of people have invested in a certain box that allows the radio feed and television feed to sync up during the broadcast just so they can let the harmonious sounds of Fish on the radio describe the action on the court.

But make no mistake about it, Indiana basketball is an *event*. It's something you plan your calendar around. There will be some fans who may try to say that it used to be that way for them when Bob Knight was roaming the sideline, but it's just not the same anymore. They'll tell you that they may catch an IU game here or there, but it's no longer the event it used to be. Our experience is that those people are beginning to fade away. It may have been 30 years since Indiana last won a national championship, but you certainly wouldn't know it by the way Indiana fans show up whenever IU plays at home or on the road, or how the Twitterverse is alive every time Indiana has a basketball game. Indiana has a rabid fan base that is focused completely on the Hoosiers when IU takes the court.

This opening chapter takes a look at the way some people incorporate Indiana basketball into their daily lives. Which of these methods of watching Indiana basketball best describes your own personal situation?

Watch It at Assembly Hall

Think of Indiana University basketball and you picture candy-striped warm-up pants.

You think of the five national championship banners, Martha the Mop Lady, and the *William Tell* Overture at the under-eight-minute timeout.

You think of Branch McCracken, Bob Knight, and most recently Tom Crean. You remember the last undefeated college basketball team in history, the 1976 Indiana Hoosiers.

You think of one of the most iconic, blueblood, elite college basketball programs in America.

And you think of Assembly Hall.

For 46 years, Assembly Hall has been one of the most revered basketball arenas in the country, a place where the Hoosiers have won 84 percent of their games and where crowds of 17,400 rabid fans have made the arena a daunting atmosphere for opposing teams.

"I don't think there's any place quite like it anywhere else in the country," said retired longtime *Bloomington Herald-Times* sports editor Bob Hammel. "I think it's just the configuration where it looks like its red all the way up to the ceiling on both sides. I'm not sure of any other place that I've been where you just really have the feeling like you're taking on the multitude and not just the home team."

Indiana home games have always been a tough ticket, and there continues to be a waiting list for season tickets. The best chance to see Indiana play in Assembly Hall is to buy either a three-game or six-game package that is offered for games played when the students are out for Christmas break in late December and early January. IU has the largest student section in the nation in Assembly Hall, boasting 7,200 seats, and when students are on break there's a much better opportunity for other fans to see IU play.

A three-game package in the main seating area in 2016 ran for $132 per adult. A six-game package was double that at $264.

Some think that's a small price to pay to see games in the iconic arena.

As the venue has gotten up in years, however, and with other schools building new, sterile, state-of-the-art arenas every year, the question of what to do with Assembly Hall has loomed large.

Rebuild or renovate was the question asked in Indiana circles since the mid-1990s. Ultimately, the decision was made to preserve IU's rich history in the building and give Assembly Hall a much-needed facelift. Eighteen months and $45 million later, the new-look Assembly Hall debuted in time for the start of the 2016–17 basketball season.

"I am thrilled that this project will preserve the best home-court advantage in college basketball while also greatly enhancing the total game-day experience for every fan, player, coach, and visitor," said IU director of athletics Fred Glass the day that IU broke ground on the new building.

Eric Neuburger, IU's associate athletic director for facilities and external alliances, said Indiana could not just simply kick an IU treasure like Assembly Hall to the curb. Preserving the iconic building made the most sense.

"The building is part of our character," Neuburger said. "It's our home-court advantage. It's an intimidating place to play in. You walk in and you look up, and you see two steep walls of fans looking down on you, and that's like no other place. We feel like it has become the most unique basketball facility in the country, and that's what we didn't want to lose."

Indiana coach Tom Crean said that Assembly Hall is vital to the future of the Indiana program. "All over the country, people know what an intimidating environment Assembly Hall can be," Crean said. "It's one of our greatest assets, and we're excited to see improvements made to our legendary facility that will dramatically improve the Hoosier fan experience."

And it's not just the IU men's team that is benefitting from the Assembly Hall facelift but the women's program under the direction of Teri Moren, too.

While there was a waiting list for season tickets for IU men's basketball, fans of the women's game in 2016 could get season tickets that were $42 for 14 home games, or $3 per ticket. Seniors over age 65 could get the same package for $1 per game. The same $14 season package was available for youth tickets under age 18.

Many believe the Indiana women's team is clearly on the upswing, and fans have a chance to get in on the ground floor. "I think with the Cook Hall practice facility and the renovated Assembly Hall, and all that we've done the last eight years in women's basketball, I think our program could be a sleeping giant," said IU deputy athletic director Scott Dolson, who as of 2016 was in his 26th season working in the IU athletic department. "I think we're really close, and I'd be shocked if we don't see our women's basketball program consistently going to NCAA tournaments and then knocking on that door and ultimately getting those recruits and getting a Final Four and maybe hanging that banner up. I can see that happening. We've got the resources in place to make that happen."

Don Fischer remembers fondly the dedication game he attended at Indiana's Assembly Hall in its inaugural season in 1971.

Bob Knight was in his first season as the Indiana coach, and Digger Phelps was making his debut as the head coach at Notre Dame. The teams met on December 18 in IU's new basketball facility.

Final score: Indiana 94, Notre Dame 29.

Fischer has been the play-by-play voice of Indiana football and basketball for 44 seasons, beginning with the 1973–74 basketball season. But that game, he attended as a spectator. "I don't even remember how I got the ticket or why I was there, but I was working in Terre Haute at the time and came to Assembly Hall for the dedication game," Fischer said. "All I remember is how magical the entire arena seemed back then, and then two years later I found myself broadcasting in that facility. And I still have the same feeling today that I did all of those years ago when I walk into Assembly Hall. It's just a very, very special place."

The building has a storied tradition. The first event held there was a Homecoming Variety Review featuring Bob Hope and Petula Clark on October 23, 1971. Its design was based off a Cattle Auction House, and the land where it was built was originally the Faris family farm through 1950.

It was the home court of three Indiana basketball national championship teams in 1976, 1981, and 1987. Going into the 2016–17 season, IU's all-time record at Assembly Hall was 551–106.

Through 2016, Chuck Crabb was in his 41st season working for IU Athletics. His current position is assistant athletic director for facilities. He is probably best known for being the public address announcer for Indiana basketball for the past 40 years. Chills have been known to run down the spines of IU basketball fans when Crabb announces "The Indiana Hoooooooooooooooooosiers!"

Crabb was a junior at Indiana in 1971 when Assembly Hall opened its doors. He remembers that, when Assembly Hall was built, it was the final structure that trumpeted athletics' relocation from the center of the Bloomington campus (Seventh Street) to the current athletics footprint that is bordered between 17th Street to the south, the bypass to the north, Dunn Street to the west, and Fee Lane to the east.

"We moved to where a lot of people said was 'halfway to Martinsville,'" Crabb said with a smile. "We moved out to the edge of the bypass, and there were three structures in particular that made up the new home of athletics on our campus. It was the [Gladstein] fieldhouse that was used temporarily for basketball, it was Memorial Stadium, and it was finally the Assembly Hall in the 1971–72 season. All the sports as the program existed at that time were pretty much accommodated by those facilities."

At the time that Assembly Hall opened in 1971, Indiana athletics had a total of 10 sports. Today it has 24. But in 1971, the men's soccer program had yet to be established (it started in the fall of 1973). Women's athletics was added in 1975, and other sports along the way.

There's no way to overstate the financial impact that Assembly Hall has had over the years. It has supported the existence of so many of IU's athletic programs. Most years, Assembly Hall ranks in the top 10 nationally in average attendance. In fact, its lowest attendance average in the building's history was still 17th nationally.

At some point, however, the big attendance wasn't enough. In the early 2000s, IU, in search of revenue streams to help fund those programs, first introduced advertising signage into Assembly Hall.

"It takes a significant amount of revenue to support a program of our size," Crabb said. "And advertising done in a tasteful manner has not had an earth-shattering impact on how that building is seen. It's been done tastefully, either with static signage or maybe an advertising bug in the corner of a video image."

For the most part the first 45-plus years of Assembly Hall came and went with very few changes. The arena got a new basketball floor in 1976 and again in 1995. In 2005 it got a new $1.99 million scoreboard/video board. But the changes to that point were very cosmetic.

That changed with the current renovation. Thanks to a $40 million gift from alumna Cindy Simon Skjodt, Indiana was able to renovate rather that rebuild. In honor of that landmark gift made by Simon Skjodt and her philanthropic organization, IU announced in 2013 it would rename Assembly Hall the Simon Skjodt Assembly Hall.

In addition, athletics received a $5 million gift from IU alumnus Mark Cuban to establish the Mark Cuban Center for Sports Media and Technology that will be housed on the west side of the Simon Skjodt Assembly Hall.

The renovation was able to blend the old with the new in the arena.

From the outside the most significant change is to the south lobby that has received an extreme facelift. On the interior, floors have been replaced, concession stands and bathrooms remodeled, and escalators added—four in the south lobby and two in the north. The old zig-zag ramps will still be used, but only in the north lobby.

All the seats in the arena have been replaced except for the bleachers at court level. The only part of the seats that was not replaced was the cast-iron arm rests. Everything else about the seats was replaced, and all the seats are now red. A few seats were removed to accommodate changes in press seating, but there won't be a noticeable difference in the arena's 17,400-seating capacity.

The Hall of Fame portraits that once hung in the lobby have been digitized and adapted into an interactive display in the south atrium. Assembly Hall also has a new video board that is three times wider and has all the bells and whistles so that fans can enjoy better replays.

"There is a significant wow factor when people walk into that building," Crabb said. "It's entirely different than what they experienced for the first 45 years of the Assembly Hall."

It only takes a moment for fans to realize the difference when they enter the south lobby. "I just think it's the sheer size," Crabb said. "Instead of coming in under a 12-foot-high ceiling as they come through those six entry doors on the south lobby, there is 70 feet of clear space overhead. Directly ahead of them is a connecting bridge that goes in front of the Spirit of '76 suite. There are touchscreen LED video presentations that they see. The old arena now has a very modern look to it."

Neuburger believes the best part about the new Assembly Hall is that Indiana was able to renovate without changing the atmosphere. "I think people are hit with the fact of how familiar the building is and how new it is at the same time," he said. "Everything has been touched in some way but nothing anyone would have wanted to stay has been disrupted in any way. It's still the masterpiece of a building that everyone expects to see when they come to Assembly Hall."

One major improvement has to do with restrooms in the arena. Before the renovation, there were 184 toilets in Assembly Hall. In the new Assembly Hall there are 314. The biggest percentage difference is how many restrooms there will be for women. Before the renovation, there were 123 men's and 61 women's toilets. In the new arena, there are 154 men's and 134 women's. So while the facilities for men increased by 33 percent, for women, it's up 119 percent. In addition, there will be 16 all-gender restrooms where there were none before.

Improvements to cellular reception and Wi-Fi have also been significant in recent years. "People want to sit in the arena now, pull out their smartphones, and watch the multitude of ESPN family apps or BTN apps that are available for either the game they're watching or other games," Crabb said. "We have a statistics program that allows people to follow the game and see the box score just the same as our media people on press row."

Most of all, the renovation has allowed the university to preserve a venue that has wonderful memories for longtime Indiana fans. "Alumni take great pride when they come back to the Bloomington campus and they want to come to facilities that are clean, modern, and a wonderful experience to enjoy," Crabb said. "We've been very fortunate with this half-mile square that we call the IU Athletics Complex to accommodate upwards of 5,000 to 6,000 vehicles on a football Saturday or a basketball weekend. That means tailgate opportunities, it means a great opportunity to come into the stadium or the arena and cheer on the cream and crimson. And it means being a part of a very proud Hoosier Nation." (Authors' note: this story, written by author Terry Hutchens, appeared in the 2017 *Visit Bloomington* magazine.)

• • •

There's something extremely unique about the opportunity to see a game at Assembly Hall. The season ticket holders may or may not take the experience for granted, but the fans who are able to get tickets for the games when the students are on break or against cupcake opponents in November and December often tell you that they only get one chance a year to be in the arena and it's something that is always a major treat.

They love the atmosphere that's filled with tradition. They love all the bells and whistles that the newly renovated arena is able to provide. And they love being in the moment, knowing that there are fans across America and the world who would happily trade places with them on that particular day.

See, if you're an Indiana basketball fan, there's just nothing quite like Assembly Hall.

If you haven't been there for a game, it's a No. 1 Bucket List item for the IU basketball fan.

Watch the Game in Bloomington

If you can't watch the game in person in the Simon Skjodt Assembly Hall or if the game is on the road, the next best thing to being there is to catch the Hoosiers with dozens of your soon-to-be friends at one of the many bars or eating establishments in Bloomington where the game will be shown on multiple television screens.

Sure, you could watch it at home in the privacy of your living room, too, but seeing the game with a large group of IU fans on Indiana turf can be a special experience—especially on big game days in the non-conference season or the majority of games during the Big Ten season, the bar scene in Bloomington is clearly the place to be.

Some places have drink and food specials with special incentives in place if you're showing your true IU cream and crimson colors that day. Some people have a regular group of IU fans with whom they gather at a local bar for every game. It's their own version of having a season ticket. It's just that their season ticket is in front of the television at one of Bloomington's favorite establishments.

Julie Warren, of VisitBloomington.com, highlighted some of the best places to watch Indiana basketball. Here are some of the top locales in Bloomington where rabid IU fans will turn out to support the Hoosiers:

Nick's English Hut

423 East Kirkwood Avenue | (812) 332-4040
An IU tradition. Try the stromboli and some sink the biz fries.

Yogi's Grill & Bar

519 East 10th Street | (812) 323-9644
Features a wide variety of beers on tap, along with
mini corn dogs and buffalo chips.

The Tap

101 North College Avenue | (812) 287-8579
Serves about a million craft brews, awsome pickle fries, and tuna tacos.

BuffaLouie's

114 South Indiana Avenue | (812) 333-3030
The best wings in town. Kid friendly too.

Kilroy's Sports Bar

319 North Walnut Street | (812) 336-6006
Strictly an under-30 crowd—the place to go to mingle with IU students.
Drink specials regularly and pepperoni-stuffed breadsticks to die for.

Not on VisitBloomington.com's list but also worth checking out in Bloomington are: Opie Taylor's on Walnut on the Square, Hoosier Bar & Grill, Mother Bear's Pizza, Scotty's Brewhouse, Upland Brewing Company, the Uptown Grill, Bear's Place, Coaches Bar & Grill, Kilroy's Bar & Grill (different than Kilroy's Sports Bar), the Alley, and AMVETS Post 2000 out on West Airport Road.

And there are many more. Perhaps you have your own favorite spot, too.

Soak Up the Atmosphere in Cook Hall

Whether you watch the game live in Assembly Hall or at one of Bloomington's many bars and restaurants, a good pre-game stop is Cook Hall, Indiana's practice facility that is just to the east of IU's home court.

It's the ultimate fan experience for someone wanting to take a trip down memory lane with the Hoosiers. There are interactive displays as well as banners hanging everywhere with your favorite IU players of all time from every decade represented.

If you haven't been to Cook Hall and you want to check it out on game day, make sure to allow yourself plenty of time. You'll be glad you did.

Coauthor Bill Murphy has given tours to the general public of Cook Hall in the past. In the next few pages, he takes you on the same tour. Here's a look at Cook Hall through the eyes of IU historian Bill Murphy:

As you walk into Cook Hall and Legacy Court, look up. As you gaze upward, you will see huge pictures of Indiana basketball greats. This is the place where Indiana honors its former great players. If you notice in Simon Skjodt Assembly Hall, the Hoosiers honor teams, not individuals, with the multiple banners that hang in the north and south ends of the arena. But in Cook Hall, the pictures are in full view, inviting you to step back and relive the memories of the best that Indiana basketball has to offer.

The pictures that hang from the rafters represent a Who's Who of Indiana University Basketball. As you walk in from the right side, the first one you see is George McGinnis, a player who in one season set the bar high for every IU player who would follow. You see folks like Jay Edwards, and you think of his rainbow three-pointers and last-second heroics that were a big part of IU basketball in the late 1980s. You see Kirk Haston, and you can picture Tom Coverdale lifting the big man from Lobelville, Tennessee, off the ground after he hit that shot to beat No. 1 Michigan State at the buzzer in 2001. You see the "Splendid Splinter" Jimmy Rayl who scored the most points ever by an IU player in a game with 56—and he did it twice, both in Big Ten play. You see more recent players like Victor Oladipo, Yogi Ferrell, and Cody Zeller side by side with all-time greats like Don Schlundt, Archie Dees, Steve Alford, and Isiah Thomas. You see plenty of women's players, too—Cindy Bumgarner, Jill Chapman, and a more recent player like Tyra Buss. You even see Martha the Mop Lady. But just looking above, you're immediately filled with memory after memory of the greatest players in Indiana history.

You can ask yourself these questions: Which ones were from the same city or the same high school? Which ones were brothers or high school teammates? Which ones were record holders? And on a more personal note, which ones did you actually see play or maybe had just heard about?

The next thing that catches your eye is the cylinder of champions, where Indiana's five national championship trophies are located.

But that's just the tip of the iceberg. Look to your left and there is the wall of champions. At the bottom is a net and ball and a 1940 picture featuring captain Marv Huffman. One above that, and it's 1953 and Branch McCracken is being carried off after the win. Take a closer look. Can you locate Don Schlundt and Bobby Leonard? The third from the bottom is a famous picture from 1976 of Bob Knight, Quinn Buckner, and Scott May. Then we see a 1981 picture of Isiah Thomas and Ray Tolbert. Finally it's 1987 and the picture of Steve Alford, Todd Meier, and Daryl Thomas, plus Keith Smart's famous 23 jersey and a picture of "The Shot."

But there's more. In the display cases, straight ahead, a rich and storied history comes alive. There is Hallie Bryant's Harlem Globetrotters jersey. Tom Van Arsdale's NBA All-Star jersey, and a pair of Walt Bellamy's Atlanta Hawks basketball trunks. Look up and see Archie Dees' two Big Ten Most Valuable Player Trophies, as he became the first player in Big Ten history to do this. Looking further, there is Don Schlundt's 1953 Big Ten MVP Trophy, his 1954 Big Ten Champion Belt Buckle, and his famous road-red No. 34 jersey and pants. There's Ernie Andres' Indiana Basketball Hall of Fame plaque. There's a game ball from the March 10, 1906, Indiana-Purdue game which Indiana won 30–27, and Dean Barnhart's 1909 letter sweater, which would be the very first year Indiana University would award "I" letters for basketball. There is the Big Ten's all-time leading scorer Calbert Cheaney's jersey and his Player of the Year trophy.

And that's just what you find on the main level. We can walk upstairs and see Wayne Radford's jersey, Jimmy Wisman's jersey. Maybe a little bigger than it is supposed to be. (Anyone remember that picture on the cover of the *Indianapolis Star* of the Wisman grab by Bob Knight?) Scott May's Eastman Player of the Year Award, a box score from the NCAA title game against Michigan in 1976 to complete the undefeated season, and a plaque to the undefeated champions. Only 1,000 of these were made. Move to your left and see a list of the men and women who have served as head basketball coaches for Indiana University men's and women's teams.

There is a wonderful timeline of Indiana basketball that goes completely around the second floor. As you walk around the timeline, here are some of the questions you might want to ponder: Starting in 1901, who was Indiana's captain and leading scorer? Who was the first IU player to score 20 or more points, and against whom? Who became Indiana's first player to score 30 points in a game? In 1959, how many points did Indiana score against Ohio State to set a record? Tom and Dick Van Arsdale's stats were remarkably close in scoring and rebounding for their careers. Just how close were they? Remarkably, there has only been one triple-double in IU history. Who accomplished the feat, and what categories did he do it in? And the list goes on and on.

So what do we know about Cook Hall?

Cook Hall was a gift to Indiana University from Bill and Gayle Cook. It is a 67,000-square-foot, multilevel facility that features practice courts, locker rooms, player lounges, a strength and conditioning area, coaches' offices, and meeting/video rooms. With the addition of Cook Hall, IU's men's and women's basketball teams now have two regulation-size basketball courts, allowing access 24 hours a day. There is also a shared athletic training suite, featuring state-of-the-art hydrotherapy equipment and a video analysis system to promote the health and recovery of student-athletes. Cook Hall also boasts comprehensive cutting-edge digital technologies to streamline operations and enhance instruction and training of student-athletes.

Cook Hall is also home to the Pfau Shine Legacy Court, where we first walked in. This is a unique museum/exhibit space. As we have already seen, it gives one a unique ability to see the rich history of Indiana basketball, chronicled by photographs, artifacts, trophies, and interactive touchscreen kiosks that celebrate IU's championship teams and its rich traditions.

Cook Hall was completed on March 15, 2010, and the dedication ceremony took place on April 25, 2010. Quinn Buckner, Scott May, Amy Metheny, Felisha Legette-Jack, Tom Crean, Jori Davis, and Jordan Hulls spoke at the dedication.

It is now a celebrated destination spot for Indiana basketball fans to get immersed in their favorite topic—the Indiana Hoosiers.

Watch the Game Anywhere in the Country

There's something about gathering with friends—or even total strangers—and supporting IU that can make for a special game-day experience when you're outside the state of Indiana.

No matter what state you're visiting or what state you happen to live in, there is likely a bar not that far away that has a weekly gathering of Indiana basketball fans who meet regularly to cheer on the Hoosiers. That's what happens when you have a university that ranks in the top three in the nation in terms of living alumni. Couple that with a blue-blood, historically special basketball program, and you have a recipe for some diehard fans who want to turn out and cheer for their team.

Visiting New York City on game day and looking for a place to watch the Hoosiers? There are lots of places to choose from. One of the favorites is Traffic Bar. Google "Traffic Bar and the Christian Watford shot to beat Kentucky in 2011," and you'll know all you need to know about this spot. It's located at 986 Second Avenue and can be found at www.trafficbarnyc.com. Owner and IU grad Joey Morgan knows how to treat Indiana fans, and you'll feel like you're back on Kirkwood Avenue in B-town in no time.

Maybe you're in Chicago and want to catch the Hoosiers. The Kirkwood Bar & Grill is one spot, and it takes its name from Kirkwood Avenue in Bloomington. It's at 2934 North Sheffield Avenue and can be found at www.kirkwoodbar.com. Looking for a wild spot where hundreds of IU fans gather in Chicagoland to watch the Hoosiers? You have to check out Joe's on Weed Street. Located in the former North End warehouse district, Joe's Bar is the self-proclaimed Chicago sports bar home of the Indiana Hoosiers. There are hundreds of TVs and projection screens and a huge room in the back that's always reserved for IU fans on game day. Joe's is located at 940 West Weed Street in Chicago and can be found at www.joesbar.com.

In Arizona? There are lots of possibilities in the Phoenix/Mesa/Tempe/ Glendale area. There's Padre Murphy's in Phoenix proper and the Red Owl Sports Grill in Tempe. In Glendale, check out Max's Sports Bar. In Surprise, you'll find Fuzzy's Southwest Sports Grill, and in Mesa it would be R.T. O'Sullivans.

There is a very active IU Alumni Association group in Colorado. Their official watch site is Blake Street Tavern in Denver. If you're in Boulder, check out The Lazy Dog Sports Bar & Grill. In Colorado Springs? That would be Old Chicago's on Commerce Center Drive. Finally, in Fort Collins, it would be Taps Sports Bar & Grill.

If you're in Florida, go to iuaa.com, the Indiana University Alumni Association page, and pick from one of the seven or eight Florida chapters and inquire through them where the locals view IU athletics. There is as much of a concentration of IU alumni in Florida as any- where in the country (outside of the state of Indiana), and the places to watch IU play are too numerous to list.

If you're in Atlanta, the spot where the IUAA meets is the Hudson Grille.

The state of Kentucky provides a couple of IU's biggest basketball rivals, but that doesn't mean there aren't places in the state where IU fans gather to watch their team play. In Louisville, there's Hoops Grill & Sports on Strawberry Lane and also on Westport Road. There's also Buds Tavern. In Owensboro, there's Maloney's Pizza and Wings on Highland Pointe Drive.

Live in Golden Gopher country? There's a Park Tavern location in St. Louis Park on Louisiana Avenue South.

In 2012 Indiana played in Portland, Oregon, in the NCAA Tournament, and fans showed up in droves in the Pacific Northwest. There are three spots that we know of to watch IU in Portland: The

Cheerful Bullpen on SW Taylor Street, The Cheerful Tortoise on SW Sixth Avenue, and Jolly Roger on SE 12th Avenue and Madison.

Listen to Fish

I t's game day and you're driving somewhere, so you can't watch the Hoosiers on TV and you can't find a place to stop and watch the game for a few hours and take a break from the road.

The ultimate backup plan always involves the voice of Indiana University football and basketball Don Fischer. If you have Wi-Fi access and an app on your smartphone or tablet, listening to a familiar voice call the Hoosiers is only a few clicks away. There are lots of options on the market. The best thing to do if you don't already have one is to google "radio apps" and see what you come up with. You'll probably see a list that includes names like TuneIn Radio Pro, iHeart-Radio, Pandora Radio, Stitcher Radio for Podcasts, Slacker Radio, Xtend Fm Radio, or SiriusXM Internet Radio.

Or, if you're within earshot of Indiana, you may be able to find a station on the IU Radio Network. Learfield Communications holds the exclusive rights as Indiana University's official radio outlet.

If you're in any of the following places or near them, these are some of the cities where you'll be able to pick up IU basketball on the radio: Batesville, Bedford, Bloomington, Boonville, Columbus, and Eminence, Kentucky. There are also outlets in Evansville, Fort Wayne, French Lick, and Indianapolis. There are spots in Jasper, Jeffersonville, Kendallville, Kokomo, Ligonier, Linton, and Loogootee. It goes as far south as Louisville, Kentucky, too, and places like Madison, Marion, Michigan City, Mount Vernon, Richmond, and Salem. And there are spots in Seymour, South Bend, Tell City, Terre Haute, and Vincennes.

In other words, if you're driving in and around Indiana on game day, there's a good chance you'll find a signal—at least in the daytime—where you can pick up the Hoosiers and listen to Fish on the radio.

Simply put, Fish is the best.

Fischer has been the voice of Indiana University football and basketball for more than four decades and shows no signs of slowing down.

Many IU fans say they will turn off the television sound and listen to Fischer call the games on the radio. This can become a challenge with a delay between the TV broadcast and the live radio call, but there is actually equipment you can purchase to get the two synchronized. A good number of Indiana fans would quickly pony up the money to make that happen.

To many people, Fischer is Indiana basketball.

When former Indiana football coach Terry Hoeppner was first introduced to the IU media after being named Indiana's football coach in December 2004, one of the things he said was that he was looking forward to working with Fischer. He said he had listened to Indiana basketball broadcasts all his life and could think of countless times when he had picked up a weak radio signal broadcasting IU basketball on a recruiting trip and always felt like he was listening to a trusted friend.

That's how Indiana fans think of Don Fischer.

Fischer has called more than 1,800 games, including three of Indiana's national championships (1976, 1981, and 1987) and 10 Indiana football bowl games. That's a pretty impressive feat right there, considering the Hoosiers' football team has only played in 11 bowl games in history. The only one Fischer didn't call was the 1967 IU Rose Bowl team—And he only missed that by six years.

The first football game that Fischer called was also Lee Corso's first game as the head football coach at Indiana. It was 1973. IU lost to Illinois that day, 28–14. The Hoosiers would go 2–9 that season and lose their final seven games in a row.

As for basketball, his first game was Indiana vs. the Citadel on December 1, 1973. In his first three seasons broadcasting the Hoosiers,

IU captured the Big Ten title all three years and had an amazing 48–2 record in conference games over that stretch. For his third season, he called the last unbeaten season in college basketball history when the 1976 Hoosiers went 32–0 en route to winning the national championship.

He called Indiana games for 27 of Bob Knight's 29 seasons at IU. It wasn't always easy, but it was usually interesting. One of the responsibilities he had was broadcasting Bob Knight's radio show. Anyone who listened to that knew it was an adventure for the broadcaster, too. Fischer initially took questions for Knight until one evening when a belligerent caller made Knight angry. In a commercial break, he said he was done taking phone calls. So, instead, listeners would submit questions in writing, and Fischer would pick and choose which ones he used. Sometimes he just made up his own questions and used names from his high school yearbook to go with them.

After a while, Knight began doing the radio show from his home. Sometimes he would be eating while he had the show on his speakerphone and would make comments with food in his mouth. One time, Knight began choking on a chicken bone in the middle of a live radio show. Another time, in the middle of an answer, a toilet was heard flushing loudly. Once, when Knight was doing the show from his office at Assembly Hall, he stepped away at one point to take a shower. The most memorable time, however, came one night while the IU coach was doing the show from his garage, where he was cleaning a gun. As he was cleaning it, it fell on the floor and discharged, making a loud bang on the airwaves.

For Fischer, it was simply part of the job when working with Bob Knight. Since Knight's dismissal in September of 2000, Fischer has worked with IU basketball coaches Mike Davis, Kelvin Sampson, interim coach Dan Dakich (for seven games), and Tom Crean. In football, along with Corso, Fischer has worked with Sam Wyche, Bill Mallory, Cam Cameron, Gerry DiNardo, Terry Hoeppner, Bill Lynch, Kevin Wilson, and Tom Allen.

Fischer has been named Indiana's Sportscaster of the Year so many times by the National Sportscasters and Sportswriters Association that they should just name the award after him. He has won it more than 20 times. In 2004 he was inducted into the Indiana Sportswriters and Sportscasters Hall of Fame, and he added the Indiana Broadcasters Association Hall of Fame designation to his impressive résumé in 2010.

Fischer's career began in 1968 when he called his first high school football game for WOLI-FM in Ottawa, Illinois. He had told the station manager that he had play-by-play experience because he needed the job, but it was clear very quickly to everyone that he had not. The station manager was waiting for him when he got back to the station after that first game and gave him three weeks to figure things out or he was going to fire him.

Fischer sought out veteran sportscaster Art Kimball and took a crash course in broadcasting. When his three weeks were up, Fischer had improved enough that the station manager allowed him to continue. And the rest—as they say—is history.

Fischer has been asked many times when he will stop broadcasting Indiana athletics. He has said he'll know when the time is right, but he doesn't think he's slowing down just yet. Still, Indiana fans should never take for granted the treasure they've been able to enjoy in having Fish on the call of Indiana football and basketball since 1973.

Indiana basketball coach Tom Crean paid Fischer the highest of compliments on the first radio show of the season in 2016, Crean's ninth year working with the "Voice of IU."

"Don is the greatest announcer in the history of college basketball," Crean said.

You're not going to find many Indiana fans who disagree.

See the Hoosiers Play on the Road

We've talked about how much fun it is to be in Assembly Hall and to experience Indiana basketball live. The next best thing is going on the road with the Hoosiers into hostile territory and supporting IU basketball there.

One of the things that makes Indiana basketball special is that, no matter where IU plays, there are always a great number of fans in attendance wearing the cream and crimson and cheering on the Hoosiers. It doesn't matter if it's a December tournament in New York City, an NCAA Tournament game in Portland, a trip to the Lahaina Civic Center for the Maui Invitational in November, or a Big Ten road game at one of nine possible destinations each season.

When IU travels, there are always a small number of tickets that can be obtained in a section right behind the visitors' bench. These are normally reserved for players' families, former players, IU administrators, or friends of the staff. So those are much more difficult to get. Usually, you have to know someone to get your hands on those tickets.

But to just get in the building is usually a much easier proposition. There are very few arenas in the country that are sold out just about every game. Assembly Hall is one of them, but there are some places in the Big Ten where it's not difficult at all to get a ticket. Ever seen the Hoosiers play at Northwestern? Everyone should do it at least once. The gymnasium is often turned into an IU home game away from home where thousands of IU fans are in attendance, and oftentimes make it almost a neutral court. Live close to Piscataway, New Jersey? There are usually plenty of good seats available at Rutgers for the IU-Rutgers game, too. Same is true in Nebraska. The others are more difficult, but not impossible. Sometimes it's a matter of paying the scalper's price or getting the tickets online from a ticket service.

The bottom line is, if you want to make it happen, it can be done.

See the Hoosiers
Play in Hawaii

In the same vein as going to a Hoosiers road game, a trip to the Lahaina Civic Center in Maui or a game in Honolulu can be a once-in-a-lifetime experience to see your Hoosiers in action.

Indiana is part of a rotation that generally gets a trip to Maui every four or five years. The Maui Invitational folks love having Indiana on the island because the Hoosiers always sell out their individual allotment of tickets.

If it's the Maui Invitational, the Lahaina Civic Center is a little cracker-box of a gym that holds fewer than 3,000 fans. It's a fun and intimate atmosphere to watch IU basketball. You feel as if you're in a small high school gym where you can hear every word that is spoken from the players and the coaches. When Bob Knight was the IU coach, you can imagine what some little ears were treated to in that building.

But it's not just Maui. IU has played games on Oahu, as well. In November 2016 the Hoosiers played Kansas at the University of Hawaii in the Armed Forces Classic. IU also played in the Rainbow Classic in 1974 and 1979 and in the United Airlines Tipoff Classic in Honolulu in 1997.

If you want a chance to watch the Hoosiers in shorts and a flowered shirt and then hit the beach right after the game, this is the place to do it.

Players and Coaches

Calbert Cheaney's exhibit in the Indiana Basketball Hall of Fame

To really know Indiana University basketball is to know its history. And IU basketball is filled with a rich hardwood history.

There are too many players to count who have worn the cream and crimson and gone on to do good things in the professional ranks. The Indiana coaching tree is an impressive one, too, with two names—Branch McCracken and Bob Knight—who stand above the rest, with a total of five national championships and 15 Big Ten titles between them.

The Sheriff and the General. Two of the best that college basketball has ever seen.

But first let's begin with the players.

As mentioned, it's difficult to talk about the best Indiana basketball players of all-time because there are so many to choose from. More than 40 players have earned All-America status while at IU. More than 15 have been honored as the Big Ten's most valuable player. IU has had players win the Wooden Award and the Naismith Award.

So when you try to narrow the field to showcase some of the best of the best of Indiana history, you're no doubt going to leave out some high quality players. Here's our attempt to give you a taste of some of IU's finest basketball players of all time. When looking at star players of the past, we should begin with those inducted into the Hall of Fame first, so our first six are all Indiana University players in the Naismith Memorial Basketball Hall of Fame.

The Hall of Famers

Walt Bellamy

Bellamy was born on July 24, 1939, in New Bern, North Carolina, and attended J.T. Barber High School. He first came into contact with Indiana University in 1956, when his high school coach, Simon Coates, came to Bloomington during some postgraduate work at IU. He would invite a young Walt Bellamy along to come see the place before Walt's senior year.

While in Bloomington, Bellamy was able to play basketball with IU players Wally Choice, Hallie Bryant, and Gene Flowers. He would say that "The competitiveness of it was fascinating to me. The cama-raderie, along with the fact that such an esteemed coach as Branch McCracken came out to acknowledge my presence, was the a culmi-nation of all the things that led me back to Indiana. I had a rich and rewarding experience at Indiana." Bellamy would indeed come back to Bloomington to play for the Hoosiers and McCracken. Bellamy would headline a decade of the best centers any Big Ten team had ever put together. The decade began with All-American Bill Garrett, followed by three-time All-American Don Schlundt. The Big Ten's first two-time MVP Archie Dees succeeded Schlundt. Then Bellamy came in after Dees.

Growing pains would show in Bellamy's first season, his sophomore year, as Indiana would finish 1958–59 with a record of 11–11 and a fifth-place finish in the Big Ten. Bellamy would average 17.4 points

Walt Bellamy with Coach McCracken (Indiana University Archives, P0020158)

and 15.2 rebounds in his first year as a player at Indiana, giving Hoosiers fans a hint of what was to come.

In Bellamy's junior year, IU would put together one of its greatest seasons under Coach McCracken with an overall record of 20–4, finishing second in the Big Ten and winning its last 12 games, holding a national ranking of seventh. Bellamy upped his average point total to 22.4 and rebound at a 13.5 clip that season, being named both All-America and first-team All–Big Ten. In addition, after his breakout junior season, Bellamy would be a member of the gold-medal 1960 U.S. Olympic team.

In his senior year, Indiana finished 15–9 with a fourth-place finish in the Big Ten. Bellamy averaged 21.8 points per game and set an IU record for rebounds with an average of 17.8, including an IU and Big Ten record of 33 rebounds in his last game as a Hoosier. Bellamy was again selected as an All-American and first-team All–Big Ten. He was named Indiana MVP all three seasons. Bellamy went on to become the first Hoosier taken No. 1 in the NBA Draft.

Bellamy played his rookie year for the Chicago Packers and was named NBA Rookie of the Year after averaging 31.6 points and 19.0 rebounds, numbers topped by only one other person in NBA history— Wilt Chamberlain. In his NBA career, he would play for the Packers, Zephyrs, Bullets, Knicks, Pistons, Hawks, and Jazz. He finished his NBA career as one of only eight players ever to score more than 20,000 points and have 14,000 rebounds.

Bellamy was elected to the Basketball Hall of Fame on May 10, 1993, and passed away on November 2, 2013, at the age of 74.

Quinn Buckner

William Quinn Buckner was born August 20, 1954, in Phoenix, Illinois. Buckner's father was a member of the undefeated 1945 Indiana football team. Quinn was a high school All-American in both football and basketball at Thornridge High School in Dolton, Illinois, a south Chicago suburb. He led the Thornridge basketball team to two straight state championships, and in his senior year they went undefeated at 33–0. That year, he averaged 25 points, 11 rebounds, and six assists per game while shooting 55 percent from the floor and 71 percent from the free throw line. Quinn was called "the most exciting prep basketball player in Illinois."

Buckner came to Indiana to play both football and basketball. Bob Knight said of Buckner, "He's unquestionably one of the best athletes in the nation, and we certainly feel he is one of the very best

The Mighty Quinn (Indiana University Archives, P0052978)

basketball players." He would go on to say, "His feelings about team-work and team play really fit in well with the kids we have recruited. His talent should go very well with the talent we have on hand." Buckner would start two years at defensive back in football and four years in basketball.

It was a truly remarkable feat. In Buckner's freshman year, he stepped off the gridiron and a week later started on the hardwood. During his freshman year at IU as a point guard, he led his Hoosiers to a 22–6 record, a Big Ten title, and a spot in the NCAA Final Four. Indiana would finish that year losing to UCLA in the semifinals and defeating No. 4 Providence in the consolation game 97–79. For the year, Buckner averaged 10.8 points, five rebounds, and handed out 82 assists.

Buckner's sophomore year saw Indiana again win a share of a Big Ten championship. The Hoosiers completed the season with a record of 23–5 and the championship of the CCA (a short-lived postseason alternative to the NIT for teams that didn't make the NCAA tourny). Buckner's point average dipped to 8.2, but his assists climbed to a total of 150 as he solidified his role as floor general.

Buckner's junior year was indeed a special one as he led Indiana to its third Big Ten championship in a row. Indiana finished 31–1, becoming the first team in Big Ten history to go through a round robin Big Ten schedule undefeated at 18–0. Buckner was selected as an All-American and All–Big Ten first-team while scoring 11.8 points a game and dishing out 177 assists.

Buckner's senior year would top his junior. Not only did Indiana win a fourth straight Big Ten title, they went undefeated in the Big Ten (18–0) and overall. He was again selected as an All-American while averaging 8.9 points and dishing out 133 assists. In the NCAA championship game, Buckner played 39 minutes, scored 16 points, grabbed eight rebounds, and dished out four assists. Buckner would go from the NCAA championship to the 1976 Olympics and a gold medal, and then be drafted in the first round of the 1976 NBA Draft by the

Milwaukee Bucks with the seventh overall pick. He went on to play for the Bucks, Celtics, and Mavericks.

While playing for the Boston Celtics in 1984, he won an NBA championship to go with his Olympic gold medal, NCAA championship, and Illinois High School championship. Yes, indeed, he was the "Mighty Quinn," who in 2015 would be inducted into the Basketball Hall of Fame.

Everett Dean

Everett Dean was born on March 18, 1898, in Livonia, Indiana. He went to school in Salem, Indiana, and came to Indiana University in 1917. His first game at Indiana took place on January 2, 1918, in Vincennes, Indiana, as Dean and his Hoosiers teammates beat the Vincennes YMCA 47–16. Dean, just a sophomore, scored four points in the game.

That was the start of his basketball career, but not his career as an athlete at Indiana. Although tiny Salem did not have a football team and Dean had never played the sport, he did catch a pass and score a touchdown in Indiana's 24–7 season-opening loss to Kentucky. In basketball Dean led Indiana past Ohio State 37–31 in the biggest performance of his sophomore year with 17 points. Dean scored in double figures five more times in his first year. Indiana finished the 1918 season 10–7, sixth in the Big Ten. On March 3, 1919, Dean outscored the entire Notre Dame team (as well as the rest of his teammates) with 15 points in the Hoosiers' 29–11 victory.

In Dean's junior year, Indiana advanced to fourth in the Big Ten, finishing 13–6 overall. Dean averaged 9.6 points per game. By his senior year, Dean had made a name for himself as one of the nation's best players. Indiana finished 15–6 with Dean averaging 11.1 points a game. Everett Dean was then named Indiana's first ever All-American. During his Indiana career, he outscored the other team on seven occasions. The *Indiana Daily Student* described Dean in this way: "He is a man around whom the whole play of the crimson varsity revolves. His

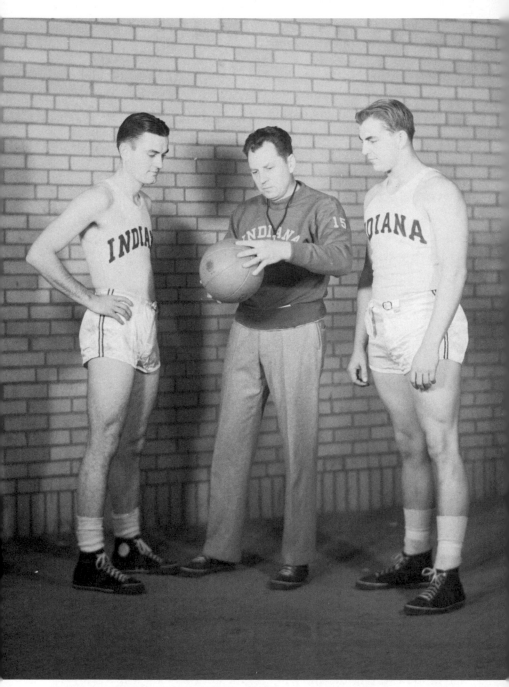

Coach Everett Dean imparting instructions (Indiana University Archives, P0020897)

size, speed, basket-eye, and hard work make him an invaluable scorer in that remarkable offense which Coach Lewis has developed. His early season work makes him loom as All-American material."

As a senior, Dean, who was a serious student, won the Big Ten Medal of Honor for academic and athletic excellence. After he graduated from IU, Hall of Fame manager Connie Mack offered him a baseball contract. But Dean turned down Mack to coach basketball at Carleton College, where he coached for three years before coming back to IU in 1924 at the age of 26 to become the head basketball coach at Indiana.

While coaching at Indiana, his overall record was 162–93. He gave Indiana its first Big Ten championship in basketball in 1926 and then won it again in 1928 and 1936. In 1938 Dean left Indiana for Stanford, where he would win the 1942 NCAA championship. Dean is the only coach to be in both the Naismith Basketball Hall of Fame and the College Baseball Hall of Fame. Coach Dean died on October 26, 1993, at the age of 95.

Bobby Leonard

Bobby Leonard was born on July 17, 1932, in Terre Haute, Indiana. Leonard would grow up in an area of Terre Haute called Shantytown. They lived in a one-bedroom house with an outhouse. His first job was to empty the chamber pot in the morning.

Leonard attended Terre Haute Gerstmeyer, entering high school as a 5'4" freshman. By his senior year he had grown to 6'3". Leonard hit a 20-foot jumper to send Terre Haute into overtime against Fontanet in the sectionals, a preview of things to come at IU. Leonard scored a career high of 52 against the Blackhawks in the morning game of the final sectional day. Terre Haute went on to win the sectionals that night.

Leonard became a wanted man among college basketball coaches. Notre Dame, North Carolina State, Kentucky, and Indiana were all vying for Bobby. While Kentucky offered the most, IU coach Branch McCracken attracted Leonard as much as anything else

about IU. Coach McCracken talked to Leonard's high school coach, Howard Sharpe, and after their talk, Coach Sharpe told Leonard that McCracken and IU were who he should play for.

At Indiana during his freshman year, he met Nancy Root, whom he would later marry. Leonard would later say that Coach McCracken was "a special guy. He was like a father to me." His freshman year, McCracken had Lou Watson bring the freshmen down to scrimmage the varsity. After the first quarter, the freshmen were ahead, and McCracken told Watson to take the kids back upstairs.

During Leonard's sophomore preseason, he won McCracken's free-throw contest; the winner got to go with McCracken and his wife, Mary Jo, to the Nashville House in Brown County for dinner. McCracken told Leonard how good the chicken dinner was at $1.75, but Leonard being Leonard, he ordered the steak dinner at $3.50, much to Branch's surprise. During Leonard's sophomore year, Indiana finished the season 16–6, good for fourth in the Big Ten, while Leonard finished second on the team in scoring with 14.5 points a game.

In 1953, Leonard's junior year, Indiana started the season ranked 19th in the nation. Indiana lost two of its first three games by a total of three points, but would go on to win 17 in a row before losing at Minnesota by two. At the end of the season, Indiana's record was 23–3, with the three losses coming by a grand total of five points. Along the way, Indiana defeated No. 19 Minnesota at home and No. 4 and then No. 10 Illinois at home and away, giving the Hoosiers a 17–1 conference record, the best ever in the Big Ten at the time.

Leonard was Mr. Outside for the Hoosiers, scoring at a 16.3 clip. In the NCAA Championship game, Leonard drove toward the basket with 27 seconds to go and the game tied. While he missed the basket, he drew a foul from Kansas guard Dean Smith. He hit the second of the free throws to win the game for Indiana and the NCAA title 69–68. He would be named All-America that year.

His senior year, Leonard led Indiana to another Big Ten championship and a 20–4 record. He would again be named All-America with a 15.4 scoring average, but Indiana lost a chance at a second straight national title when Leonard was called for a charge after making a basket. Notre Dame then scored, and the Hoosiers lost 65–64.

After graduating, Leonard was drafted by the Washington Bullets. He went on to play for the Minneapolis/Los Angeles Lakers before ending his career with the Chicago Packers. Leonard would coach fellow Hoosier Walt Bellamy with the Chicago Packers, but gained fame as the second coach of the ABA's Indiana Pacers. Leonard coached the Pacers to three ABA titles and became a voice on Pacers Radio with his familiar three-point call of "Boom, Baby." On February 14, 2014, Bobby Leonard was selected to the Basketball Hall of Fame.

Branch McCracken

Branch McCracken was born on June 9, 1908, in Monrovia, Indiana. McCracken was a high school star at little Monrovia High School, where his team won 78 of its 84 games his sophomore, junior, and senior years. Coach Everett Dean talked about recruiting McCracken to Indiana: "We didn't have any trouble recruiting Mac, although several other universities wanted him. He wanted to come to Indiana, and he was a great player." Like his coach, Everett Dean, McCracken, who had never played football in high school due to Monrovia being too small for a football team, would score a touchdown in football for IU before ever making a basket for the Hoosiers.

The *Daily Student* wrote about McCracken: "His height, ranginess, and cleverness, the three attributes of a good center, are so manifest in Branch McCracken that he already is one of the leading members of the squad. He has all the natural attributes of a good netman, Coach Dean believes, and is expected to bear watching, in spite of his experience. McCracken's drive, long frame, and keen eye for the hoop caused him to be feared by all opposing pivot men. His strong suit is his ability to get the tip-off and to get through the guards for many follow-up shots."

Everett Dean called McCracken "rough and tough." McCracken never missed a game; even when slowed by injuries, he planted himself near the foul line with his back to the basket. It was from there he would pass off to players cutting by him. His other option was to keep the ball to himself and roll to the basket. "Once we saw what he could do, we let him go," Dean went on to say. "He was one of the first college centers who played the pivot the way it's played today."

McCracken's sophomore year Indiana was 15–2, and he won Coach Dean's second Big Ten championship, leading the Hoosiers in scoring with a 10.1 average. McCracken's junior year, Indiana suffered through a 7–10 record, finishing eighth in the Big Ten. During McCracken's senior year, Indiana would move back into the upper half of the Big Ten to fourth place. McCracken would receive All-America honors while averaging 12.1 points a game. He finished his

Branch McCracken—always coaching, always teaching (Indiana University Archives, P0021439)

career as the Big Ten's all-time leading scorer with 366 points, having scored more than a third of all of Indiana's team points in that three-year period.

In McCracken's first Big Ten game as a sophomore, he outscored Chicago by himself 24–13. McCracken would set many firsts for the Hoosiers and college basketball. Indiana's national title in 1940, coaching the first African American player in Big Ten basketball, Bill Garrett, and coaching the first televised regular season college basketball game. In 1960 McCracken was elected to the Basketball Hall of Fame, and the Court of Assembly Hall was named McCracken Court. McCracken passed away in Indianapolis on June 4, 1970, a Hoosier legend.

Isiah Thomas

Isiah Thomas was born on April 30, 1961, in Chicago, the youngest of seven boys. Thomas grew up often competing against players much older than himself. "My brothers got me started playing when I was three," Thomas recalled. Even as a small boy in kindergarten at Our Lady of Sorrows, he would suit up for the seventh- and eighth-grade team more or less as a water boy. However, by the time he was in fourth grade, he wound up playing on that same team as a starter. Thomas picked jersey No. 11 because of his admiration for Sammy Puckett, an older player at his school who always wore No. 11.

At Westchester St. Joseph High School in Chicago, Thomas became an All-America player. Indiana won the battle for Isiah's services mainly because Coach Knight was, in Thomas's mind, very similar to his mother in his mannerisms. During the summer before Thomas would attend IU, he played for Coach Knight in the Pan American games. Thomas played a vital part on that team; in fact, Thomas would be the leading scorer in the title game win over Puerto Rico, with 21 points. While playing for the United States Pan American team, Thomas wore a different number for the only time in his life, No. 12.

Upon entering Indiana University, Thomas made an immediate impact. During his freshman year, Indiana captured the Big Ten title with a 13–5 record, going 21–8 overall. Thomas averaged 14.6 points a game that season, while also handing out assists at the rate of 5.5 a game.

Thomas would save his best for his sophomore year. Once again, he led Indiana to a Big Ten championship with a 14–4 record, 26–9 overall. Indiana won a second NCAA championship under Knight and a fourth for the school. In their opening NCAA tournament game against Maryland, Thomas and Indiana were nearly perfect. Indiana defeated Maryland 99–64. Thomas scored 19 points, handed out 14 assists, and did not commit a turnover in what many called a time-capsule game. In the national championship game, he scored 23 points against North Carolina in Indiana's 63–50 victory. Thomas was named the Most Outstanding Player of the NCAA Tournament. In his first

Isiah scoring—"a little child shall lead them." (Indiana University Archives, P0021882)

two years, Thomas had brought IU two Big Ten titles and a national championship.

After his sophomore season, Thomas declared for the NBA Draft. He became the second overall pick in the draft when selected by the Detroit Pistons. Thomas played for the Pistons from 1981 to 1994, leading Detroit to two NBA titles in 1989 and 1990. Much like the 1981 NCAA tournament, he was named MVP of the 1990 NBA Finals. Thomas was a 12-time All-Star and two-time All-Star Game MVP.

After his playing career was over, Thomas coached the Indiana Pacers from 2000 to 2003 and the New York Knicks from 2006 to 2008. During his college career, Indiana fans became very familiar with the Bible verse from Isaiah 11:6, "and a little child shall lead them."

The Best of the Rest

Steve Alford

Steve Alford was born on November 23, 1964, in Franklin, Indiana. It is said that at the age of three, when his father was a coach for the local high school basketball team, Alford learned to count by watching the numbers on the scoreboard at his father's games. His mother sent out an announcement proclaiming Steve to be Mr. Basketball for the year 1983.

Alford would play for his dad, Sam, at New Castle, Indiana, which boasts the largest high school gym in the nation. As a high school freshman, Alford scored just over a point a game, but by his sophomore year he pushed that mark to 18.7 per game. By Alford's senior year in 1983, he was scoring at a clip of over 37 points per game and would indeed be named Indiana's Mr. Basketball.

After his freshman year at IU, Alford would be selected to the 1984 U.S. Olympic team that won a gold medal in Los Angeles, where he averaged 10.3 points, shooting at 64.4 percent from the field, and ranked second on the team in assists.

Steve Alford's picture-perfect shot (Indiana University Archives, P0044789)

Alford averaged 22 points a game as a senior at Indiana, while scoring a career-high 42 points against Michigan State in a 84–80 IU victory. In the NCAA Championship Game, Alford would set a NCAA championship record at the time of seven three-pointers in the game. Indiana's 1987 NCAA championship was their fifth in the school's history, and Alford would become Indiana's first four-time team MVP.

Alford left IU as its all-time leading scorer with 2,438 points. In the Legends of College Basketball, named by the *Sporting News*, Steve was No. 35 on their list of the 100 greatest Division I college basketball players. Steve was drafted by Dallas and play for both the Mavericks and Golden State Warriors, where he scored 744 points and handed out 176 assists in his career.

Alford would go on to coach at Manchester, Missouri State, Iowa, New Mexico, and UCLA. Over his coaching career, his teams have gone 572–272 for a .660 winning percentage in 25 years of coaching.

Damon Bailey

Bailey was born on October 21, 1971, in tiny Heltonville, Indiana. Some would say he was born to Hoosier greatness. Bailey's legend grew when, as an eighth grader, coach Bob Knight started the recruiting process that would eventually land Bailey at IU. According to John Feinstein in his book *A Season on the Brink*, after watching Damon in the eighth grade, Knight said, "Damon Bailey is better than any guard we have right now. I don't mean potentially better. I mean better today."

Bailey's legend would grow during his high school years. Averaging over 23 points a game in his freshman year, he led Bedford North Lawrence High School to the state finals. Bailey took BNL back to the state finals as a sophomore, and during his senior year, he took his team one step further by leading it to the state championship with a 63–60 win over Concord High School, a game in which he scored 30 points in front of 41,046 fans at the Hoosier Dome. Bailey would finish his high school career playing in three state finals, winning one championship, and scoring a state record 3,134 points, reaching double figures in all 110 games he played in. Bailey was named Indiana's Mr. Basketball, was the consensus 1990 National Player of the Year, and left IU fans anxious for what the next four years would bring.

During his first three years at Indiana, Bailey, being the consummate team player, set aside his scoring prowess to help Indiana to 87 victories. Indiana captured Big Ten titles in both his freshman and junior seasons and went to the Final Four in his sophomore year. Bailey averaged 11.3 points over the three-year span.

In his senior season of 1993–94, Bailey led the team in scoring with 19.6 points a game. He was drafted by the Indiana Pacers in the 1994 NBA Draft but would have his rookie year cut short after the team recommended surgery. He would be cut at the start of his second season. Although Bailey would never play in a regular season NBA game, his fame will forever live on for Hoosiers fans.

Kent Benson

Benson was born on December 27, 1954, in New Castle, Indiana. Benson was sought after following his Mr. Basketball senior year at New Castle High School. Notre Dame, Kentucky, and Indiana waged a fight for his services. Indiana held the edge as Benson had been a spectator at the state tournament and joined in the roaring crowd at Assembly Hall as a triumphant Indiana team came into the Hall on their way to the locker room. Victors of the NCAA Mideast Regionals, Indiana was Benson's choice, and he would thrill Hoosiers fans for the next four years.

During Benson's freshman year, a year which saw him score at a 9.3 clip and rebound nearly eight per game, Indiana finished 23–5 in a tie with Michigan for first in the Big Ten. Benson was named the MVP in the CCA tournament won by IU. Benson's sophomore and junior years would be with arguably Indiana's greatest teams of all time. In his sophomore year, Indiana went 31–1. Benson averaged 15 points a game and was named All-America and All–Big Ten. During Benson's junior year, Indiana was a perfect 32–0, Big Ten and NCAA champions. Indiana was ranked No. 1 from the beginning to the end of the season. Benson's average increased to 17.3 points and 8.8 rebounds. He was again selected All-America and All–Big Ten, and was the MVP of the Final Four.

Benson found himself the only starter left for the 1976–77 season. He led the Hoosiers and played hard, but the Hoosiers were young and finished fourth in the Big Ten with a 16–11 record. Benson missed the last four games of the season due to back surgery. For his senior season, he averaged 19.8 points and 10.5 rebounds a game. He was again named All-America, and in 1977 he was the first player taken overall in the NBA Draft, by the Milwaukee Bucks. Benson also played for Detroit, Utah, and Cleveland. During an NBA career that spanned 11 years, Benson averaged 9.1 points, 5.7 rebounds, and 1.8 assists a game.

Butch Carter

Butch Carter was born on June 11, 1958, in Springfield, Ohio. He attended Middletown High School and was named Ohio's Player of the Year in 1976. During Carter's sophomore year, Indiana finished second in the Big Ten. In Carter's junior year, Indiana finished fifth in the Big Ten, but they were invited to New York and the NIT. In the tournament, Indiana would have to face two Big Ten teams that had finished ahead of Indiana in the Big Ten, Ohio State and Purdue. In the semifinal game, Indiana beat Ohio State 65–55. The championship pitted Purdue against Indiana. The game went back and forth. Purdue's Joe Barry Carroll missed the front end of a one-and-one with six seconds left, and Indiana came down with a chance to win it. Carter raised up from the top of the key and buried the jumper to give IU a 53–52 win.

In Carter's senior year, IU won the Big Ten championship, edging out Ohio State in the final game of the season. Carter's two free throws sent the game into overtime, allowing Indiana to pull out a win and the title. Carter averaged over 11 points per game for his senior year.

The Los Angeles Lakers made Carter their second pick in the 1980 draft. He played eight years for the Lakers, Pacers, Knicks, and 76ers, scoring 3,137 points, with 546 rebounds and 683 assists. Upon retiring, Carter coached the Toronto Raptors for two seasons.

Calbert Cheaney

Calbert Cheaney was born on July 17, 1971, in Evansville, Indiana. He was not the highest recruit for Indiana in 1989. In fact, Cheaney was not the highest-rated recruit in Indiana. Lawrence Funderburke, as well as Pat and Greg Graham, were all more highly thought of. In fact, it looked as if Cheaney would stay home and play for the University of Evansville Purple Aces and Jim Crews. Cheaney had played his high school ball at Evansville Harrison and at the last minute opted for IU.

However, when the season started on November 25, two freshmen started for IU. Funderburke was not a surprise. However, the other was Calbert Cheaney, who surprised many, but not for long. In that first game at Assembly Hall against Miami of Ohio, Cheaney went 9-for-11 from the field and scored 20 points in a 77–66 Indiana victory. In his freshman year, Cheaney led Indiana in scoring with a 17.1 average.

As a sophomore, Cheaney led IU to a 29–5 record and a Big Ten title. He was selected All-America, scoring an IU record 734 points for a 21.6 average while taking the Hoosiers to the Sweet Sixteen in the NCAA tournament. In Calbert's junior year, Indiana finished 27–7 and went to the Final Four.

Cheaney may have saved his best for last, however, as he led Indiana to a 31–4 overall record as a senior and won another Big Ten title with a 17–1 mark. Cheaney was selected not only All-America, but named the College Basketball Player of the Year, averaging 22.4 points a game. In his four years, he scored a total of 2,613 points to become Indiana's and the Big Ten's all-time career scoring leader.

Cheaney was the first pick for the Washington Bullets and the sixth overall pick in the 1993 NBA Draft. During his 13-year NBA career,

Calbert Cheaney sets the Big Ten scoring record (Indiana University Archives, P0051655)

Cheaney played for Washington, Boston, Denver, Utah, and Golden State, averaging 9.5 points, 3.2 rebounds, and 1.7 assists per game. Cheaney was the second IU player after Steve Alford to win the Indiana MVP award four straight years.

Archie Dees

Archie Dees was born on February 22, 1936, in Ethel, Mississippi. The 6'8" forward-center played at Mount Carmel High School in Mount Carmel, Illinois. He was named a high school All-American during his senior year. Dees attended Indiana to play for Branch McCracken and would be the third of four great centers over a decade at IU—following Bill Garrett and Don Schlundt and preceding Walt Bellamy.

Dees scored 2,823 points at Mount Carmel, making him one of the all-time leading scorers in Illinois high school history. With Mount Carmel on the Illinois-Indiana border, Dees saw Indiana games on TV, which played a part in his recruitment at IU. But that wasn't the most important reason, according to Dees. "I thought Branch McCracken was one of the greatest coaches who ever lived," he said. "He was a legend. It was an honor to play for him." Dees talked about the offense McCracken ran at Indiana: "I could run, and that's a big advantage I had over other big guys. I was in the best shape of my life, and it was a tribute to McCracken. I was never in that kind of shape in the pros. It was the perfect offense for me. I came to the right school at the right time."

Dees' first game at IU was a preview of what the next three years would bring. With all the pressure of the world on young Archie to replace three-time All-American Don Schlundt, he scored 21 points in a 93–74 Indiana win over Ohio University. Game 2 looked even better as Archie scored 21 points with 22 rebounds in a win over Kansas State. Indiana finished Dees' first year with a 13–9 record.

After Dees' 1956–57 junior season, Hoosiers fans couldn't wait for his senior season. Their brilliant center was the Big Ten scoring champ, MVP, and an All-American. But in a total shock to all Hoosiers fans, Indiana would lose six of its first seven games. Dees was still scoring at his familiar pace, but Indiana was not clicking. However, IU won 11 of its last 15 games, including their last five, to capture the Big Ten title.

Dees finished his senior year at Indiana as the first Big Ten player to be honored two years in a row as the league's Most Valuable Player. Dees

again led the Big Ten in scoring and was also selected as All–Big Ten and All-America. He finished his career at Indiana with a 22.7-points-per-game average, which ranks second all-time history for IU players with more than one season, and he also grabbed 914 rebounds.

The Cincinnati Royals picked Dees as their first pick, the second player taken overall in the 1958 NBA Draft. He signed a $25,000 contract that included a $4,000 signing bonus. Dees' NBA career included stops at Cincinnati, Detroit, Chicago, and St. Louis, averaging 8.1 points and 4.8 rebounds in an injury-plagued career. After retiring from the NBA, Dees joined with fellow All-American Don Schlundt to form perhaps the tallest insurance agency of all-time. Dees passed away on April 4, 2016.

Steve Downing

Steve Downing was born on September 9, 1950, in Indianapolis, Indiana. He came to Indiana in the shadow of his friend and teammate from high school, George McGinnis. Downing, along with McGinnis, led Indianapolis Washington to an undefeated state championship in 1969. Downing's first year at IU was a roller coaster of a season. Along with McGinnis and Joby Wright, Downing led Indiana back to respectability with a 17–7 record after two last–place finishes in the Big Ten.

His most memorable accomplishment came in an 88–79 victory when he recorded the only triple-double in Indiana basketball history. Downing had 28 points, 17 rebounds, and 10 blocked shots.

Downing's junior year came under the coaching of 31-year-old Bob Knight. Indiana finished the season ranked No. 17 in the country with an overall record of 17–8. Its third-place conference finish was the highest since the 1967 team finished in a tie for first. Downing finished the year averaging 17.5 points and 15 rebounds a game.

As a senior, Downing was selected as Big Ten MVP and named All-America, as well as a member of the Final Four all-tourney team. In 1973 Downing was Boston's No. 1 draft pick. Injuries limited his NBA career to just 24 games over two seasons, yet in 1974 he would be a member of the NBA champion Boston Celtics.

Bill Garrett and Don Schlundt

These two All-America centers are grouped together because both were drafted by NBA teams, although neither would play in the NBA for various reasons.

Bill Garrett was born on April 4, 1929, in Shelbyville, Indiana. Don Schlundt was born on March 14, 1932, in St. Joseph County. In 1951 Garrett was selected by the Boston Celtics in the second round of the draft, becoming the third black player ever drafted by an NBA team. Schlundt was picked by Syracuse in the second round of the 1955 NBA Draft. Shortly after Garrett was drafted, he was called to military service.

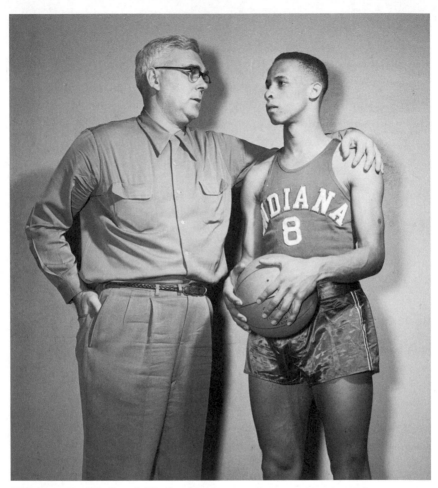

Bill Garrett with Coach McCracken (Indiana University Archives, P0038009)

When Garrett returned from his tour of duty, he was cut from the Celtics' roster. He spent time with the Harlem Globetrotters before becoming the head coach of Crispus Attucks High School in 1957. Schlundt never really considered an NBA career because he was married and knew he could make more money for his family by selling insurance.

Both of these players' lives crossed in various ways. Garrett's last year at IU was the 1950–51 season, while Schlundt's first year at Indiana began in the 1951–52 school year. Bill Garrett represented both a first and last in college basketball. Garrett was the first regular African American basketball player in the Big Ten. And he would be the last 6'3" center to win All-American honors.

Garrett had won the Mr. Basketball award in the state of Indiana in 1947 while leading his Shelbyville team to the 1947 state championship. Garrett was indeed an Indiana Mr. Basketball, not only in high school but at IU as well. Garrett was not only a pioneer for African Americans in the Big Ten, he would lead the Hoosiers in scoring all three seasons.

Garrett passed former teammate Lou Watson as Indiana's all-time-leading scorer with a career total of 792 points. After Garrett's career with the Globetrotters, his coaching of Cripsus Attucks brought him continued success. Garrett led Attucks to the 1959 Indiana High School state championship, becoming at the time the first man to both play for and coach a state championship team. Bill passed away on August 7, 1974, from a heart attack and was buried in Crown Hill Cemetery in Indianapolis.

Schlundt succeeded Garrett as the center on Indiana's basketball team. Don came to IU by way of a great high school career at Washington Clay High School in South Bend, Indiana. Indiana center Jim Schooley hosted Schlundt on his visit to IU. Don very much wanted to be in the fraternity that Schooley was in (Theta Pi Beta), so they meshed well. In fact, Schlundt told Coach McCracken he would come to Indiana with one condition: that he could room with Schooley.

Schooley's assessment of Schlundt was that, "Don was a natural guard." Dr. Marvin Christie described him as a "big boy who could handle himself like a guard," which was very unusual back then. Don could feed his teammates and set them up for a pass when they would go for the bucket. Don was very quick with his feet and he would sidestep his defender when going to the basket to avoid a charging foul. He could play McCracken basketball, which is to say he could run the floor as well as the little guys who could play Hurryin' Hoosier ball.

Schlundt was able to play as a freshman because of the temporary rules allowing freshmen to play due to the Korean War. During his freshman year, Indiana finished 16–6 and fourth in the Big Ten, and Schlundt led IU in scoring with 17.1 points per game. It was during his sophomore year that he and Indiana achieved the ultimate glory. Indiana's season was off to a slow start after a win over Valparaiso. Indiana lost its next two games—to Notre Dame by one (71–70) and to Kansas State by two (82–80)—both on the road. After that, Indiana won its next 17 games. Schlundt scored 39 points at Ann Arbor and would follow with 33 points in games against Michigan State, Butler, and Illinois.

In the 1953 NCAA tourney, Schlundt racked up 23 against DePaul, then helped knock off Notre Dame, scoring 41 points in an unstoppable performance. In the Final Four, Schlundt totaled 29 against LSU in a 80–67 win that put Indiana into the final. Then, in the championship game against Kansas, Don led all scorers with 30 points in a 69–68 victory that gave the Hoosiers their second national championship. Schlundt received many honors for the season, including All-America, All–Final Four, All–Big Ten, and Big Ten MVP.

During Schlundt's junior year, Indiana would repeat as Big Ten champs while Schlundt would repeat as All-America and All–Big Ten. His senior year was a disappointment from the team's aspect, as Indiana finished 6–14. But for Schlundt, the honors kept coming in. For the third year in a row, he was an All-American and the Big Ten's leading scorer, with a 26 points per game average.

By the time Schlundt's career ended, he was Indiana's and the Big Ten's scoring leader with 2,132 points. In his final game at Indiana against Ohio State, Schlundt matched his career high of 47 points and set Big Ten records by hitting 25-of-30 free throws in an 84–66 win. Don Schlundt passed away from stomach cancer on October 10, 1985, in Indianapolis at the age of 53.

Eric Gordon

Eric Gordon was born Christmas Day, December 25, 1988, in Indianapolis, Indiana. Gordon played his high school ball at Indianapolis North Central High School, earning Mr. Basketball honors in 2007. After committing to Illinois, Gordon switched to IU. Although he played only one season at IU, Gordon led Indiana and the Big Ten in scoring that season with a 21.5 average.

Indiana finished 25–8 with Gordon, good for third in the Big Ten. The 6'4" guard was named Big Ten Freshman of the Year and third-team All-America. After Gordon's one year at IU, he entered the NBA Draft. He was the Los Angeles Clippers' No. 1 pick in the 2008 draft and the seventh overall pick. Gordon's career has taken him to the Clippers, Hornets, Pelicans, and Rockets so far, averaging 16.5 points a game overall.

Greg Graham

Born on November 26, 1970, in Indianapolis, Indiana, Greg Graham played at Indianapolis Warren Central High School. He came to Indiana after an outstanding all-star high school career and was a member of one of the most heralded recruiting classes in IU history in 1989.

On February 21, 1993, at Assembly Hall, Graham would have his greatest game as a Hoosier against in-state rival Purdue. On that Sunday afternoon, Graham led all scorers with 32 points. But it was how they came about that was so unusual. Graham connected on 2-of-3 three-pointers and was just 2-for-7 from the field. However, he would shoot 28 free throws that day, connecting on 26 of them. As Coach Knight said afterward, "We were using our 'Greg Graham Shoots Fouls' offense today, so we had to leave him in." The "Greg Graham Offense" resulted in an Indiana 93–78 victory.

Graham, a 6'4" guard, finished his Indiana career in the top 15 for scoring at IU with 1,590 points. He was selected by the Charlotte Hornets in the first round as the 17th overall pick of the 1993 draft.

Graham played five years in the NBA for Charlotte, Philadelphia, New Jersey, Seattle, and Cleveland, averaging 4.5 points a game.

A.J. Guyton

A.J. Guyton was born on February 12, 1978, in Peoria, Illinois. He played at Central High School in Peoria and chose to attend Indiana in 1996 near the end of Coach Knight's career at IU.

Guyton said of his Indiana career, "We had a lot of good wins. Those were the best four years of my life. I wouldn't change a thing. I would go back to Indiana and do it all over again." Guyton ended up with 2,100 points, the fourth most in Hoosiers history. He was honored as an All-American, All–Big Ten, and Big Ten MVP in his senior year.

Guyton was selected by the Chicago Bulls in the second round of the 2000 NBA Draft. He played for both the Bulls and Warriors in his two years in the NBA. After a few very successful years of coaching, as of 2016 Guyton had accepted a position as an assistant coach with the Windy City Bulls of the NBA's Development League.

Kirk Haston

Born on March 10, 1979, in Lobelville, Tennessee, Kirk Haston led Perry County High School in Linden, Tennessee, to a 37–0 record and a Class A state championship his senior year. In 1998 Coach Knight brought the Tennessee Mr. Basketball to an Indiana team that finished third in the Big Ten. As a freshman, Haston scored nearly 10 points a game. After that season, on May 5, 1999, Haston's whole world was turned upside down. Haston had just finished his finals and had returned home when he noticed he had missed a few phone calls from his Granddad. He called his Granddad back only to learn that his mom had been killed by a tornado that had gone through his hometown.

Haston returned to Lobelville the next day and had been home for no more than 10 minutes when a knock on the door revealed Coach Knight and all of his assistant coaches. Knight took Haston into the kitchen and listened as the memories of the young man's mother flowed. Then Knight told Haston that he was going through some tough times, but he knew that he could handle it because of how his mom had raised him. Knight leaned forward and said, "I know you have that kind of toughness in you because your mom had that kind of toughness in her."

In the summer of 1999 Knight kept Haston busy, sending him on the Big Ten All-Star Tour. He also sent both Haston and his Granddad to work at coach Rick Majerus' basketball camp at the University of Utah.

By Haston's sophomore year, Indiana and Coach Knight faced controversy near the end of the season when Knight was fired by the university. Haston was selected as an Academic All–Big Ten player while averaging 15.3 points a game. He was also selected All-America and All–Big Ten.

Haston left Indiana after his junior year and was drafted as the NBA's 16th overall player in the 2001 NBA Draft by the Charlotte Hornets. Haston's NBA career was brief, as he averaged 1.2 points in 27 games. In 2010 Haston returned to his high school alma mater. As of 2017, Haston was still coaching there and had led his alma mater to three state championships.

Alan Henderson

Alan Henderson was born on December 2, 1972, in Morgantown, West Virginia. He played his high school career at Brebeuf Jesuit Preparatory School in Indianapolis, Indiana. In 1991 Henderson was named to the McDonald's All-America team while leading his high school team to the state finals. Henderson travelled down south from Indianapolis to join a loaded team in Bloomington as a 6'9" forward.

Henderson made his Hoosiers debut with 20 points and eight rebounds against 11th-ranked UCLA. For his freshman season, Henderson averaged 11.6 points and 7.2 rebounds a game. In 1993, Henderson's sophomore year, the Hoosiers won the Big Ten title with a 17–1 record, while posting a 31–4 overall mark. Indiana spent the entire season ranked in the top 10, never dropping lower than No. 4

and finishing the regular season ranked No. 1. Henderson had torn his ACL in practice before the Purdue game that year and would miss the final six games of the Big Ten season. He tried to play in the NCAA tournament but wasn't effective. He finished the year averaging 11.1 points and 8.1 rebounds.

In Henderson's junior year, Indiana finished 21–9 while he averaged 17.8 points and 10.3 rebounds. In his senior year, Indiana again finished third in the Big Ten while he won All-America honors with 23.5 points per game—the most ever for a Knight player at IU—and 9.7 rebounds a game. Henderson left IU as the school's all-time leading rebounder with 1,091 boards, three more than Walt Bellamy's 1,088.

Henderson was selected in the first round, the 16th overall player, in the 1995 NBA Draft by the Atlanta Hawks. He would also play for Dallas, Cleveland, and Philadelphia in the NBA. In 1998 Henderson was selected as the NBA's Most Improved Player. For his career, Henderson scored 5,094 points and collected 3,249 rebounds.

Jared Jeffries

Born on November 25, 1981, in Bloomington, Indiana, Jared Jeffries started at Bloomington North High School. Selected as both a McDonald's All-American and Indiana's Mr. Basketball, Jeffries led Bloomington North to the Indiana high school finals in 2000 before losing to Marion High School.

Jeffries joined the Hoosiers in 2000 at the time Bob Knight departed and coach Mike Davis took over the reins of the IU program. During Jeffries' freshman year, he started every game and averaged 13.8 points and 6.9 rebounds. In addition, Jeffries was named the Big Ten Freshman of the Year.

As a sophomore, Jeffries, the 2000 Gatorade National Player of the Year, became the go-to man in the Hoosiers offense and the stopper inside on the IU defense. Indiana entered the NCAA tourney as co-champions in the Big Ten. Against No. 1 Duke, Jeffries provided Indiana with a huge spark, hitting for 24 points and gathering 15 rebounds in the Hoosiers' stunning victory. The Hoosiers would lose in the NCAA Championship Game, but Jeffries had a stellar season. He was named All-America, All–Big Ten, and Big Ten MVP.

Jeffries was the 11th pick in the 2002 NBA Draft, by the Washington Wizards. He also played for the New York Knicks, Houston Rockets, and Portland Trail Blazers. Jeffries scored 3,003 points, collected 2,563 rebounds, and handed out 798 assists in his career. Jeffries became a personnel scout for the Denver Nuggets, and in 2013 he was the host of a fishing show on TV.

Scott May

Scott May was born on March 19, 1954, in Sandusky, Ohio. After an outstanding high school career, May came to IU in what turned out to be one of the best recruiting classes ever. May's grades were not what they needed to be, so he was declared academically ineligible as a freshman, By his sophomore year, however, he and the team were ready to go on one of the best runs in IU and Big Ten history. Indiana would go 23–5 in May's sophomore year, tie for the Big Ten title, then lose to Michigan in a one-game playoff to determine which school would represent the Big Ten in the NCAA tournament. They lost by eight at Champaign, Illinois, on March 11, 1974. The loss sent IU to the newly formed CCA Tournament, which Indiana would win, and began a new journey that would last for two years. May averaged 12.5 points his sophomore year, but greater things were on the horizon.

In May's junior year, Indiana appeared unbeatable. They would run through the pre-conference season unbeaten, then go 18–0 for a record in the Big Ten season. IU would beat Purdue by one on the road, but lost in another way. May fractured his arm in the first half of the Purdue game and was lost to Indiana at that point.

On March 20, 1975, Indiana played a rematch with Kentucky in Dayton, Ohio, to see which team would go to the Final Four. The Hoosiers were 31–0. Knight would start May, who played with a huge cast on his arm. May was not the same player, and without a healthy

Scott May connects as Indiana rolls (Indiana University Archives, P0043394)

May, Indiana lost 92–90. On the year, May averaged 16.3 points and 6.6 rebounds a game. May was selected All-America, All–Big Ten, and the Big Ten's MVP.

In 1976, nothing would deter the Hoosiers from their goal. In the NCAA Championship Game, Indiana defeated Michigan for a third time to capture the title behind May's 26 points and eight rebounds. On the year, Scott May was named National Player of the Year, All-America, All–Final Four, All–Big Ten, and Big Ten MVP. He was also named Adolph Rupp Trophy winner, Helms Foundation Player of the Year, AP College Player of the Year, UPI Player of the Year, and Sporting News College Player of the Year.

May was the overall No. 2 pick in the NBA Draft by the Chicago Bulls and named to the All-Rookie first-team in 1977. May played for the Bulls, Bucks, and Pistons, as well as in Europe. For his NBA career, May averaged 10.4 points a game, 4.1 rebounds, and 1.7 assists. Today, May owns more than 2,000 apartments in Bloomington.

George McGinnis

George McGinnis was born on August 12, 1950, in Indianapolis. McGinnis started at Indianapolis Washington High School in both football and basketball, dominating in both sports as few ever have. In McGinnis's senior year, along with teammate Steve Downing, McGinnis led Indianapolis Washington to an undefeated season and an Indiana state championship in basketball. Along the way, McGinnis gathered Mr. Basketball honors for the state of Indiana. McGinnis and Downing remained teammates as they headed south from Indianapolis to Bloomington and IU.

It was a time in college basketball when freshmen were ineligible to play, so Hoosiers fans had a long year's wait before they could see this Superman of youth grace the hardwood with his talent. But once McGinnis could play, Hoosiers fans knew it was worth the wait. The Hoosiers' first opponent was Eastern Michigan, and McGinnis did not disappoint the Hoosier faithful, leading Indiana to a 99–82 victory in

front of a capacity crowd. McGinnis scored 26 points while collecting 11 rebounds. In his second game, McGinnis's 26 points and 10
rebounds helped Indiana snap Kansas State's 17-game home winning
streak with a 75–72 victory. In the Kentucky game, McGinnis had 38
points and 20 rebounds.

In his one year at IU, McGinnis was selected All-America and All–Big
Ten. He left Indiana with a season record of 29.9 points per game and
an impressive 14.9 rebounds per game.

After the death of his father, McGinnis decided to turn pro and leave
Indiana University. The Indiana Pacers turned to the hometown hero,
and it was a match made in heaven. McGinnis helped lead the Pacers
to two ABA championships, being named the MVP of the 1973 ABA
playoffs. He was selected the MVP for the ABA in 1975. McGinnis left
the Pacers and the ABA to join the NBA's Philadelphia 76ers, becoming a three-time NBA All-Star, making the All NBA first-team in 1976.
In his career, McGinnis played for Indiana, Philadelphia, Denver, and
then Indiana again. McGinnis averaged 17.2 points and 9.8 rebounds
in his stellar professional career. Today, McGinnis still works for the
Pacers.

Jon McGlocklin

Jon McGlocklin was born on June 10, 1943, in Franklin, Indiana.
McGlocklin led Franklin High School in scoring and became an all-
state player in 1961. He joined the Van Arsdale twins—Dick and
Tom—as well as Steve Redenbaugh and Al Harden to form a very
solid recruiting class from Indiana high schools for coach Branch
McCracken.

As a junior, McGlocklin scored at least 20 points in six of Indiana's last
eight games, averaging 15.7 on the season.

McGlocklin's senior year would be one of the most enjoyable seasons
in IU history. Coach McCracken looked at McGlocklin as an extremely
versatile player who could do well at guard, center, and forward. At
guard, he would give the Hoosiers a big man and a stronger scoring

potential, both from inside and outside. McGlocklin teamed so well with the Vans he was called the third twin. During his senior year, McGlocklin finished with a 17.2 scoring average and 4.1 rebounds a game.

After graduating from Indiana, McGlocklin was selected in Round 3, the 24th pick overall in the NBA Draft, by the Cincinnati Royals. McGlocklin spent three seasons with the Royals before being traded to the San Diego Rockets. Then, in 1968, McGlocklin would be picked up by the Milwaukee Bucks, the second overall pick in the NBA's expansion draft. McGlocklin became an NBA All-Star in 1969 for the Bucks and became a starting member of the NBA champion Bucks in 1971. McGlocklin had his No. 14 retired by the Bucks after his career, in which he averaged 11.6 points and 2.4 rebounds a game. McGlocklin became the voice of the Bucks for 25 years and started the MACC Fund to fight childhood cancer.

Victor Oladipo

Born on May 4, 1992, in Silver Springs, Maryland, Victor Oladipo played at the famous De Matha Catholic Program in Hyattsville, Maryland. Oladipo's senior year saw him average 11.9 points, 10.3 rebounds, and 3.6 blocks per game. Oladipo led De Matha to the city championship. Oladipo was selected to the Washington Post 2010 All-Met First-Team. He was ranked No. 144 overall in his class. Indiana coach Tom Crean saw something others didn't and recruited Oladipo, and his efforts paid off.

As a freshman, Oladipo started five games, the first against Penn State on December 27. He collected 14 points, four rebounds, three steals, and two assists in 27 minutes. For Oladipo, his freshman year averages were 7.4 points, 3.7 rebounds, and one steal in 18 minutes a game. It became clear that, even as a freshman, he was one of IU's better players.

In Oladipo's sophomore year, Indiana would improve its win total by 15 games, including a game in Bloomington against No. 1 Kentucky, a game Indiana won on a last-second three-pointer, giving Indiana a one-point win. Oladipo continued his overall improvement, scoring at a 10.9 clip and becoming not only the best defender in Indiana but one of the best defenders in the Big Ten. He was voted by many to be the most improved player during his sophomore year. Indiana advanced to the Sweet Sixteen in the NCAA tournament by defeating New Mexico State and VCU.

Oladipo's junior year was full of hope for both Indiana and Oladipo. ESPN reporter Eamonn Brennan wrote, "In two-and-a-half seasons in Bloomington, Oladipo has morphed from a raw athletic specimen to a defensive specialist/energy glue guy—he became a hit with IU fans for holding his hand in front of his face after dunks at home, typically after a steal he himself created—into a sudden, stunning, bona fide collegiate star." He ranked third in the nation in field-goal percentage at 61.4.

In a February 2 game at home against No. 1 Michigan, Oladipo guarded four different players on 45 possessions, allowing just four points. Indiana won its first outright Big Ten title since 1993. Oladipo started all 36 games, averaging 13.6 points, 6.3 rebounds, and 2.1 steals per game. Oladipo's performance and year were so outstanding that he was named the Sporting News Men's College Basketball Player of the Year, the National Co-Defensive Player of the Year, and first-team All-America. He would also be named to the Big Ten first-team and was the Big Ten Defensive Player of the Year.

Oladipo was the second player picked overall in the 2013 NBA Draft by the Orlando Magic. Oladipo recorded his first NBA triple-double on December 3, 2013, against the Philadelphia 76ers with 26 points, 10 rebounds, and 10 assists. Oladipo set a career record 14 assists to go along with 30 points, and nine rebounds in a double-overtime victory over New York. Oladipo finished second in the Rookie of the Year voting. On March 18, 2015, Oladipo scored a career high 45 points against the Cleveland Cavaliers. Oladipo was traded to the Oklahoma City Thunder on June 23, 2016.

Jimmy Rayl

Jimmy Rayl was born on June 21, 1941, in Kokomo, Indiana (with, many would swear, a basketball in his hand). Jim played at Kokomo High School in Indiana. Rayl was a real high school hero in every sense of the word, he led Kokomo to the championship game in 1959, losing to Indianapolis Crispus Attucks. Rayl was named the Trester Award winner and Indiana's 1959 Mr. Basketball. But Rayl's most memorable high school game probably came in his senior year at New Castle in front of a standing-room-only crowd of 2,200 in the old New Castle gym. Standout shooters Ray Pavy of New Castle and Rayl of Kokomo were both going for the scoring title, with Rayl holding a nine-point lead heading into the game. The shootout was everything it was supposed to be. New Castle won 92–81, but Rayl won the scoring title as he shot 18-of-33 for 49 points, while Pavy scored 51 points.

Rayl came to Indiana, and in his own words, it was a match made in heaven. Rayl loved to shoot, and McCracken loved for the 6'2", 140-pound guard to shoot. In Rayl's first game at IU, he scored 12 points, connecting on six baskets in a Hoosiers win over Indiana State. However, on the year, Rayl averaged just four points a game with a high of 13 against Minnesota. But his next year at IU was a completely different story. Rayl started the season against Drake with 14 points and then poured in 34 against New Mexico State. The scoring in big numbers was on.

Archie Dees told of coming back to Bloomington and playing Horse with Rayl. "I've never seen anything like it. Rayl would only play me netters. I could make my shots any way I could—hit the rim, off the backboard, whatever. But for Jim, netters meant his had to be swishes. If it hit the rim, it didn't count. But I never beat him, ever. Like I said, I've never seen anything like it." Former IU guard Sam Gee said, "I saw Bobby Leonard, Steve Alford, all those guys. Rayl was the best. He was a pure shooter." Bobby Leonard said of Rayl, "He had the best variety of shots I've seen. He could really shoot."

During Rayl's junior year, the scoring continued to mount. On the season, Rayl set the IU scoring mark of 29.8 points a game (since passed

High-scoring Jimmy Rayl puts in two versus Purdue (Indiana University Archives, P0029318)

by George McGinnis at 29.9 a game). The highlight of Rayl's junior year came against Minnesota at Bloomington on January 27, 1962, in an overtime game. Minnesota took a one-point lead with seven seconds left. Rayl brought the ball upcourt and crossed the midcourt stripe. Rayl, knowing time was running out, let fly a shot from 30 to

35 feet away. The ball hit its mark, and IU won 105–104. That, however, is only half the story. By hitting that shot, Rayl scored his 56th point, setting a new IU and Big Ten mark.

During Rayl's senior year, he averaged 25.3 points a game. He scored 20 or more points in 19 of the 24 games that season. Again, Rayl provided highlights for Indiana fans and caused Michigan State fans to rejoice that he was graduating. At East Lansing, Rayl dropped 44 points on the Spartans in a 96–84 Hoosiers victory. Then, on February 23, 1963, Rayl lit up the Spartans for 56 in Bloomington, setting a record of most points in a regulation game and setting a record for most shots taken in a game with 48 shots.

In 1963 Rayl was drafted by the Cincinnati Royals in the third round of the NBA Draft. Rayl started his post-Indiana career with the Goodyear AAU team out of Akron, Ohio, and celebrated a championship with them. In 1968 the ABA was formed, and the new league's Indiana franchise wanted to feature as many Indiana natives as possible.

Rayl signed with the Pacers for $15,000 and $17,500 for his second year. In his first year, he averaged 12 points a game with a high of 32. In his second season, he averaged 8.9 points a game. In retirement, Rayl worked for Xerox in Indianapolis.

Ray Tolbert

Born September 10, 1958, in Anderson, Indiana, Ray Tolbert played at Anderson Madison Heights, where he would be an Indiana All-Star, a McDonald's All-American, and an Indiana Mr. Basketball.

Tolbert came to Indiana in 1977. His freshman year saw him contribute right away as Indiana looked for a big man. In a game against SMU in Indianapolis, Tolbert chipped in 14 points. On January 19 in Bloomington, he scored 24 points and grabbed eight rebounds as IU defeated Ohio State. For his freshman year, Tolbert scored 10.1 points a game with 6.7 rebounds.

Tolbert's sophomore year saw the Hoosiers winning a championship, just not one fans were used to. It wasn't the Big Ten, where they finished fifth. It wasn't the NCAA championship—they didn't make it there. It was the NIT. For the year, Tolbert averaged 10.3 points and 7.2 rebounds a game.

But what a year Tolbert's senior year would be. The season began slow, with IU starting out 7–5. Indiana would turn things around to finish 26–9 and grab first place in the Big Ten with a 14–4 record. Indiana won its first NCAA game over Maryland 99–64 behind Tolbert and Landon Turner, who combined for 46 points and 15 rebounds. Indiana would go on to win its fourth NCAA championship with Ray Tolbert, Randy Wittman, Isiah Thomas, and Landon Turner leading the way. For the season, Tolbert averaged 12 points and 6.4 rebounds while being named the Big Ten's MVP.

In 1981 Tolbert was selected by the New Jersey Nets in the first round, the 18th pick overall. In Tolbert's NBA career, he played for the Nets, Supersonics, Pistons, Knicks, Lakers, and Hawks while scoring 928 points. Tolbert lives today in Fishers, Indiana, where he is a varsity assistant at Fishers High School.

Bill Tosheff

Born on June 2, 1926, in Gary, Indiana, Tosheff captained basketball, football, baseball, and track at Gary Froebel, where he was all-city and all-conference in basketball.

Tosheff traveled south to Bloomington to play for Branch McCracken and IU from 1948 to 1951 after spending time in the army during World War II. In his very first college game, Tosheff was the second leading scorer with 10 points in a 61–48 Indiana victory over DePaul. Tosheff was a consistent scorer for IU from the outset, scoring 8–11 points in each of his first six games.

Tosheff's high as a sophomore was 18 points, which he did twice, both times against Purdue, as Indiana swept the season series with the Boilermakers. Indiana finished fourth in the Big Ten in 1948–49.

In Tosheff's junior year, Indiana finished third in the Big Ten, finishing 17–5 overall and being ranked 20th in the nation at the end of the season. Tosheff averaged 8.3 and 7.5 his first two years, but his playmaking was just as important.

In Tosheff's senior year, Indiana moved one notch closer to first in the Big Ten, finishing second with an overall record of 19–3. On the year, IU finished ranked No. 7 in the country. Tosheff's big games scoring-wise this year came against Iowa where, as against Purdue his sophomore year, he scored the same point total both games: 19 points.

In 1951 Tosheff was drafted by the Indianapolis Olympians. He played for the Olympians as well as for the Milwaukee Hawks. In 1952 Tosheff was named NBA Co-Rookie of the Year. In 1988 Tosheff founded the pre-1965 NBA Players Association in order to secure fair pension plans for the NBA players who were active before 1965. Tosheff helped to close a loophole that said players before 1965 had to have five years of service, while after 1965 players only needed three years of service to get the NBA pension.

On October 1, 2011, Tosheff died from cancer at the age of 85.

Dick and Tom Van Arsdale

The twins have to be mentioned together. They were born on February 22, 1943, in Indianapolis, Indiana. They were identical twins in every sense of the word. They attended Emmerich Manual High School in Indianapolis, where they starred not only in basketball, but also in baseball and track. They led Manual to two sectionals, two regionals, and one semi-state championship. Their senior year, they took Manual to the state championship game only to lose to Kokomo in overtime.

They both made all-state and All-America high school teams. They shared the Trester Award, given to athletes who best combined mental attitude, scholarship, and athletic ability. The twins shared Indiana's Mr. Basketball for 1961. Dick finished first in his class with straight As; Tom finished third with one B. Tom was 15 minutes older than Dick.

The twins declared their intentions to enroll at Indiana University after their senior year. McCracken called it one of his greatest recruiting jobs ever. But it wasn't really that hard; the recruiting had been set in motion long before, as the Vans enjoyed watching Don Schlundt and Bob Leonard lead the 1953 Hoosiers to the national championship.

The Vans came to Indiana after their stellar high school career and began their IU career on December 1, 1962, against Virginia before a sold-out crowd of 10,344 Hoosiers fans. For the thirty-something generation, to understand the popularity of the Vans, first put it in context of Damon Bailey, or for today's generation, maybe Cody Zeller. But they were *big*, much bigger than their 6'5" frames. Well, in that first game sharing the spotlight with seniors Jimmy Rayl and Tom Bolyard, the Vans showed they were worth the wait. Dick had 11 in that game, and Tom had nine. That was some day, bucket fans. Not only did IU win 90–59, Rayl would begin his senior year with 35 points. To top the day off, Phil Dickens brought the "Old Oaken Bucket" in for fans to see as IU had defeated Purdue 12–7 to return the bucket for the first time since 1947.

The Vans' first IU team finished 13–11 with a Big Ten third-place finish. Their sophomore year, Tom scored 299 points for a 12.5 average, while Dick scored 292 for a 12.2 average. Tom's top game of 26 came against Michigan, while Dick's top was also 26 points, against Wisconsin.

The Vans' junior year was a tough year record-wise, as Indiana lost its two top scorers—Jimmy Rayl, who was second in the Big Ten in scoring; and Tom Bolyard, who was third in the conference. In their second game as juniors against Notre Dame, a 108–102 victory at Fort Wayne, Tom and Dick both scored career highs on the same night. Both hit 15 field goals, but Dick hit 12 free throws to Tom's four, giving Dick a career high of 42 points, while Tom's was 34.

McCracken said of the Vans, "They're two of the finest we've ever had. Last year they had all the pressure in the world on them, but they came through like champions. This year, I'll be greatly surprised if they're not greater yet. They're smart and they were learning all the time last season. That experience will show. Both are hitting much better from the outside, and their ability to connect from outside should make their driving game more effective." On the year, Dick averaged 22.3 points, while Tom scored at a 21.3 average. Dick was named to the All–Big Ten first-team, Tom to the second-team.

As the Vans began their senior year, McCracken would say of his two stars, "I think the twins are in for their best season yet. They've been tremendous the last two seasons, but that experience makes them more poised and able to use finesse where they might have been inclined to use strength before." The Vans' last season was also McCracken's last season, and they closed this chapter in Indiana basketball on a high note. Indiana finished the 1964–65 season with a 19–5 record in the Big Ten, good for fourth place, and were champions of the Memphis State Invitational. Indiana won their first nine games and were ranked as high as second in the nation. They finished the season winning their last three games, including the Vans' last home game against Purdue, 90–79. Tom had 19 and Dick had 14 in their last home game. Dick scored 21 and Tom 18 in their last game at IU, a win at Wisconsin. Tom and Dick were both selected All-America and All–Big Ten.

Tom finished the 1964–65 season with a 18.4 average, while Dick averaged 17.2. In their careers at Indiana, Tom scored 1,252 points, while Dick scored 1,240. Tom gathered 723 rebounds, while Dick had 719. In 72 games as Hoosiers, Tom averaged 17.4 points and 10 rebounds a game, while Dick averaged 17.2 and 10.

Dick was selected in the second round, the 10th overall pick by the New York Knicks. Tom was selected in the second round, the 11th overall pick by the Detroit Pistons. Dick started as a small forward for three years for the Knicks. Tom started at guard for the Pistons, and both wore No. 5. Both Tom and Dick were selected NBA All-Rookie First-Team in 1966.

The twins—Tom (25) and Dick (30) Van Arsdale—two-time Indiana MVPs (Indiana University Archives, P0021965)

In 1968 Dick was the first pick of the Phoenix Suns in the expansion draft, the first overall. He played his next nine years in the NBA for the Suns and is remembered as the "Original Sun," scoring the first points in Suns history. While a Sun, he made three NBA All-Star teams and the NBA All-Defensive Second-Team in 1974. Dick is a member of the Phoenix Suns Ring of Honor, and his No. 5 was retired by the Suns. During his 12 seasons, Dick scored 15,079 points for a 16.4 average.

Tom played three years in Detroit. During his third year, he was traded to the Royals, where he teamed up with his hero in high school, Oscar Robertson. While playing for Cincinnati, Tom, like Dick, made three NBA All-Star teams. Tom went from the Cincinnati Royals/Kansas City-Omaha Kings to the Philadelphia 76ers. From there he went to the Hawks, and finally, during his 12th and final season, Tom teamed with Dick in Phoenix, where he took the No. 4 jersey. During his 12 years, Tom scored 14,232 points for a 15.3 average.

The twins live with their families in Phoenix. Dick suffered a stroke in 2005 and now does works of art.

D.J. White

Born August 31, 1986, in Tuscaloosa, Alabama, D.J. White was a high school standout at Hillcrest High School. White, recruited by Mike Davis at Indiana, became Davis' prize recruit. White was a Parade Magazine All-American, and Alabama Gatorade Player of the Year in high school. In 2005 White was selected as Big Ten Freshman of the year. As a senior, White was named the 2008 Big Ten MVP while finishing second in the Big Ten in scoring with a 17.4 average. White led the Big Ten in rebounds with 10 a game. He also led the Big Ten in field-goal percentage. White was named second-team All-America. He became the first Indiana player since Alan Henderson to average a double-double. White finished his career at Indiana with 1,447 points and 748 rebounds.

White was drafted in the first round of the NBA Draft, the 29th over-all pick, by the Detroit Pistons before being traded to Oklahoma City. White also played for Charlotte and Boston, averaging 5.9 points a game.

Randy Wittman

Randy Wittman was born on October 28, 1959, in Indianapolis, Indiana. Wittman played at Ben Davis High School. Wittman became the first Ben Davis player to be selected to the all-state team and become an Indiana All-Star, as he averaged 23 points a game, making him one of the most sought-after players in the nation in 1978. During his senior year, he shot 58 percent from the floor and 73 percent from the line. Wittman's backcourt teammate at Ben Davis was Tim Wilbur, IU's football hero in the Holiday Bowl.

Wittman's freshman year saw him play the role of point guard. At 6'6" and being a lethal outside shooter, he was a great asset for the Hoosiers. Wittman was a very important part of Indiana's NIT championship in 1979.

In Wittman's sophomore season, Indiana was ranked No. 1 for the prescason, and it looked as if the Hoosiers could contend for the NCAA title; however, in IU's fifth game, Wittman went out of the game early in the second half, never to return all season long due to a stress fracture in his foot. This was a major blow to the Hoosiers because Randy had led Indiana in minutes played the season before.

In Randy's third year, what had been prophesied for the year before came true in 1981. In the NCAA Championship Game, Wittman was 7-of-13 from the floor and 2-for-2 from the line for 16 points in Indiana's 63–50 victory over North Carolina. On the season, Wittman was named Academic All–Big Ten while scoring 10.4 points per game.

During Wittman's final year, he led IU in scoring with 19 points a game. Along the way, he picked up All-America, All–Big Ten, and Big Ten MVP honors.

Wittman was picked in the first round of the NBA Draft by the Washington Bullets. He was then traded to the Atlanta Hawks, where he played for five years before joining the Sacramento Kings for one season, ending his playing career back home in Indianapolis for the Pacers for three seasons. In his career, Wittman scored 4,034 points for a 7.4 average, and handed out 1,201 assists. After his playing career ended, Wittman began coaching, first as an assistant for the Pacers, then the Timberwolves, and then as head coach for the Cleveland Cavaliers. He went back as an assistant for the Timberwolves, and then the Magic, before dipping into the head coaching waters again with Minnesota, then the Wizards before becoming an assistant one more time.

Mike Woodson

Born March 24, 1958, in Indianapolis, Indiana, Mike Woodson played at Indianapolis Broad Ripple High School. As a Ripple Rocket, Woodson's skill shined through as he averaged 28.6 points a game as a senior. Those skills landed Woodson a spot as a member of the all-state team, as well as a member of the Indiana All-Star team, where he was the leading scorer in the team's annual summer battle against the Kentucky High School All-Stars.

During his freshman year at IU, Woodson scored 500 points for an 18.5 average. In his sophomore year, he scored more than 20 points 14 times on the season, and he became only the second Hoosier to score over 1,000 points by his sophomore year. He was selected second-team All–Big Ten for the second year in a row. Woodson was also voted to the Indiana and Gator Bowl Classic all-tournament teams. Woody led Indiana in scoring with a 19.9 average in his second year in Bloomington.

In 1979, Woodson's junior year, Indiana fell to fifth in the Big Ten, yet there was a little surprise in store for this Hoosiers team. It would occur in the last regular season game, when IU travelled to Champaign, Illinois, to play No. 1 Illinois. Woodson hit on 18 of 27 field goals, connecting on 12 of 14 from the line for an outstanding

48-point performance to lead Indiana to a 72–60 upset of the top-ranked team in the nation. The victory vaulted Indiana into the NIT tournament where Indiana won all four tourney games, including wins over Ohio State and Purdue. On the year, Woodson was named All-America and All–Big Ten while averaging 21 points a game.

Woodson entered his senior year needing 402 points to pass Don Schlundt as Indiana's all-time leading scorer and 322 points in the Big Ten to pass Michael Thompson's Big Ten mark. But in the fifth game of the season at Lexington, Kentucky, Woodson hurt his back. He played in the next game, scoring 19 in a win over Toledo. However, it was found after the game that he had a herniated disk, requiring surgery. Woodson missed much of the rest of the season. After missing 15 games, Woodson returned at Iowa with six Big Ten games left. He scored 18 points to lead Indiana over Iowa. Next, behind Woodson's 24, Indiana beat Minnesota. Indiana went on the road up north, defeating both Michigan State and Michigan as Woodson scored 24 against the Wolverines. Indiana won its last two to win the Big Ten title. Woodson won the Big Ten MVP playing in only six Big Ten games out of 18. He also was selected All-America and All–Big Ten.

Selected in the first round, the 12th overall pick in the 1980 NBA Draft by the New York Knicks, Woodson began his NBA career. Besides the Knicks, Woodson's time in the NBA saw him play for New Jersey, Kansas City, Sacramento, the Los Angeles Clippers, Houston, and Cleveland. Overall, in 11 years in the NBA, Woodson scored 10,981 points for a 14-point average, rebounded 1,838 for a 2.3 average, and dished out 1,822 assists for a 2.3 average. When Woodson's playing career was over, he began coaching in the NBA. His first step as an NBA assistant coach was in Milwaukee. After three years, Woodson moved on to Cleveland for two years, then Philadelphia for two, and Detroit for one. At that point, Woodson moved on to becoming the head coach for the Atlanta Hawks, a job that lasted six years. Woodson moved on to New York as an assistant for one year before taking over the head coaching responsibilities for two years. In 2014 Woodson became an assistant for the Clippers, where he was as of the 2016 season.

Cody Zeller

Born October 5, 1992, in Winona, Minnesota, Cody Zeller played his high school basketball in Washington, Indiana, for Washington High School, as did his two older brothers. Zeller played on a state championship team three times. Zeller was named both Indiana Mr. Basketball and a 2011 McDonald's All-American. He was also selected Gatorade Player of the Year for Indiana and a member of the Parade All-America team.

When Zeller chose to play at Indiana University, he became the 26th Indiana Mr. Basketball to do so, but even more than that, he provided Indiana a bridge from the greatness of the past to a return of that greatness in the future. Papers called Zeller's commitment to Indiana, "The savior of Indiana basketball."

As a freshman, Zeller was the leading scorer for the Hoosiers 15 times that year. For the season, Zeller led Indiana in scoring with 15.6 points, adding 6.6 rebounds. Zeller was the Big Ten Freshman of the Year, as well as second-team All–Big Ten.

Zeller's sophomore year saw him named as the preseason "Player of the Year" and IU rated as No. 1 in the nation. It was the last regular season game of Zeller's career at IU that may have been his most notable. Indiana was down by five points at Michigan with just 54 seconds to go when Zeller went for six straight unanswered points for a 72–71 victory. Zeller finished with 25 points and 10 rebounds as Indiana won its first outright Big Ten title in 20 years. During his career, Zeller set an IU record by making 59.1 percent of his shots during his two-year career. For the season, Zeller led the team in scoring and rebounding with 16.5 points and eight boards.

Zeller was selected as the fourth overall pick in the 2013 NBA Draft by Charlotte. After his first year in the NBA, Zeller was named to the NBA All-Rookie second-team. In his second year, he scored a career high 23 points in a win over the Bucks. So far in his three years in the NBA, Zeller has averaged 7.94 points a game and 5.64 rebounds while hitting on 49.5 percent from the field and 74.1 percent from the line.

And Then There Were the Coaching Legends

When talking about the best of the best of Indiana basketball coaches, there are two names that are a cut above the rest—Branch McCracken and Bob Knight. Indiana has five national championship banners hanging in the Simon Skjodt Assembly Hall, and McCracken and Knight can lay claim to them all.

Branch McCracken

Branch McCracken would win Indiana's first two national championships in 1940 and 1953. He would also lead Indiana to four Big Ten titles in 1953, 1954, 1957, and 1958. McCracken was one of nine children in a family of five girls and four boys. His father was a road contractor. "We were a big family, and every one of us had to work," said McCracken's younger brother Bill. "My sisters had to work—we all had to work. It was rough, but we enjoyed it. If we had a quarter in our pocket when we went away to play a basketball game on the road, we were set. A hamburger cost a nickel. A Coke cost you a nickel. If we had 25 cents, we were in good shape."

McCracken would play basketball. Yes, indeed, he would play basketball. He and his brothers played basketball in their barn with their neighbors, the Woodens. McCracken, as an 11-year-old sixth-grader, would land a spot on the eighth-grade basketball team.

After honing his basketball skills for three years at the eighth-grade level, McCracken entered high school ready to establish himself as a force to be reckoned with. He made Monrovia's high school team as a freshman forward in the 1922–23 season. As "Mac" entered his sophomore year in 1923–24, both he and Monrovia began to turn the heads of high school observers from not only the state of Indiana, but the Tristate area of Indiana, Ohio, and Kentucky to participate in the famous Tri-State Tournament held in Cincinnati, Ohio. In the first year of the tournament, Monrovia knocked off several larger schools as they pushed their way to finish second in the tourney.

McCracken would go from Monrovia to Indiana to play both football and basketball. He would score a touchdown in football before ever scoring a basket in basketball. "I loved the game of basketball and I had enough confidence in myself that I thought I could make any team in the country," McCracken said. "When freshman practice started, there were a lot of boys who came out for basketball who had quite a reputation. Some of them were all-state in high school, and I didn't know just how good they were going to be, but after the first scrimmage, I knew right then that if they were good enough to play at Indiana University, then I could make the team too."

It would not take long for McCracken to see that he belonged. Starting at center for the Indiana Hoosiers, in the fourth game of his sophomore season, he would lead IU to a 32–13 victory over Chicago. McCracken outscored Chicago himself as he hit on 11 field goals and two free throws for 24 points. He would conclude his sophomore season on a Big Ten–champion team, ending up in a tie for second in the Big Ten individual scoring race.

McCracken opened his junior year with IU in the new Fieldhouse on December 8 with Washington. Stamping himself forever in Indiana history, McCracken became the first person to score in that arena. Years later on February 23, 1960, McCracken would walk off that same court a winner in the last game played in that fieldhouse.

McCracken finished his playing career in 1930 as the Big Ten and Indiana's all-time leading scorer. He would accept the job as Ball State's head basketball coach. He would, in addition to coaching, turn down an offer from the Green Bay Packers to play football and instead played professional basketball for Osh Kosh, Fort Wayne, and Indianapolis. At Ball State, McCracken would twice win the Small College Coach of the Year in both 1931 and 1938.

Coach McCracken would return to his beloved Indiana in 1938 as head coach, taking over for his old coach Everett Dean. In his first six years at Indiana, McCracken would finish second all six years with a combined record of 99–29, while capturing Indiana's first national title in 1940. In 1953 McCracken and the Hoosiers would win their second national championship with a record of 23–3. Indiana would finish the Big Ten season with a record-setting 17–1 mark. In his 24 years at the helm of Indiana, McCracken would win four Big Ten titles, two national championships, and finish in the top half of the Big Ten 20 out of 24 years, including finishing first or second 12 out of his 24 years.

McCracken received many honors at IU, including as a player being All–Big Ten in basketball from 1928 to 1930, a Helm Foundation Basketball All-American in 1930, and was selected to the Naismith Memorial Basketball Hall of Fame in 1960. He would also be named to the Helms Hall Coaches Hall of Fame in 1958 and the Indiana Basketball Hall of Fame in 1963, and was a charter member of the Monroe County Hall of Fame in 1976 and the IU Athletics Hall of Fame in 1982.

Branch McCracken and John Wooden would be the only two consensus All-Americans to coach a NCAA championship team in basketball.

During the 1948–49 season, McCracken and Indiana would break a barrier in the Big Ten by playing the first African American player, Bill Garrett.

After the 1942–43 season in which Indiana finished with a record 18–2 and a second-place finish in the Big Ten, McCracken would leave coaching at Indiana to go to war. His son Dave would say, "Dad didn't have to go—he was too old." McCracken's wife, Mary Jo, said, "He didn't have to go, but he felt that if his boys were going, so would he. He also didn't have to go overseas, but he believed that he could make his best contributions there. Mac went to North Carolina originally, but at that time the Air Force was having a terrible problem with their pilots freezing at their controls both in training and in combat. Because Mac had always been used to relaxing under severe pressure, he was sent to Chicago to teach a refresher course. He taught that course both in the United States and abroad, and later after the war, he received many letters from flyers who said that course had saved their lives, for they were able to relax, and not tense up under the stress of combat."

One story best typifies McCracken's intensity and desire to win. During the 1949–50 season, Indiana would begin the season with 10 straight wins. Dr. Marvin Christie would recall the game that broke that streak and McCracken's reaction. "The game was tied at 67, and Michigan had the ball underneath their basket with six seconds left. Michigan would inbound the ball and, after a couple of seconds, shot and missed. The ball bounced out deep into the backcourt. When Michigan recovered the rebound, I looked up and there were still six seconds left on the clock. Michigan shot again and finally scored as the buzzer went off. A good 15 seconds must have transpired. McCracken leaped up from the bench to rush to the scorer's table. The official scorer jumped up and ran across the court as McCracken approached, yelling that Indiana had been robbed. The Michigan coaches approached McCracken. By that time, McCracken had taken us off the court and we were headed to the locker room. The Michigan coaches couldn't have been nicer. They told McCracken we will play an overtime, but McCracken would hear none of it. Then they said they wouldn't count the game and we could play again at a neutral site, but again McCracken said no. When McCracken got upset, you couldn't control him. He just wasn't going to play them again, he was so mad. I think he thought the loss might motivate us even more the rest of the season. We ended up third in the Big Ten that year."

McCracken's intensity was great, but so was his passion for IU, and so was his desire to compete. His son Dave would recall, "Dad was in the hospital and the doctor had told him he would have to quit coaching or he would die. The doctor came out and told Mom and me what he had told dad. We both were afraid to go into his room, but we went in anyway. To our surprise, Dad was in a great mood. We asked if he understood what the doctor had said, and he said with a smile, 'Yes. How many people know how they are going to die?'"

Coach Branch McCracken with the 1953 national championship team
(Indiana University Archives, P0023227)

McCracken also had a deep love for his players. Max Walker recalled one such time. "Branch and Mary Jo came up and said to me that they wanted to help me on the crib death of our son," Walker said. "They knew it was a very bad time, and as a student I did not have the money to get my son back to Milwaukee. They told me that they would take care of all the funeral expenses. That meant so much to me."

McCracken would earn another nickname from his nephew. The young man could not remember McCracken's name, but he knew it had something to do with a tree, so McCracken's nickname from that young man for the many years to follow was "Twig."

McCracken was the epitome of excitement on the court. His son Dave would recall the time when McCracken charged onto the court to dispute a call. The official looked at McCracken and told him it would cost him a technical foul for every step it took him to get back to Indiana's bench. McCracken looked to the bench and summoned two players to come out and carry him back to the bench. No technical was assessed.

Dick Sparks said, "Branch's deep-throated voice was a huge asset to him. When giving the referees a piece of his mind, he could belt out his complaint while not looking at the referee, thus avoiding a technical foul."

Larry Cooper added, "We played in the Fieldhouse, and the floor was set up knee-level. Coach had a towel, and he wrapped the end of that thing with tape. He would slap that towel on the court, and it didn't matter what kind of noise was in the Fieldhouse, he would slap that towel down and look at you and tell you what he wanted right now."

One referee found a unique way of controlling McCracken's rants. When asked how he got McCracken, who was vehemently objecting to a call, to sit down so quickly, official Jim Enright said, "Nothing to it. I just said 'Now, Branch, you've made your point and you'd better sit down. You know, this game's on television and your fly is open.'"

Jim Schooley recalled, "When Mac got a little too excited about a call, Ernie Andres would grab his belt to keep him from wandering too far out on the court and getting a technical foul."

Dick Sparks talked about McCracken's intensity. "Branch and Lou [Watson, McCracken's longtime assistant], made you work hard in practice," he said. "If you were slacking, be ready for the wrath of God."

Ray Pavy said, "Branch had such a presence. One time years after I had played, I was sitting with Herman Wells at a basketball game. We were at Assembly Hall watching Knight's team. Knight was going crazy on a call. President Wells said to me, 'There's not much difference between Knight and the Bear [Branch]. Knight has nothing on Branch." Pavy added, "Branch's greatest talent was making you believe you were the best shooter in the world."

Although McCracken could be tough, he had a huge heart. Pavy would say, "Branch loved all his boys. He was a big bear, but he was mellow inside. After I was hurt, Branch, with Herman Wells, made sure every one of my classes was on the first floor."

Former player Pete Obremskey recalled McCracken's benevolence. "Branch was responsible for paying seven years of my education. So to me, he walked on water. Of course, when I was playing for him, I didn't feel that way."

The late Indiana great Walt Bellamy valued the relationship he had with Coach McCracken. "Coach McCracken touched all student-athletes," he said. "I felt prepared. Did he holler and throw chairs? No, but he certainly was effective in preparing men to play basketball and to be successful in life."

McCracken would tell the following story about himself: After a game, a fan asked McCracken, "Why did they call a technical foul on IU?" McCracken replied, "Indiana had too many men on the floor." The fan asked him, "Who was the sixth man?" And he responded, "Me."

McCracken's playing of Bill Garrett would break the color line of Big Ten basketball. McCracken told the *Indianapolis News* and the *Lafayette Journal & Courier*, "There's no rule against colored athletes, but if somebody has to be the first to use them, it's going to be me." He would go on to say, "It wasn't as hard a thing for me as it was for Bill. All the pressure was on him, but he was an exceptional guy. He handled discrimination on and off the floor without changing expression." Bill Garrett would say of McCracken, "He made you grow up real fast, just by the way he handled the players as far as getting themselves ready. I think it was one of the greatest attributes he had as a coach."

Archie Dees talked about McCracken's leadership, saying, "Mac was definitely a leader. He led every player, every person that came in contact with him to greater heights than they could ever hope to achieve. He was a born leader."

Ernie Andres remembered McCracken's impact on the team from his very first year as a coach. "I was Mac's first captain," he said. "It was obvious he intended to win at Indiana. He had a winning attitude about him. He didn't believe in doing anything halfway. Everybody who played for McCracken respected him. He would work you as hard as anybody, yet at the same time he would do anything for you to try to help you, and it didn't just mean on the basketball court, but in school or in life in general."

Bobby Leonard recalled, "Branch had a way about him. Branch was a winner and he instilled winning into the ballplayers, there's no doubt about it. There wasn't a night that you went on the floor that you weren't ready to tear someone apart. You went out there to win a ballgame—that was Branch. With Branch, you had such great admiration for him, and we were so close to him that you didn't want to feel in your own mind that you had let him down."

Bill Garrett would say of McCracken, "He had a solid way about him. His manner demanded respect. The overall respect he had from his players was amazing."

Close friend and teammate Jim Strickland remembered a very aggressive but kind McCracken. "He was the most aggressive man I ever met in my life," he recalled. "He liked to go at it and go at it fast....Branch's biggest concern was his boys. He worried more about his kids on the team—more than any coach I have ever known. He would follow them after they got out of school and was a huge help to them."

Indiana Hall of Fame coach Everett Dean remembered McCracken in this way: "Mac loved the game and he lived it. He had quite a spirit. He was an easy man to coach because of his attitude."

One of Indiana's all-time greats, Don Schlundt, would say of McCracken, "Without Branch, I would not be who I am today. He made me a better person. It was just the way you respected the man."

Archie Dees remembered McCracken's use of psychology against whomever he would play next. "He would walk up to me and say, 'This guy is tough. He's strong,'" he said. "He used this on me, telling me he didn't want me to get hurt. He would start on Wednesday, and by Saturday, I couldn't wait to get out there and get a look at this guy. I really wanted to get at him. I was really ready to play. The crazy thing was that he did this so well that it not only worked my sophomore and junior years, but I would listen even as a senior. I would always listen to him."

Longtime friend Bill Unsworth gave what may be the best account of Branch's deep competitive nature with a story of how hard he would take a loss. "He had been beaten by Minnesota at Minnesota by one point," he recalled. "On the plane coming back from Minnesota, he would say, 'My goodness, if you could just get beat by 30 or 32 points, you could go to sleep at night with no stress, realizing that you had a club that wasn't going anywhere. It would make all the difference in the world sleeping or not sleeping.' The following year, Indiana was invited to the University of Cincinnati to dedicate its new Fieldhouse. Well, the day of the game at noon, there was a lunch given by the University of Cincinnati in honor of Branch for playing on that Monrovia team that won back-to-back championships in the High School Tri-State Tourney that was held in Cincinnati each year. As fate would have it, Cincinnati would beat IU that day by 32 points. Mac got on the team bus and said, 'My, my, if you could just get beat by one point, you would know you had something. How can anyone sleep if you get beat by 32?'" McCracken just did not like to lose.

Jim Strickland recalled a story of how Branch inspired everyone. "We were at Illinois and a group of us had gone down to the locker room before the game. We would leave when the boys came in to get dressed. We didn't notice that one of our party had fallen asleep in the corner of the locker room behind the lockers. We were standing outside, and we heard Branch pounding on the table and firing the boys up. The next thing you know, the team bust through the doors and following them was our friend, as ready as the boys. If Mac had given him a suit, he would have played. I never knew Mac to do anything he didn't think was in the best interest of IU and his boys. He was so completely dedicated to Indiana University."

The lack of social networking did not inhibit Branch in keeping track of his players and their activities. Tom Bolyard would recall, "There were five or six coffee shops on the square in downtown Bloomington, and Branch would go to each one, sit down, and have a coffee with everyone. He built up quite a network. As a player, you could not go anywhere or do anything in the community without Branch knowing about it. People would call Branch up and say, 'Hey, so-and-so are here—should they be?' And if they weren't supposed to be there, Branch would be there shortly after. He just knew everything. We as players knew you couldn't get away with anything." Branch would give the players' professors three-by-five cards, and they were to write down if a player missed class or if any of them were having any kind of problem in class.

Tom Van Arsdale offered these thoughts on what Coach McCracken stood for: "Just from the standpoint of what he stood for—the tradition that he had developed over the years at Indiana. The way he treated me was an influence on me, and I think it taught me that it is important to treat your fellow man with respect and kindness, and you can still be effective doing that."

To Tom Bolyard, "He was like a father. Between classes, if I had a break, I went to his office, had a Coke, and talked, not only about basketball, but schoolwork, life, what I was going to do when I got out of school. I tell you, he was just like a father to me. I probably couldn't have made it without him."

Bobby Leonard would say of McCracken, "He took me as a wild kid off the streets of Terre Haute and taught me a lot of values. I had never been baptized. Branch took me to a church and had me baptized when I was 19 years old. You don't get any greater feeling for a man than I have for Branch McCracken. There is no greater feeling."

Jimmy Rayl recalled getting married in 1966 and sending Branch and Mary Jo an invitation. "I didn't really know if he would be able to come or not, but that day, there he was with Mary Jo, sitting right up front with a huge smile on his face. It meant a lot."

Larry Cooper remembered how Branch helped him through a rough time in 1965. "At the start of my senior year," he said, "a good friend whom I played with for two years at Hutchinson Community College at Kansas was killed in a car crash. Coach released me from the final drill before the start of fall practice and allowed me to return to Kansas City for my friend's funeral. This may sound like a minor thing, but it meant a lot to me at the time."

McCracken expected all his players to be 15 minutes early. If you weren't, you were late. McCracken made it a habit before each practice to greet each player with a personal comment to let his players know how important they were to him as a person. They would echo the comment, "We were his kids."

McCracken was famous for saying to his players, "Get up—you're not hurt!" Rayl recalled, "One day in practice, Dave Porter fouled me on a fast break and sent me flying into the gooseneck goalpost we had. I went sliding down it. Branch rushed over to see if I was all right. He didn't say, 'Get up!' that day."

Tom Van Arsdale would comment on McCracken's famous saying of "Get up—you're not hurt": "Branch was a rough-and-tumble man. One day in practice, the team was running fast-break drills and he got run over by one of us, I don't remember who it was. As Branch was flat on his back, the entire team circled him and yelled, 'Get up—you're not hurt!' As it turned out, he was injured, and we all felt terrible. Branch was a great man, and we all loved him."

Ray Pavy talked about McCracken's coaching genius: "It was a remarkable thing that two coaching greats, McCracken and Wooden, came from the same area. They both understood the game so well, and both used a press on defense to speed up the game—McCracken a man-to-man press, and Wooden a zone press. But their idea of speeding up the game was due to their feeling that, 'Our talent will beat your talent.'"

Tom Bolyard remembered McCracken's game-day strategy would consist of his coming into the locker room and saying, "'Jim, I need 20 shots out of you. Bolyard, I need 20 out of you.' Then he would turn to Tom and Dick Van Arsdale and say, 'I need 12 shots out of both of you.'"

Archie Dees, the first two-time Big Ten Most Valuable Player, would say of McCracken, "He was just a born leader. It was an honor to play for him. It was the type of situation that you never had to question, 'Was he telling you the right thing?' Whatever I was told, I would do without any reservation, and I think that is one of the most important things in being a coach."

When playing for a demanding coach like McCracken, things were not always smooth. Once, Bobby Leonard was called into McCracken's office for one of the famous McCracken talks to straighten a player out. "He called me in his office," he recalled. "He told me, 'When we get through, if I ever have to call you in again, I'll lock the door, and only one of us will come out.'" Leonard promised he would change, but before he left, he stopped at the door and said, "I guess I know which one of us will come out." And then he ran down the hall.

Marvin Christie said McCracken was 100 percent dedicated to IU. He remembered McCracken saying, "I can win a national championship with players from Indiana."

The famous broadcaster Dick Enberg would say of McCracken, "To the core, there was no doubt that Branch was an Indiana man."

In 1955 McCracken wrote a book, *Indiana Basketball*, the first chapter of which revealed what aspect of coaching he felt was most important. The chapter, "The Coach, His Psychology, and His Players," would deal with just that part of coaching dealing with team spirit, driving desire, self-discipline, and pride in one's self.

A Bucket List of Indiana University Basketball Coaches

Rank/Coach	Big Ten Titles
1. Bob Knight	11
2. Branch McCracken	4
3. Everett Dean	3
4. Tom Crean	2
5. Lou Watson	1
6. Mike Davis	1

In 1965 McCracken would retire after 32 years of coaching, the last 24 of them at IU. In 1963 Branch had started a summer basketball camp in Angola, Indiana. This camp would serve as an outlet for his desire to teach the game of basketball. He would also stay at IU and work with student teachers as a supervisor.

Branch McCracken remains the youngest coach to win an NCAA basketball championship by more than three years. He was 31 years, nine months, and 21 days old when the 1940 Indiana Hoosiers beat Kansas for the title.

The floor of Assembly Hall would be renamed after Branch McCracken on December 18, 1971. The Monrovia Junior High–Senior High School main gymnasium would be named after McCracken, as well.

The 1966 Indiana Basketball Guide would pay a lasting tribute to Coach McCracken titled "Thanks, Mac." It began:

The start of a new era in Indiana basketball prompts a look back at the McCracken Era of IU. A peek at those golden years at Indiana and the record achieved by those exciting Hoosier teams emphasizes the debt of gratitude basketball fans of the state and nation owe to the Sheriff.

For example: two National Collegiate Championships, three Big Ten titles, and a share of a fourth. His teams placed either first or second in the Big Ten 12 of his 24 seasons; teams placed out of the top five in the conference only four times in 24 years; a 354–74 winning percentage and a 210–116 mark in Big Ten play; a career coaching record at both Indiana and Ball State of 457–215; a winning margin over every other Big Ten team (Chicago 6–0; Michigan 24–9; Michigan State 20–7; Wisconsin 25–10; Purdue 28–15; Northwestern 21–10; Iowa 24-16; Ohio State 27–17; Minnesota 19–16; and Illinois 19–17).

It was a time of great excitement, of great play, and not least, great coaching. All eras must come to an end, and there will be other great days ahead. But none will forget the great contributions of Branch McCracken to Indiana University, its basketball program, and basketball fans everywhere; from then, "Thanks, Mac. Well done."

McCracken would win his last battle off the court as he secured the Indiana head basketball job for his longtime assistant coach, captain, and former player Lou Watson.

McCracken would live just five short years after retiring from coaching at Indiana. He would die in Indianapolis at the IU Medical Center on June 4, 1970, of a heart ailment just five days short of his 62nd birthday.

McCracken himself would write his best tribute when he wrote in his book, "A coach is not paid in money or winning teams, but in the men his players become." McCracken was passionate, caring, fiery, and a Hoosier through and through.

Bob Knight

First we had the Sheriff, and now we have the General.

Bob Knight was born on October 25, 1940, in Massillon, Ohio, to Carroll "Pat" Knight and Hazel Knight. Pat Knight worked as a freight agent for the Wheeling–Lake Erie Railroad. He would walk four miles to work every day and back again each night. Bob Knight's mother, Hazel, was a school teacher. Bob was an only child and adored by both his parents. Bob Knight's grandmother, Sarah Henthorne, would move into the house before Bob was born. His grandmother would teach young Bob how to make his bed every morning, and she would be the one to provide young Bob with hugs and physical affection. Although Knight was born in Massillon, he would grow up in Orrville, Ohio, and attend Orrville High School.

Knight was a good student who loved and tried all sports. He was an infielder and a better-than-average hitter in baseball, which, according to Knight, was probably his best sport. He would spend his summers playing softball nearly every night. However, base running was not his best strength. In junior high his coach would admonish him for the lead he took at first base. "I was never very quick, so the lead I took was very short. My coach said to me, 'Boy, I want to tell you something. You can't steal second by keeping one foot on first.'" Another time his team was in a tournament game, and the score was tied 0–0. Knight would get three straight hits, and each time he would be thrown out trying to steal. When Knight connected on his fourth hit, someone from the crowd yelled out, "Chain him down!" This would draw a roar from the crowd and Knight.

At Orrville High School, Knight would develop into a star basketball player who would average nearly 25 points a game in his junior and senior years. Both Knight's grandmother and father wanted him to become a lawyer.

Knight would be recruited by coach Fred Taylor to attend Ohio State. He would become part of Ohio State's greatest recruiting class ever, which included the great Jerry Lucas and John Havlicek, to go along with Mel Norwell and Gary Gearhart. These recruits would lead Ohio State to three straight national title games, winning in 1960 and losing to the Cincinnati Bearcats the next two years. Knight would recall what his father had told him in Bob Hammel's book, *Knight with the Hoosiers*, "I can remember my dad telling me that he sure thought Fred was the guy who should be my coach. My dad didn't know anything about it, but he really liked Fred, and he told me he'd really like to have me play for him. And he would feel that way all the time I played for him. My dad also wanted me to play somewhere close so he could watch me play." Despite all this, there were times that Bob did not feel the same way, for according to Coach Taylor, Knight would "set the NCAA record for the number of times he quit the squad."

In his career at Ohio State, Knight would start four or five times his junior year and two or three times his senior year. A story told by his assistant coach Frank Truitt spells out his frustration. "It was the NCAA championship game against Cincinnati in 1961, with just under two minutes remaining in the game," Truitt recalled. "Bob went into the game, he got the ball in the left front court, faked the drive to the middle, then made a crossover dribble and drove to the right for a basket to tie the game. He ran over to me and yelled, 'I should have been in this game a long time ago!' I yelled back, 'You hot dog, you are lucky to be in the game at all!'"

Knight would graduate with a degree in history and government. In 1962 at the NCAA finals in Louisville, Knight would meet Harold Andreas, one of Ohio's best high school coaches. Knight's plan was to teach a year and then go to law school and become the lawyer that both his grandmother and father wanted him to be. During this time, he would interview for the head basketball and line coach in football job at Celina, Ohio. However, he really wanted to just concentrate on basketball, so he would end up taking an assistant coaching job for Coach Andreas at Cuyahoga Falls.

After one year at Cuyahoga Falls, Knight was to be a graduate assistant at UCLA as arranged by his former coach Fred Taylor. George Hunter, the head coach of basketball at Army overheard Knight talking to Coach Taylor about the position when he stopped in and offered Knight an assistant job at Army. Knight took Hunter up on his offer only to arrive at West Point and find that Hunter was no longer coaching there. Tates Locke, an assistant to Hunter, had taken over the head coaching duties and would honor Hunter's offer to Knight. Years later, Knight would show his loyalty to both Andreas and Locke by hiring them as assistants at IU.

Knight's intensity for the game would show while an assistant for Locke. One game Knight came into the locker room and told Coach Locke, "They're going to start the second half shooting some free throws, and one other thing. I won't be sitting with you the second half. They threw me out." Knight had debated a close call at the end of the half, way too much.

In 1965 Tates Locke would leave Army to take a job at Miami of Ohio, and Knight would sign a one-year contract for $6,000 to be the head coach at Army. At the age of 24, Knight would become the nation's youngest major-college coach.

Knight would be the head coach at Army for six years, compiling a record of 102–50. He would lead Army to four NIT Tournaments, finishing as high as third in 1970.

In the spring of 1971, Indiana head coach Lou Watson would resign and leave an opening for the head coaching position at Indiana University. Knight had come to a crossroads of his own after his Army team suffered its first losing season (11–13) in his six years at West Point. Knight had rejected offers from schools like Florida, Texas Tech, and Wisconsin, who had prematurely announced they had hired Knight as their head coach. Indiana would come calling the year before finishing the season 17–7, yet there was great unrest with the team, leading to Coach Watson's resignation. Indiana athletic director Bill Orwig would talk Knight into coming to Bloomington as the new head coach. One early story about how Knight caught the attention of his team involves coaching great Mike Krzyzewski. Speaking to a basketball class taught by Knight, Krzyzewski asked if there were any questions. Steve Downing raised his hand and said, "I don't have any questions. I just want to say how happy I am to see somebody who played four years for the coach and lived through it." It took time for Indiana fans to get used to Knight's patient offense after watching the Hurryin' Hoosiers of Branch McCracken. In one of the early games, guard Bootsie White was bringing the ball up the court when a fan yelled out, "Shoot the ball, Bootsie." White went past the Indiana bench and said to Knight, "Don't worry, chief, I don't hear 'em."

As much as some fans hated the new style of play, the fact that Indiana would finish Coach Knight's first season with a 17–8 record and a third-place finish in the Big Ten with an NIT invitation began to bring fans around. In year two, a team led by Downing, Ritter, Green, and a freshman named Quinn Buckner would finish 22–6, first in the Big Ten, and third in the NCAA Tournament. At this point, fans were fully behind Knight and his new style of play. It's funny how winning will have that effect on people.

The first-place finish in the Big Ten during the 1973 season would be the first of four in a row. In 1974 Indiana would tie with Michigan for the Big Ten title. Because at that time only one school from each conference could go the NCAA tourney, a one-game playoff between Michigan and Indiana would take place in Illinois to see who would represent the Big Ten in the tourney. Indiana would come out on the short end of a 75–67 score. After the game, Knight would say without any question the Wolverines deserved to win and represent the Big Ten in the NCAA.

Knight wanted the opportunity to play in the NIT, but the administration had committed the Hoosiers to play in the new Conference Commissioners Association (CCA) tournament to be played in St. Louis. Knight and the team didn't want to go, but when it became clear that they were going, Knight would say, "If we have to go, then let's win the damned thing." The Hoosiers would barely beat Tennessee, 73–71, and Toledo, 73–72, in overtime to set up a championship match with USC. During the championship game, a USC player palmed the ball. Knight jumped up and yelled, "He carried the ball, he carried the ball!" He was hit with a technical foul, after which he said to the referee, "You don't have any idea what the hell you're doing." Knight collected his second technical at that point and was tossed from the game. As the game progressed, Knight would offer advice to his assistants from the stands. At that time, coaches tossed out of a game could sit in the stands. Knight was so upset at what had happened, he seriously considered resigning as head coach of Indiana after only his third season. Indiana would emerge on March 18, 1974, as CCA champions, defeating USC 85–60 despite the technical fouls on Knight.

The next two years at Indiana may be the greatest in Indiana history. The 1975 team would win the Big Ten outright, setting a record by going undefeated in a round robin schedule (18–0). On the way to an undefeated regular season, Indiana would dispatch number No. 7 Kansas, No. 15 Kentucky, No. 11 Notre Dame, No. 17 Michigan, No. 17 Minnesota, No. 20 Purdue, No. 17 UTEP, and No. 13 Oregon State. Indiana was running over everyone. Then, with three games remaining, Indiana would find itself without leading scorer and All-American Scott May, who had fractured his left arm in the first half of a win over Purdue. Indiana would go on to win its last three regular-season games and the first two of the tourney, until it faced a rematch with Kentucky. In a coaching move Knight would later say was his worst ever, he chose to start May, cast and all. The game was extremely physical, to the point of getting out of hand, and Kentucky prevailed to end Indiana's dream season at 31–1.

Indiana would begin Knight's fifth season ranked No. 1 and would stay atop the polls for all 17 weeks. It was a season for all time. Highlights included a fourth consecutive Big Ten title and duplicating the record of going 18–0 in the conference, an undefeated regular season, and victory in the NCAA tournament to seal the Hoosiers' third national championship in basketball. Knight would be recognized as National Coach of the Year; Scott May, Kent Benson, and Quinn Buckner would be All-Americans. Scott May would also be the College Player of the Year.

Indiana finished 32–0, defeating No. 2 UCLA, No. 8 Notre Dame, No. 14 Kentucky, No. 17 St. John's, and No. 16 Michigan twice.

But perhaps more impressive in the NCAA tourney, IU would defeat in order: No. 17 St. John's, No. 6 Alabama, No. 2 Marquette, No. 5 UCLA, and in the championship game, No. 7 Michigan. Add it up and that would be 11 ranked opponents that the team with the target affixed firmly on its back had been able to knock off week after week. It was quite an impressive feat and clearly, a season of a lifetime.

The 1977 season would see the return of junior Kent Benson, but gone were five important seniors, and Indiana would fall off to a 16–11 record and a fourth-place finish in the Big Ten. In 1978 IU would bounce back to a 21–8 record and a second-place Big Ten finish. After a 22–12 record and a fifth-place finish in the Big Ten in 1979, Indiana would be invited to the NIT and win the championship by one point over in-state rival Purdue on a last-second shot by Butch Carter.

The NIT championship was extremely satisfying to Coach Knight, who had coveted such a title to go along with his 1976 NCAA championship.

Coach Knight's career had experienced many highs and lows over the years, but there were a few positives that remained constant. One constant would be that he ran a squeaky clean program. Also his players graduated from Indiana; Indiana was a consistent winner; and his players were fundamentally sound.

In the summer between the 1979 NIT championship and the 1979–80 basketball season, Coach Knight coached the United States Pan Am team in Puerto Rico. Included on that team were three of his own players—Mike Woodson, Ray Tolbert, and incoming freshman Isiah Thomas. Although Knight and the United States would come home with the gold, Knight would also return with more controversy.

The problem started when the Brazilian women's team entered the gym where the U.S. team was practicing. Coach Knight asked his assistant Mike Krzyzewski to go over and ask the Brazilian team to be quiet. At this time Puerto Rican security guard Joe Silva stepped in to challenge Coach Knight's authority. Silva explained to Coach Knight, "Hey, man, this is my gym. When you're in Puerto Rico, you do as I say. They can come in [referring to the Brazilian team], they've got a right to be here." It was then that events began to escalate. Silva poked Knight directly in the right eye, causing Knight to duck his head and raise his left hand, touching Silva's right cheek. In response, Silva grabbed Knight's arm, shouting that Knight had hit him and in doing so had hit a Puerto Rican policeman. So Knight was under arrest. Much to the dismay of the assistant coaches and the players, Knight was put in a car and taken away. While the charges against Knight were dropped, Silva would bring civil charges of his own against Knight.

Meanwhile, the U.S. team was being targeted both on and off the court, to the extent of being threatened with harm, as Captain Mike Woodson was told, "We have guns. If the game is close, we're going to shoot down onto the floor." While no shots were fired, the United States won by a score of 113–94. The U.S. would be led by Mike Woodson and future Indiana star Isiah Thomas, who scored 21 points, had five steals, and handed out four assists.

Bob Knight would fly back to the United States the next day. He would be tried in absentia and convicted of aggravated assult and was sentenced to nine months in prison and a fine of $1,000. Later Knight wrote a letter to Puerto Rican Governor Carlos Romero-Barceló, trying to explain his side of the story, ending with "most sincere apologies if anything I have done or said has been interpreted as being offensive to the people of Puerto Rico," putting an end to the incident.

Beginning in 1980, Indiana would finish first in the Big Ten in three of the next four years. This would include the 1980–81 season, which would end with Knight's second NCAA championship. The season would not start out looking like a banner year, as Indiana opened the season with a 7–5 record, including losses to the only ranked teams it would play: No. 2 Kentucky, No. 9 Notre Dame, and No. 8 North

Carolina. Indiana would right the ship and go on to win the Big Ten title outright, winning its last 10 games, including the five from the NCAA tourney. The Hoosiers would be led by Big Ten MVP Ray Tolbert, All-American Isiah Thomas, and future Big Ten MVP Randy Wittman. In the tourney, they would destroy No. 18 Maryland 99–64 after spotting them the first eight points of the game. They returned to Bloomington to host the Mideast Regionals, then moved on to the Spectrum in Philadelphia for the finals, dispatching LSU in the semifinal game 67–49. Indiana would enact revenge on the North Carolina Tar Heels to capture Knight's second NCAA championship.

Indiana was back in first with a record of 24–6 in 1983. Knight would lead the United States Olympic team to victory in Los Angeles in the summer of 1984. He put one of his own players, Steve Alford, on the team. A great story on Knight came out of his three-month, bootcamp-style training when Michael Jordan, knowing Alford still had three more years with Knight, told Alford, "One hundred dollars, you'll never last four years at Indiana." Isiah didn't last four years, Jordan reminded Alford. "Isiah was a special case," Alford replied. "Take the bet!" Jordan said. "I'm telling you, man, you'll never go the whole three years." Alford, laughing, said, "Okay, I'll bet you." And, as they say, the rest is history as Alford would last four years with Knight, ending his senior year with Knight's third and last NCAA championship. But there would be other roads to travel before that path was taken. In the 1984–85 season, Knight would again face controversy of his own making. First, on January 27, 1985, Knight would pull Steve Alford aside before the morning walk-through to tell his sophomore guard, "I am going to sit you down today. You're just going to watch, you're not going to play. I want you to watch the freshmen," Knight would say. "Watch how they play defense. Watch how they move."

Alford would not be the only one to sit down. All the starters, with the exception of Uwe Blab, would do the same. Indiana would lose the game to Illinois 52–41.

Knight would address the move on Monday's radio show saying, "When someone talks about Steve Alford, you almost have to start with me in terms of people who support him and like him and want to see him do as well as he can. I recruited him...I picked him to play on the United States Olympic team."

The criticism of Knight that year wouldn't stop there. On February 23, Knight became very angry at two calls in a row, and on the second call picked up a chair from the team bench and threw it across the floor past the free throw line. Purdue would win that game in Bloomington, 72–63. Knight would apologize publicly the next day. "I am certain that what I did in tossing the chair was an embarrassment to Indiana University. That was not my intention, and for that I'm deeply sorry." Knight would be suspended by the Big Ten for one game and put on "probationary status for two years. All in all, 1984–85 was Indiana's most difficult season under Knight, finishing seventh in the Big Ten with a losing record of 7–11.

The next year would be the year of John Feinstein's book, *A Season on the Brink*. Knight would agree to do the book because he wanted to show that a college basketball program could win championships while following the rules and requiring its players to go to class. Knight would say to his players after a home loss to Michigan State, "I never thought I would see the day when Indiana basketball was in the state it's in right now." The Hoosiers would finish second in the Big Ten, one game behind Michigan.

In 1987 Indiana basketball was back all the way. However, along the way, players found, as they knew all along, life with Knight is never dull. On Knight's birthday, he kicked the team out of practice, and they were faced with the problem of what to do with the cake they had for his birthday. Should they give it to him on his birthday or wait for a better day? Courage won out, and they gave him the cake, and he was very pleased with it. In January, Knight ran into Michael Jordan, who told him about the bet with Alford, telling Knight, "Tell Steve I owe him $100." Knight would respond, "Don't pay it. He

Coach Bob Knight with Steve Alford (Indiana University Archives, P0044659)

hasn't made it yet." As the season progressed, Indiana would win the Big Ten championship in a tie with Purdue.

Indiana would go into the NCAA tourney and would win two tourney games in Indianapolis, then travel east to Cincinnati, win two there, and go to New Orleans for the Final Four. Knight would show his coaching genius and beat UNLV at its own game—a running game. The Hoosiers would beat No. 1 UNLV 97–93. On March 30, 1987, Indiana under Knight would win its third NCAA title on a last-second shot over Syracuse, 74–73.

Knight's and Indiana's fortunes would slip in 1990 to seventh place. However, Indiana would come roaring back to finish first in two of the next three Big Ten seasons, including a fifth trip to the Final Four in 1992. In 1993 Indiana would win its 11th and final Big Ten championship under Knight. In Knight's last six years, Indiana would finish second once, third three times, and fifth twice in the Big Ten.

Knight would give his idea about Indiana University and Indiana basketball in the book *Indiana University Basketball, A Winning Tradition*:

> What's important at Indiana University is not what a player does while he is here.
>
> Very few schools have combined athletics and academics as successfully as Indiana, yet we take as much pride in the accomplishments of our players after they have left IU as we do on all their achievements here in school. All but two of our four-year players have completed or are finishing degrees. Our players have all gone on to successful careers in professional basketball, business, or in some cases, coaching. Those who have completed their professional playing careers have now launched very successful second careers.
>
> I have always made it clear that an education is the top priority for our players; basketball is secondary. But, just as the University offers exceptional educational opportunities in all fields, it also offers a basketball program without equal. No other school in the country enjoys the tremendous support like that given by our students, the community of Bloomington, and the State of Indiana.
>
> The best endorsement of Indiana basketball is the number of former players who come back to attend practices, watch games, encourage the kids, and help in any way possible with what the present team is doing. Their desire to give something back to the program in this way and their belief in what we're doing here says it all.

On July 25, 1981, just months after winning the 1981 national championship, Landon Turner, who was on his way to a day of fun at Cincinnati's King's Island, an amusement park in Ohio, would be involved in a terrible car crash that would leave the would-be senior All-American paralyzed from the chest down.

Knight, who was away on a fishing trip in Idaho, would return right away to be at Turner's side. While Turner was still unconscious, Knight would stand over his bed saying, "Landon, Landon." Someone would ask coach Knight to holler at Turner as if they were at basketball practice. Knight reportedly said, "Are you sure you want me to do that?" He would do so, though, but Turner still was unresponsive. Coach Knight would start the Landon Turner Trust Fund by contributing $60,000 of his own money and getting then Indiana governor Otis Bowen and many other dignitaries to help, as well as many thousands of Hoosiers fans across the nation.

Knight's kindness would make an impression on Turner's parents, who would write, "I don't think anyone could send their son to a school better than Indiana University. We never had any reservations about sending Landon. Once you become a part of the IU basketball family, you always remain a part of it. Coach Knight is very loyal to not only the players in the current program, but to past players and their families as well. He has a good heart. I wish everyone knew the Bob Knight the Turner family knows."

Knight was always helping people but did not want credit for it. One time he was at an AAU game in Bloomington when future recruit Pat Graham hurt an ankle. After the game, family and friends had gone back to see Pat, but Knight would wait until everyone was gone to check on Graham, not wanting anyone to see him.

Scott May would say of Knight, "Coach likes to have old players come back and watch ballgames and practices and spend time with current players. That's part of the tradition, and I'm all for that. I like to see the players putting something back into the program." Quinn Buckner would say, "The fact that you see just about all of the players return is a tribute to Coach Knight and the things he as imparted on us and the kind of people we have become."

Dr. Steve Green would have two stories about Coach Knight. He told of how in one game he came out for a rest and Tom Abernethy took his place. "Tom went on to have a really bad few minutes, and Knight was fuming. You could tell he was really mad, and as players we all kind of enjoyed seeing Coach blast another player. He was a master at it. All of a sudden he's nose to nose with me and says it's my fault. If I was in there he wouldn't have to watch that crap." So much for enjoying someone else get reamed out.

Green would also speak about another time with Knight. "Coach Knight's desire for us to excel in the classroom, as well as on the court, is basic to everything he does. He'll insure that you'll get the best education possible when you come to Indiana. And he'll be the best ally you'll have from the time you enter Indiana, throughout your career, then for the rest of your life." Green would be Knight's first recruit to Indiana.

All-American Kent Benson would talk about how Knight recruited him. "Coach Knight laid everything on the line to me," he recalled. "He didn't promise me anything except the opportunity to get a degree. It was then that I made the decision to attend Indiana."

Knight could also be very intense, not only during but after games, as described by Ray Tolbert in the book *Landon Turner's Tales from the 1980–'81 Indiana Hoosiers*:

> We had just lost at Ohio State by one point. We were so hungry, we had stopped at McDonald's and had a bunch of Quarter Pounders and fries. Coach grabbed up everyone's McDonald's bag and threw them on the ground. We had played so poorly that he didn't think we deserved to eat. I had played 40 minutes and thought, "He's not going to throw my food away," It smelled so good, and he said that we had played like this and that, and that we didn't deserve this food. He took the whole bag and tossed it out the window. Man, we were so mad.

Coach was that much of a perfectionist. There was a time when he just blew up and destroyed the I-Men's room. Coat hangers everywhere. Whatever was available to grab, he grabbed and destroyed it. We were like, "This man is nuts."

There also was a time when Knight was screaming, cursing, and said, "I want all of you such-and-such's to go in the bathroom and look at yourselves in the mirror. Take a good look at yourself and think about how you played. Well, Landon goes in there with his comb and starts combing his hair.

Coach Knight's team was not always kind to Notre Dame and Digger Phelps. But Knight could help Phelps out on occasion, like when Coach Knight and Coach Phelps were having trouble staying in front of their respective benches. So at one point Knight asked to have a conference with official Jim Bain and Phelps. "I was yelling at Tim Andree for taking a bad shot, and the official told me I wasn't allowed to cross the center line," Phelps said. "Bobby told him, 'If he wants to come across that line to yell at his kids, let him, because I might want to be down at his end yelling at mine, and I know he won't mind.'"

In Turner's book, Jim Crews tells this story about Knight. "One day Coach was sitting on the sideline on one of those plastic red chairs. The real practice was over, and everyone's kind of shooting free throws as he's sitting over there. And he says, 'Okay, everybody over here!' Coach was sitting there and everybody's kind of standing around, and he says, 'I really enjoyed practice today. Practice was really good. You guys did a great job.' All this positive stuff. He says, 'I'll see you guys tomorrow.' Well, everyone's leaving and so Landon goes up to Coach and pats him on the knee and says, 'I thought you had a good practice today, too.'"

Coach Knight would bring the motion offense to IU. He talked about how he would prepare his team for this offense: "Our offense is centered around the basic idea of working to get the good shot. The most important singular aspect of our offensive thinking is to get the ball inside against whatever defense confronts us. We do very little scrimmaging during the course of the year but concentrate on halfcourt work. It is necessary for our players to know each of the five spots in our offense, as we frequently play the guards inside and the forwards outside against a man-to-man. A lot of our practice time is spent in helping the players learn to recognize what the defense is doing. The defense will always tell us what kind of cut we should make, and we try to give the players a definite move on option to counter each change the defense can make. Our guards are responsible for running our offense, but we also call what we think will go, from the bench."

> ## Similarities between Branch McCracken and Bob Knight
>
> - McCracken won two national championships in 24 years. Knight won three in 29 years.
> - McCracken finished first or second in the Big Ten in 12 of 24 years. Knight finished first or second 16 times in 29 years.
> - McCracken finished in the top half of the Big Ten in 20 of 24 years. Knight finished in the top half of the Big Ten in 26 of 29 years.
> - Both men introduced new styles of play to both the Big Ten and the nation. McCracken brought the Hurryin' Hoosiers, while Knight brought the motion offense.

April 11, 2000, was the beginning of the end of Knight's tenure at IU. CNN Sports Illustrated would run a piece on Knight, including a claim by former player Neil Reed that he had been choked by Knight in a 1997 practice. Although Knight denied the claim, less than a month later the network ran a tape that seemed to show Knight placing his hand on Reed's neck. Indiana University President Myles Brand instituted a zero tolerance policy on Knight. In September Kent Harvey, a freshman at Indiana, encountered Knight and said to the coach, "Hey, Knight, what's up?" Then Knight, according to Harvey, grabbed his arm and informed him of his disrespect, saying, "Call me Mr. Knight or Coach Knight." President Brand said this was just one of numerous complaints against Coach Knight and asked Knight to resign on September 10. When Knight refused, Brand fired the coach. Knight's dismissal was met with rage by students on campus. That night thousands of students and others marched from Assembly Hall to Brand's house, burning the president in effigy. On September 13, Knight said good-bye to a crowd of 6,000 at Dunn Meadow, urging them to continue to support the basketball team.

Knight had an incredible run at Indiana and piled up a list of individual and team accomplishments. Consider:

- He compiled a record of 659–242, a winning percentage of .731.

- Knight was the only coach to take teams to every amateur title: three NCAA championships, an NIT title, the Pan American gold, and an Olympic gold medal.

- He was honored as be Big Ten Coach of the Year in 1973, 1975, 1976, 1980, 1981, and 1989. He won the Henry Iba award in 1975 and 1989, the Naismith College Coach of the Year in 1987, and the Coach of the Year by the Associated Press and *Basketball Weekly* in 1976.

- Indiana, in 29 years under Knight, finished with at least 20 victories in 21 seasons.

- Twelve players under Knight were named Big Ten Most Valuable Player.

- His 11 Big Ten titles tied Purdue's Ward Lambert as the most ever in Big Ten history.

- Knight took Indiana to the NCAA tournament 24 times in 29 years.

- He is one of only five coaches with 40 or more NCAA tournament victories.

- In 1991 Knight was inducted into the Naismith Basketball Hall of Fame. In 2009 he was inducted into the Indiana University Intercollegiate Athletics Hall of Fame.

Venues and Games

Indiana basketball has been home to five Hallowed Hoosier Hardwoods in history. Let's take a trip down memory lane and find out a little bit about each of the venues that IU basketball has called home.

Original Assembly Hall

The original Assembly Hall was really not a sporting arena—it was a small, one-story, wood-framed structure. Built in 1895 for a cost of $12,000, the building could seat 600 fans for a basketball game. (That's barely enough room for all the assistant coaches on the bench today.) The original Assembly Hall was also not only a game venue, but a practice site and the gymnasium for physical education classes.

Indiana's first game in the original Assembly Hall was played on February 8, 1901, against the Butler Bulldogs. Indiana would lose to Butler 24–20 to run its record to 0–2. Indiana would play three

The original
Assembly Hall
(Indiana University Archives,
P0020431)

games at Assembly Hall that year, winning against Wabash in the final contest, 26–17, on March 8, 1901. By 1902 Indiana would play four games at Assembly Hall and post a 2–2 record.

Indiana played the final game in the original Assembly Hall on January 5, 1917. The opponent was Rose Poly (later changed to Rose Hulman) and marked Indiana's fifth straight victory, which came in dominating fashion, 35–9. Indiana led at halftime 21–6, and Severing Buchman outscored the entire Rose Poly team 10–9.

Presidents William Howard Taft and Teddy Roosevelt, as well as presidential candidate William Jennings Bryan all spoke in the original Assembly Hall. The building itself was demolished in 1938.

A picture of the original Assembly Hall now hangs in the new Assembly Hall.

Men's Gymnasium

Since the original Assembly Hall was falling into disrepair, both the students and faculty marched for a new gymnasium for the athletes. The alumni and university personnel also lobbied for a new gymnasium. When C.P. Hutchins came to IU in 1911, he hired E.O. "Jumbo" Stiehm as football coach and athletic director. They would then take part in a major upgrading of the Indiana athletics program. It was decided to build a new gymnasium in 1914 at a cost of $250,000. The construction of the new Men's Gymnasium would take a little over a year, and the 240-by-328-foot Tudor Gothic structure was completed in 1916. The first game in the new gymnasium would take place in January 1917.

January 19, 1917, was a day of festive excitement as Indiana University celebrated its 97th birthday with a Founders' Day observance. The celebration was led by university president William Lowe Bryan, who called off classes for the day. That night the Hoosiers hosted the Iowa Hawkeyes in the new gymnasium. Coach Guy Lowman had his team ready to play, and Indiana won one of the lowest-scoring games in IU history. Winning 12–7 with 2,400 fans watching, IU led at halftime 5–4. The new gymnasium would remain the home of Indiana basketball for 12 seasons.

Indiana played its final game in the Men's Gymnasium on March 3, 1928, against Big Ten rival Michigan. Indiana defeated Michigan 36–34 to close out the history of the Men's Gymnasium. In that game, future Hall of Fame coach and player Branch McCracken scored 14 points for IU.

Today, you can walk into Wildermuth Intramural Center, walk up the stairs, enter the Men's Gymnasium, and see where Indiana played from 1917 to 1928. Take a basketball, shoot on one of the four goals up there, and transport yourself back in time to 1917. You're a Hoosier hero!

The Original Indiana Fieldhouse

On Thursday, December 13, 1928, Indiana University dedicated the New Indiana Fieldhouse against Pennsylvania, winning the game 34–26. Future Indiana head coach and All-American junior Branch McCracken led the Hoosiers in scoring with nine points. Even though the dedication game was on December 13, the first game in the New Fieldhouse was actually December 8, a 31–30 loss to Washington, in which McCracken also became the first player to score in the New Fieldhouse.

In the game-day program for the December 13 dedication, an article by Vern Boxwell titled "The Fieldhouse for All" described the purpose of the New Indiana Fieldhouse:

> Indiana University's whole physical education program for men will profit through the new Fieldhouse under the plans for the Athletic Department. The completion of this magnificent building fulfills a long need in the Indiana University Athletic Department,

Original Indiana Fieldhouse (Indiana University Archives, P0026774)

and is one of the largest and finest in the Big Ten Conference and Middle West.

All major sports at the state school are benefitted by the new addition to the athletic plant. Pat Page, head football coach, made good use of the building to develop his gridiron squad for important games, when outside practice was practically impossible because of inclement weather conditions.

During the winter months, Coach E.C. Hayes would have his track hopefuls at work in the building, preparing for the indoor and outdoor cinder path season next season. Immediately following the close of the basketball season, the portable hardwood will be removed and baseball practice will start. Tennis aspirants will also find use for the building in the early season practice. Indoor sports, such as wrestling, will be given more room in the Men's Gymnasium.

It is estimated that 13,000 cubic feet of limestone, 200,000 face bricks, and 670 tons of steel were used in the construction of the building, which is 200 by 300 feet in dimensions. The exterior construction is in rock faced ashlar Indiana limestone, and the interior is in light buff brick, with arcs of steel, the lowest of which are 75 feet from the floor. The roof is of built-up insulated type. The American blower system is employed to heat the building, and flood lights are used for illumination.

The Fieldhouse adjoins the Men's Gymnasium, and is nearly twice as large as the old building. Twelve entrances and exits, with double doors, are included. In the southwest corner is located the new training room, where bruises and injuries of the athletes are treated.

The building and its equipment are being financed entirely, at a cost of $350,000 out of proceeds from Indiana athletic contests, and athletic officials sincerely hope to have the continued and increased support of friends and patrons in paying for the building without cost to the state.

It is thought that the ultimate seating capacity of 15,000 will accommodate the maximum crowds of the future. In addition to serving as an athletic building, the Fieldhouse will be used for great general convocations and indoor exercises, such as commencement, public gatherings and conventions.

The Fieldhouse had a portable hardwood floor and a lighting system that had 47 electric lamps suspended from the ceiling. There were also seven floodlights, three of which were above the floor and two that pointed directly at each basket.

Financing for the New Fieldhouse was by First National Bank of Bloomington and the Fletcher American National Bank of

Indianapolis. So the purpose and the future of the new Fieldhouse were set. The New Fieldhouse, which would later be referred to as the Old Fieldhouse, would serve as the home court of Indiana basketball from the 1928–29 season through the 1959–60 season.

In the 31 seasons that the Hoosiers were housed in the Fieldhouse, they recorded a 234–74 record. In addition to a 9–0 start under Coach Everett Dean in 1936, they had six unbeaten years in the Fieldhouse. The 1953 champions would record the best home record with an 11–0 record on the way to Coach McCracken's first Big Ten championship and the Hoosiers' second national championship. The Fieldhouse was the place where Indiana would record their first 20-win season in 1940 (20–3). From 1938 to 1941, Indiana went on a 24-game home winning streak.

The Hoosiers broke the 100-point mark in the Fieldhouse for the first time against Tony Hinkle's Butler Bulldogs on February 2, 1953 (105–70). That same season on February 23, Indiana set a record for the most points ever scored in the Fieldhouse against archrival Purdue (113–78). All-American Don Schlundt led the way in that game with 31 points, followed by his teammate "Mr. Outside" Bobby Leonard's 16.

Indiana closed out play in the Fieldhouse by defeating the eventual national champion Ohio State Buckeyes 99–83 behind Walt Bellamy's 24 points, as all five starters scored in double figures. The win was Indiana's 11th in a row on the way to winning its last 12 games of the 1959–60 season, in which the Hoosiers finished 20–4.

A Bucket List of the 10 Most Important Games Played in the "Old" New Fieldhouse

1. January 17, 1953—IU Prevails in Clash of Titans

The Illini were not only the defending Big Ten champs, but were favored to win both the Big Ten and national championship that season.

Indiana had just won at Ohio State and was 6–0 in Big Ten play. Returning home, though, they had two problems: a sick coach in Branch McCracken and a sick shooter in Bobby Leonard, who had a sore throat and a fever. Leonard was admitted to the IU Infirmary on the Wednesday before Saturday's big game against Illinois.

The two teams were very similar. IU was averaging 82 points per game, and Illinois was right behind at 81.9. Both teams were considered the tallest two teams in the nation, with players on both teams averaging 6'4". The game had been sold out since early December.

If you didn't have a ticket and were within an 80-mile radius of Bloomington, the game was televised on WTTV. Before the game, McCracken characterized the game this way: "The team that loses this one tomorrow night is in a tough spot. It would be particularly tough for us if we lose. The winner will be in the driver's seat, and it would require a couple upsets to move the leader out of first. But it has been done in the past. No team is safe in this league, you know."

In the fourth quarter, IU would build up a five-point lead with about five minutes left in the game. To the 10,000 fans in the Fieldhouse, it looked as if the Hoosiers were completely in control. But Illinois came back to tie the game with 1:40 to play. Leonard held the ball until the final two seconds and then hoisted a shot that hit the back of the rim before bouncing over the back of the backboard to send the game into overtime.

The game would actually go into double overtime. Dick White and Dick Farley hit key free throws down the stretch in the second overtime to lift IU to a 74–70 victory.

2. December 6, 1951–The First Televised Regular Season Game in College Basketball History

One might ask why the opening game of the 1951 season against in-state opponent Valparaiso would stand out as an important game played in the Old Fieldhouse. After all, this was not a Big Ten game played with a championship on the line. It was not a game played against a national power with national rankings at stake.

No, this game is more important for its historical significance than for the outcome of the game itself. For on this day Indiana hosted the very first regular-season college basketball game ever televised in history—and this is how it came about.

The 1951 season would be a special one. It followed the seventh second-place Big Ten finish for Branch McCracken and Indiana in 10 years. It would see the dawn of the Bobby Leonard, Don Schlundt, Dick Farley, Burke Scott, and Charlie Kraak era. It would mark the 50th year of Indiana basketball, going all the way back to February 8, 1901, when Indiana played its first game against Butler, a 20–17 loss.

The idea of the broadcast of a regular-season Indiana basketball game would be the brainchild of Paul Lennon, who not only dreamed of broadcasting these games but doing the play-by-play himself. Paul would require the help of Bob Cook and Bob Petranoff. First, they had to ask the station's chief engineer, Carl Onken, if it was possible to microwave-relay signals from the Fieldhouse's Seventh Street location back to the transmitter. Next, Paul needed to get permission to broadcast these games from Indiana University president Herman Wells and athletic director "Pouch" Harrell. This permission was not easy to get, as both Wells and Harrell were worried about people staying home from the game and watching from the comfort of their family room for free. Lennon didn't hesitate, saying, "How about if we buy the empty seats at a dollar apiece?" Pulling a number out of his head, Lennon offered to pay $750 for the rights to televise the game, saying that if 750 people stayed home, it would come out the same. With that conversation, the first two steps were done. Now all that was left was to obtain sponsorship.

Lennon met with Gary Ruben, who had a new client in Terre Haute, Chesty Foods. Lennon told Ruben it would cost Chesty $2,500 a game. Two days later, Ruben called Lennon saying that Chesty would take all 11 games. With that phone call, Chesty Potato Chips became

IU basketball's first television sponsor. The first game took place on December 6, 1951, against Valparaiso. The game was a sellout, but Indiana University kept the $750.

The press box was a wooden deck above the south stand bleachers. Bob Cook did the statistics for the game. Paul Lennon did the play-by-play while also handling the commercials live, using the catchphrase, "I've got my ticket, have you got yours? This 39¢ size of Chesty Potato Chips is your ticket to tonight's game and all the other games coming up." With that, Chesty Chips flew off the selves of stores everywhere, and the company went from one shift to three overnight.

As for the game itself, Indiana defeated Valparaiso 68–59. Dick Farley led the way with 19 points. All in all, 13 Hoosiers played in the first televised game. Except for the December 22 game when the students were gone on Christmas break, the Hoosiers played before a packed house every game, and Indiana kept the $750 each time. By the 1952–53 season, Indiana would want $2,500 per game. When you venture on your bucket list to the Old Fieldhouse, on the west wall, you can see the plaque commemorating that first televised game.

3. February 29, 1960—The Final Game Played at the Original Fieldhouse

This game would be huge in IU basketball lore, not only for the opponent, but for the fact it would be the last game played in the original Fieldhouse.

Branch McCracken once said that the 1960 Indiana basketball team may have been his best at IU. That's saying something, considering that his 1940 and 1953 Hoosiers squads won national championships.

Indiana had a great team in 1960 but had lost the first three games of Big Ten play, a hole that very few teams could dig themselves out of. In 1960 only one team from the Big Ten was eligible to represent the conference in the NCAA Tournament.

On February 29, 1960, the Hoosiers played host to Ohio State. A month earlier, the two teams had clashed in Columbus and IU had led 95–91 with 1:40 to play. From that point on, however, IU turned it over twice, and Ohio State would go on to win 96–95. When they met the second time around, Ohio State was still unbeaten in Big Ten play and a favorite to win the national championship.

This was the rematch. IU, in the midst of a 10-game winning streak, was seeking revenge. Before the game, however, starter Herbie Lee had been suspended for unspecified school violations. Senior guard Bob Wilkinson told the *Daily Student*, "We can't make up for the whole season in one game, but we're going to beat them tonight and perhaps make up for that game we handed them earlier in the season."

Indiana jumped out to a 13-point lead, 23–10, and never looked back. Junior All-America center Walt Bellamy led the way with 24 points, and all five Hoosiers starters scored in double figures. Bellamy's 24 were followed by Wilkinson's 21, Long's 19, and Hall and Radovich's 13 apiece. It would be Ohio State's only loss in the Big Ten that season.

After the game, Ohio State coach Fred Taylor said, "There wasn't a thing we could do, they were just a much better club than we."

While Ohio State would win the NCAA title, Indiana would finish seventh in the nation.

And on a side note, one of the players for Ohio State that day was Bob Knight.

4. January 10, 1953—Burke Scott Rallies IU Past Minnesota

Indiana was 4–0 in the Big Ten but faced a tough challenge in Minnesota. The Golden Gophers were a top 20–ranked team and appeared primed to pull off a road upset. In the closing minutes, Minnesota led 63–62 and had the ball.

The Gophers drove for a layup but missed the shot, and IU's Bobby Leonard grabbed the rebound. He passed it out to Burke Scott, whose basket put Indiana ahead 64–63. Minnesota would come down and try to score quickly only to miss again. Again the Hoosiers got the rebound, and again Burke Scott broke ahead for a fast-break layup, giving Indiana a 66–63 victory.

Don Schlundt would lead the way in scoring with 17, followed by Dick Farley's 16, and Bobby Leonard's 15. However, Burke Scott's nine were critical, and the victory put Indiana at 5–0 in the Big Ten and a No. 6 ranking in the nation.

5. February 10, 1940—Win over Purdue Ties the Big Ten Race

Purdue was unbeaten going into the game and Indiana had just one loss. In front of a sellout crowd of 6,500 fans in Bloomington, Indiana would tie the Big Ten race by defeating Purdue 46–39. Bill Menke led the way with 12 points, followed by Vern Huffman and Curly Armstrong's eight points each.

The importance of this game would be seen later, as it paved the way for a season sweep of Purdue when the Hoosiers beat Purdue in West Lafayette for the first time in 17 years. These two wins over Purdue would allow Indiana to be picked for the second NCAA Tournament, despite finishing second to Purdue in the Big Ten standings. Indiana would go on to capture its first NCAA championship.

6. March 2, 1936—Vern Huffman Leads IU Past Ohio State

This was the final game of the 1936 season, and Indiana was out to avenge its only loss of the conference season to Ohio State.

Led by Vern Huffman, who is the only player in IU history to be named All-America in both football and basketball, Indiana defeated the Buckeyes 40–34. Huffman scored 10 points to lead the Hoosiers.

The win tied IU with Purdue for the Big Ten crown. But it was difficult to find a tie-breaker. In a quirk in the schedule that season, Indiana and Purdue did not play each other in the regular season.

7. January 16, 1939—McCracken Prevails in First Game against Purdue

Branch McCracken faced rival Purdue 43 times in his IU basketball coaching career. The first was on January 16, 1939, and the new IU coach endeared himself with Hoosiers fans as Indiana beat Purdue 39–36.

Ernie Andres led the Hoosiers with 15 points while Curly Armstrong added 11 points to the cause. The game was a sign of things to come, as McCracken-led Indiana teams would post a 28–15 record against in-state rival Purdue.

8. December 4, 1948—Bill Garrett Becomes First African American Starter in Big Ten History

Often times, the biggest games in history have little to do with what the final score may have been. IU's game in the "New" Fieldhouse on December 4, 1948, is clearly on that list. The fact that IU played a non-conference game against DePauw was of little significance.

Instead, the news was made when Shelbyville's Bill Garrett became the first African American starter in Big Ten basketball history. Indiana beat DePauw 61–48 in front of the Hoosiers faithful. On the day of Garrett's debut, he scored eight points on three baskets and two free throws. He also showed off his impressive rebounding skills as a 6'3" center.

9. March 1, 1958—Archie Dees Comes Up Big against Purdue

In March 1958 the Hoosiers were in an epic struggle with Michigan State in a quest for a Big Ten title. The two teams had tied for the championship the year before, and the March 1 contest against Purdue would be the final home game of the season.

IU had won two in a row and needed to win its last three games to ensure a fourth Big Ten championship under Branch McCracken. Archie Dees did his best to make sure IU did not lose to rival Purdue in the home finale. The All-America center scored 37 points, hitting 11 field goals and 15 free throws. Five other Hoosiers scored in double figures, led by Wilkinson's 18. Indiana won the contest 109–95 in front of a crowd of 10,500.

10. March 4, 1957—Big Second Half Lifts IU over Illinois to Tie for Big Ten Title

Indiana returned home on March 4, 1957, after a road loss at Michigan State had allowed the Spartans to move into a tie for first place in the Big Ten. Now, IU needed to beat Illinois at home in the finale to guarantee at least a share of the Big Ten title.

At halftime, it didn't look good, with the Hoosiers trailing 41–35. But in the second half IU put up a big number. Indiana scored 49 second-half points and beat the Illini 84–76. Although Big Ten MVP Archie Dees would lead the way with 25 points, seniors Dick Neal, Charlie Hodson, and Hallie Bryant would add 12, 17, and 15, respectively.

• • •

Today the Old Fieldhouse is known as Wildermuth Intramural Center or the HPER Building. In your visit to this historic, must-see, bucket list venue, you will find it located at 1025 East Seventh Street across from the Union Building.

You can visit during the hours of 6:00 AM to 11:30 PM Monday through Thursday, 6:00 AM to 9:00 PM on Friday, 8:00 AM to 9:00 PM on Saturday, and 8:00 AM to 11:30 PM on Sunday. As you walk into the Old Fieldhouse, the old court running east to west has been replaced by 10 courts running north and south. Look up, and you can still see the wooden boards on the ceiling and the old lights hanging down. On the west side near the men's locker room is the plaque honoring the playing of the first televised regular season college basketball game.

As you walk up the steps toward the Dick Enberg classroom, you will notice the beautiful limestone arches and the tiled floor and wall.

As you look at the symbols on the wall, you will notice a regal Lion, a clover, and you might be alarmed to see a swastika. What you are seeing, however, is the Sanskrit symbol standing for *su*, meaning "good," *asti*, meaning "it is," and the suffix *ka*, which transforms the phrase into a word meaning "that which is good or auspicious." This comes from the Indus Valley Civilization some 5,000 years ago and has been used by the Greeks, Romans, Celts, Buddhists, Hindus, and Native Americans. The swastika symbol was commonly used worldwide for millennia, long before it was adopted by Hitler and the Nazi Party in 1920. Remember, this building was built in 1917, well before the Nazis came to prominence in Germany.

If you go in what is called the south entrance (from the west), you will notice the crest of Indiana University also in the wall tiles. Go back into the gym and look up at the five huge windows and imagine the sun cascading through on a Saturday afternoon game. Look to the west and notice the old clock looming over the Fieldhouse, marking time and history.

Really want to complete your bucket list? Here's how coauthor Bill Murphy accomplished that one day when he was in the Old Fieldhouse. As he was wandering through the facility, he checked out a basketball, walked out to the three-point line, put up a shot, and hit nothing but net. Just as he did, a group of new students and their parents were walking through on an orientation visit. One of the women said to him, "Nice shot."

In Murphy's words, "That was a check mark on the bucket list."

The New Fieldhouse (Gladstein Fieldhouse)

By the 1940s, under the supervision of athletic director Paul "Pooch" Harrell, it became apparent that the IU athletic complex needed an upgrade. Plans were put in place to build new football and basketball homes for the Hoosiers. For financial reasons, with football being the school's biggest money-maker, it was decided a new football stadium would be built first. Indiana hoped the increased revenue would help the athletic programs in general.

The new football stadium, Memorial Stadium, would seat 52,354 and be completed and in use by 1960. Since IU did not have the money to complete both stadiums at the same time, Indiana would build a temporary home for the basketball team that would also serve as in indoor practice facility while the funds for the new Assembly Hall were obtained. As it turned out, the temporary facility would serve as the home of Indiana basketball from 1960 to 1971.

The New Fieldhouse, as it came to be called, would be built in 1960 at a cost of $1.7 million. The New Fieldhouse would seat 10,300 fans. It would have twice as much lighting as the Old Fieldhouse. Other features included wooden bleachers, folding chairs on a dirt floor, and no air conditioning. The floor was indeed dirt and sawdust with a raised basketball court. Small trailers were set up where fans could purchase soft drinks, popcorn, hot dogs, and peanuts.

As you walk into the New Fieldhouse today, if you let your mind wander, you can still smell the popcorn and hot dogs in the old gym setting. Programs were given out free to the fans. My, how times have changed. In the New Fieldhouse now, renamed the Gladstein Fieldhouse, it may be hard to imagine 10,000-plus fans crowded into it to watch Branch McCracken's and Lou Watson's Hurry Hoosiers play. If you look at the windows at the top of the Fieldhouse, you'll realize the bleachers would stop up there. If you go to an indoor track meet, the trailers with food are like those from the 1960s that fed those fans gathered around with anticipation of both a great game and great food.

If the Fieldhouse could talk, the stories would be amazing to anyone with time to listen. The Fieldhouse was just seven yours old in 1967 when more than 5,000 Hoosiers football fans paid $2 each to gather inside to watch John Pont's undefeated Indiana football team go to East Lansing and come away with a 14–13 victory over the Spartans. The game would be broadcast on closed-circuit TV to the Fieldhouse faithful. This was not the only time the Fieldhouse would be used for football that year. Just one week later, this story would unfold:

The Hoosiers arrived back in Bloomington after a very long, quiet trip following their heartbreaking loss to Minnesota. The police escort leading the team turned toward the New Fieldhouse as Pont announced to the players that this building was their next destination of the night. The players began to wonder if, after the events of the day, they were going to be practicing in the Fieldhouse with all that sawdust. Further disappointment began to set in.

When they walked into the Fieldhouse, though, much to their surprise and delight, it was filled with fans thanking them for what they had accomplished so far and providing support for the big game coming up against Purdue.

Pont went to the podium and addressed both the crowd of supporters and the team, announcing to everyone, "Tonight, we just beat Purdue!"

"And I meant it," Pont elaborated almost 40 years later. "The outpouring of support was unbelievable." And, of course, one week later the Hoosiers did beat Purdue 19–14 to share the Big Ten title and earn a trip to the Rose Bowl.

In 1965 the Fieldhouse would again be the center of attention. Branch McCracken's last Indiana team was riding high with a 12–1 record and ranked fifth in the nation. Hoosiers fans could sense a special

The New Fieldhouse in 1965 after the fire marshall's order to limit the crowd for one game (Indiana University Archives, POO51723)

season with the seven seniors leading the way: the Van Arsdales, Jon McGlocklin, Larry Cooper, Steve Redenbaugh, Ron Peyser, and the little captain with a huge heart, Al Harden. Before entertaining the Iowa Hawkeyes at home, the state fire marshall would rule that the New Fieldhouse did not have enough exits, so he would limit the number of fans who could attend the Iowa game to 3,300. Imagine telling 7,000 ticket holders that their tickets wouldn't be good for the game they were going to. The problem would be resolved but too late to save the Iowa game.

A Bucket List of the 10 Most Important Games Played in the New Fieldhouse

1. December 3, 1960—Indiana Opens New Fieldhouse with Win over Indiana State

Walt Bellamy scored 20 points, and prized sophomores Tom Bolyard and Jimmy Rayl scored 14 and 12, respectively, as Indiana opened play in the New Fieldhouse with a 80–53 win over Indiana State.

2. March 11, 1961—"Big Bell" Walt Bellamy Sets Big Ten Rebounding Record

In the end of that inaugural season in the New Fieldhouse, Walt Bellamy had a game for the ages.

IU won the game against Michigan 82–67, but it was Bellamy's final game as a Hoosier that will always hold special significance. Bellamy scored 28 points, but that wasn't even the big statistic. He also set a Big Ten record for rebounds in a game that has lasted to this day, when he pulled down 33 boards against the Spartans.

Bellamy's points would put him third on the all-time scoring list for the Hoosiers behind Don Schlundt and Archie Dees at the time. His 33 rebounds would put him first on Indiana's all-time rebounding list with 1,087. In 1995 Alan Henderson passed Bellamy on the all-time list with 1,091. However, the record probably needs an asterisk, as Bellamy's total came in 70 games over three seasons, while Henderson's mark was amassed over 124 games in four seasons.

3. January 27, 1962—Rayl Has His First Record Scoring Output

The first game between Indiana and Minnesota in 1962 had been a hard-fought Golden Gophers victory in Minneapolis, 104–100. Jimmy Rayl scored 32 points for IU in that game. The rematch, however, would be even more special for Rayl and the Hoosiers.

IU trailed at halftime 53–48 in front of 7,342 fans in the New Fieldhouse. The game went into overtime, and with seven seconds to play, Minnesota was shooting free throws down by one point. The Golden Gophers' shooter hit the first one, and Rayl said to teammate Jerry Bass, "If he makes the second free throw, call a timeout." He did make the second free throw, but instead of calling timeout, Bass inbounded the ball to Rayl and simply said, "Go."

With the clock running down, Rayl would race up court in typical Hurryin' Hoosiers, racehorse style. Rayl was such an exceptional shooter, and when he crossed the midcourt stripe, he let fire a shot from about 45 feet away. The shot would hit nothing but the bottom of the net, giving Indiana a 105–104 overtime win. Not only was Rayl the hero of the Hoosiers win, but his bucket gave him 56 points, setting a new Big Ten and Indiana single-game scoring record.

For the day, Rayl went 20-of-39 from the floor and 16-of-20 from the free throw line to pace the Hoosiers. Later, looking at a shot chart for Rayl that day, it was revealed that, had the game been played by modern rules, Rayl would have had many more points. There was no three-point line in college basketball in 1962. Some say that 17 of Rayl's field goals that day would have been three-pointers in today's game. In other words, that 56-point day could easily have been closer to 73—although if his shots had counted for three points, the game likely would not have gone to overtime.

Branch McCracken called Rayl's game, "One of the greatest exhibitions of outside shooting that I have ever seen."

4. February 23, 1963—Jimmy Rayl Does It Again

The first time Indiana and Michigan State met in basketball in 1963, Jimmy Rayl scored 44 points in a 96–84 IU victory in East Lansing.

The second time around, IU was looking for a victory that would put the Hoosiers just one game behind Illinois and Ohio State in the Big Ten title race.

Indiana roared out to a 57–45 halftime lead and coasted to a 113–94 win over Michigan State in front of 8,636 Hoosiers fans. But once again the main story was Jimmy Rayl. Rayl hit 23 field goals on 48 attempts to set a new conference record in both categories. Rayl's 56-point game, while tying his own Indiana record for one game, set the record for most points in a regulation (non-overtime) game.

For the season, Rayl scored an even 100 points against Michigan State. In the second game, Rayl came out of the game with more than three minutes to play, and fans in the Fieldhouse booed that decision by McCracken because Rayl had 56 points and only needed one more point for a new record.

Rayl joked later that he secretly hoped Bob Knight would be Indiana's basketball coach forever. It all had to do with his perception about one of his school records never being broken. Did Rayl think that no other IU player in history would ever score 56 points? That wasn't the record he was referring to. "No," he said, "because my 48 attempts in a game by one player wouldn't be broken."

What's truly amazing about that record is that Rayl is still the only player in IU history to ever attempt more than 40 shots in a single game.

One other side story involving Rayl and that season against Michigan State involved former Indiana high school standout Scott Skiles. Skiles asked Rayl if he would call Michigan State and talk to coach Jud Heathcote and put in a good word for him with the Spartans. Rayl called the office and was put on hold. A few moments later, Heathcote got on the phone and said, "Ahhhh, the great Jimmy Rayl, Indiana's all-time leading scorer."

To which Rayl replied, "Actually I'm not, coach, but if I had played Michigan State every game, I would have been."

5. February 16, 1963—Bolyard and Rayl Lead IU over Illinois

Back-to-back losses to Wisconsin and Minnesota had dropped IU out of the Big Ten title hunt, but that didn't mean Indiana couldn't play the role of spoiler.

On February 16, Illinois came to Bloomington in first place in the Big Ten and ranked No. 4 in the nation. The Illini led 50–41 at the half. The Hoosiers however, would scorch the nets in the second half, scoring 62 second-half points to defeat Illinois 103–100.

Senior Tom Bolyard would lead the way, scoring 34 points, followed by Rayl's 29. Dick Van Arsdale added 12, and brother Tom Van Arsdale had 11.

6. March 9, 1963—Indiana Plays the Role of Spoiler

In the season finale of the 1962–63 season, the Hoosiers faced the No. 3 Ohio State Buckeyes. Ohio State was in the Big Ten lead, but a loss to Indiana would drop it into a first-place tie with Illinois. This would be important because, at the time, if teams in the Big Ten tied for the championship, the team who had not been to the NCAA Tournament most recently would get the invitation. So an Ohio State loss would send Illinois to the tourney.

That was plenty of motivation for the Hoosiers in the final game of the year. In front of 10,300 screaming fans, Indiana trailed at halftime 36–34. Then the hard-fought contest went into overtime.

Jimmy Rayl had an incident in overtime that became legendary. He said Ohio State's Gary Bradds was complaining to the officials about something, and Rayl piped in with a comment of his own. "I did something I really did not do," Rayl recalled. "I yelled back at him to 'Stop complaining, you big cry baby!' Well, Bradds didn't like me saying that, so he swung at me. Luckily, he missed. He was really big. If he had hit me, it would have hurt."

Tom Bolyard and Dick Van Arsdale stepped in, and order was restored.

"The ball was thrown into me, and as I turned to go upcourt, I got hit," Rayl said. "There were nine seconds left, and we were up by one. I went down on the floor, and our fans came out on the court. I was told there were about 150 fans out there. I was really hurt, but I went to the line to shoot my free throws. I took my first shot, and the ball fell underneath the basket. I shot the second free throw a lot harder, and it went in."

Indiana won 87–85, and the fans rushed onto the floor again, this time in celebration. Rayl had suffered a separated collarbone, and if IU had had any more games that season, he would not have been able to play.

7. December 12, 1964—Quite a Collection of Talent on the Floor That Day

Indiana beat North Carolina 107–81 that day, but this was another game where it was more about something else than just the outcome.

First of all, the game would match future Hall of Fame coaches Branch McCracken and a young Dean Smith at Carolina. There were also some pretty good players on the court that day who, next season, would be named to the All-Rookie Team in the NBA. Indiana's Jon McGlocklin and Tom and Dick Van Arsdale were in that company, as was North Carolina's Billy Cunningham.

8. March 11, 1967—IU Completes Last-to-First Turnaround

Indiana went into the Purdue game that season trying to accomplish something that at one time seemed nearly impossible. The year before the Hoosiers had finished 4–10 and last in the Big Ten. A win against Purdue on this day, however, would give IU a 10–4 record and the Big Ten title.

Indiana won going away, 95–82. New Castle's Butch Joyner would lead the way with 22, while Greenfield's Jack Johnson and Michigan City's Vern Payne would have 14 apiece. The win would propel Indiana to its first NCAA Tournament appearance since 1958.

9. February 23, 1971—Steve Downing Sets a Record That Still Stands Today

One of the most amazing facts in Indiana basketball history is that there has only ever been one triple-double by a Hoosiers player. It happened in February 1971.

Indiana beat Michigan 88–79 that day to tie the Wolverines for second place in the Big Ten. Big George McGinnis from Indianapolis Washington led the way with 33 points. But it was his teammate, both at IU and from high school in Indianapolis, who stole the show.

Downing scored 28 points, pulled down 17 rebounds, and blocked 10 shots to record the only triple-double in Indiana history. Not only is the triple-double a record, but the 10 blocked shots is still the most ever by an Indiana player.

10. March 6, 1965—McCracken Coaches His Final Game at Indiana

Branch McCracken's final home game at Indiana was also his final game with the Hoosiers overall.

It was an evening game beginning at 7:30 PM and played before 9,023 fans. His son, Dave McCracken, recalled years later, "If Dad could win just one game in a season, no question about it, he would want it to be Purdue."

Indiana led throughout and eventually posted a 90–79 victory. McCracken's career had come to an end in a wonderfully victorious fashion. As he was walking off the court, he was beckoned back. With his arm around Al Harden, Branch would listen at center court as a plaque to him was read to all in attendance. McCracken was flanked by players Harden, Steve Redenbaugh, Jon McGlocklin, the Van Arsdales, Larry Cooper, and Ron Peyser. He adjusted his glasses as the emotion of the moment showed through, and he walked off the court a living legend of Indiana basketball.

As you walk into Gladstein Fieldhouse, look up and imagine a score-board that lit up a total of 49 times with 90 or more points. If you stop and listen carefully, you can hear the squeak of the tennis shoes and the pounding of bodies running up and down the court at breakneck speed.

Assembly Hall (Simon Skjodt Assembly Hall)

The idea for Assembly Hall would dawn with a schematic drawing in 1949. It would be the year actual plans were made for a basketball pavilion.

"We were also talking about a new football stadium, fieldhouse in the center of campus [now the Wildermuth Intermural Center]," said Paul "Pooch" Harrell. "From the very beginning, we were determined to have seating on only two sides, since it is difficult to sell seats in the end zone." Harrell was the Indiana man who would be most closely related with Assembly Hall. "He was the athletic director when the first plans were drawn up and would step down as athletic director in 1954 to take over the coordinator's position for Indiana's expanding complex," said assistant athletic director Chuck Crabb.

The first design for Assembly Hall would come by way of Osborne engineering, the same firm that had designed Yankee Stadium, Michigan Stadium, and Notre Dame Stadium. The design called for a standard four-sided seating arrangement. But this did not meet the ideas of Indiana officials. So what were the ideas of the Indiana officials, and why? IU officials wanted a state-of-the-art facility that would be unique from any other ever designed for basketball. After all, this was and is the Hoosier State. They wanted most of the seating on the sides, to ensure a good view of the action. At the time, backboards were solid, so those sitting behind the baskets had an obstructed view, and many times they could not tell if a basket had been made. Indiana, like many schools, installed lights atop the backboards that flashed whenever a basket was scored, much like hockey.

School officials wanted something different and were planning for seating around 20,000 fans. Coach Branch McCracken told the *Indianapolis News* in an interview in 1953, "That may be too big for us. Maybe 15,000 capacity would be big enough." Athletic director Paul Harrell found his answer in a North Carolina livestock pavilion. After they had released Osborne from designing both the football and basketball buildings and engaged the Eggers Partnership to design both, Harrell passed the pavilion design on to them as a suggestion for what Indiana officials had in mind. The school officials liked the design so much that they would use it for Memorial Stadium (the football stadium), as well. The Eggers Partnership would present the new plans in 1957 for the three structures mentioned above, and the bids were then taken. The construction figures, however, far exceeded the estimates and were rejected. So each structure was then bid separately. Assembly Hall would be dropped, and the basketball team would use the New Fieldhouse until the funds became available to build the new basketball stadium.

The year 1967 was one no IU fan will ever forget. Indiana would win four Big Ten championships: in football (the team's second ever), basketball, men's cross country, and men's swimming. It would also be the year when ground was broken for Assembly Hall on December 22, 1967, the very same day that the Cardiac Kids, the football team, left for Pasadena, California, to face O.J. Simpson and the USC Trojans in the granddaddy of them all, the Rose Bowl.

The unobstructed views of Assembly Hall are made possible by using a catenary cable system, which eliminates any support posts. The 54 cables support a total weight of 2.7 million pounds, using the principles often used in bridge construction. The cables support the long span of the room, which is 350 feet across at its widest point. This is done instead of steel trusses bearing the weight. The cables, each 1¾" thick, start at a point on the exterior wall behind the seating area and

Assembly Hall (Indiana University Archives, P0044141)

are supported mid-span on two inclined steel arches, running the length of the building.

The room decking is composed of 4,650 pre-cast concrete slabs, each measuring 3' x 6' and weighing about 600 pounds. The total weight of the building, which rests on a solid bedrock of limestone, is 127 million pounds.

The basketball court is named the "Branch McCracken Memorial Court," in honor of the basketball coach who brought Indiana its first two national titles. The court can be removed and a full 108' x 54' portable stage installed in one day.

The arena floor has an entrance which will accommodate a loaded semi-trailer truck to bring in various traveling shows. Areas under the east stands provide full stage support with individual dressing rooms, stage storage areas, two large chorus rooms, team dressing rooms, and a commissary.

The remaining part of the building, which is totally air-conditioned, provides a home for all of Indiana's intercollegiate teams except swimming. During the beginning years of Assembly Hall, offices of the Athletic Department were moved into the west main level. The red-and-blue-cushioned theater seats greet fans as they come into the new Assembly Hall.

Basketball would not be the first event in Assembly Hall when it opened on September 12, 1971. Bob Hope and British pop artist Petula Clark headlined Indiana's 1971 football homecoming on October 23. They were the first to perform in Assembly hall. The 101st edition of Ringling Brothers and Barnum & Bailey Circus would follow. The rock opera *Jesus Christ Superstar* would make an appearance in November. On December 1, 1971, it was finally the basketball team's turn, and Indiana opened its new home against Ball State, winning 84–77. On Saturday afternoon, December 18, 1971, at 2:00 PM, Indiana dedi-cated both Assembly Hall and the naming of the Branch McCracken Memorial Basketball Floor. Indiana crushed Notre Dame that day, 94–29. John Ritter would outscore the entire Notre Dame team by himself. It was the 46th and last time an Indiana player would outscore an opposing team.

Assembly Hall cost $26.6 million, and in the 45 years of its existence, it would host many performances other than basketball, including campaign speeches, commencement ceremonies, high school tourney games, and concerts, including a concert by Elvis Presley. Presley's manager, Colonel Tom Parker, had promised Elvis that he would always sing to sellout crowds. Elvis was scheduled to give a concert at a less-than-soldout Assembly Hall. The Colonel, trying to keep his promise, moved the people who had tickets in the balcony down to the main level to fill up the lower level. Parker then visited all the local hardware stores, buying up all the black plastic trash bags he could find. The black bags were then placed over all the balcony seats to make it appear as if there were not seats in the balcony. For weeks, the workers were finding pieces of plastic bags in the balcony. Promise kept, Colonel style.

Although many patrons over the years have complained about bal-cony seating, a longtime balcony patron once said, "Well, yes, I sit in the front row of the balcony, but no one ever stands up in front of me. And if that happens, we really have a story."

Sportscaster Gus Johnson would call Assembly Hall, "The Carnegie Hall of Basketball."

In 2014 Indiana University would announce a $40 million gift from Cindy Simon Skjodt and the Simon family for the renovations to Assembly Hall. Cindy Simon Skjodt would say, "I grew up going to Indiana University games and have great memories of watching basketball games with my father. The atmosphere in Assembly Hall is truly unmatched anywhere in college basketball. Everyone in our family has enjoyed incredible experiences with Indiana University. We feel fortunate for our IU relationships, and it's rewarding to give back. We hope others in Hoosier Nation who are able to do so will also give back to help make the 'Catching Excellence Campaign' a success."

The renovations of Assembly Hall focused on improving amenities to enhance the fan experience. The south lobby was restructured with a new entryway and dramatic atrium. Escalators replaced ramps in the south lobby. Throughout the arena, new branding and graphics were updated to celebrate the tradition and success of IU basketball.

Existing bathrooms and concession stands were remodeled and new bathrooms were added to Assembly Hall. A large state-of-the-art scoreboard was added. The theater seats were updated and box-seat-style seating was added above the south baseline bleachers.

Still remaining is the flagship of the Assembly Hall, the banners. The five national championship banners hang at one end and the NIT championship, Big Ten championships, and CCA championship hang on the other end.

A Bucket List of the 10 Most Important Games Played at Assembly Hall

1. February 7, 1976—Wayne Radford Saves the Day in Win over Michigan

Everyone looks back at 1976 as being IU's unbeaten national championship season, but that didn't come without a few close calls along the way.

One would be the Michigan game at Assembly Hall. IU had won the first game 80–74, but found tough sledding all day in the rematch. In fact, Michigan led the entire game. With under 30 seconds to play, the Wolverines had a four-point lead at 60–56 before Quinn Buckner hit a jumper to cut the lead in half. Michigan's Steve Grote then missed the front end of a one-and-one, giving the Hoosiers life. Indiana had a couple of shots at tying the game but couldn't until Kent Benson rebounded a miss and scored at the buzzer to send the game into overtime.

In overtime, Michigan continued to lead, but a bucket by Scott May gave IU its first lead of the game at 68–67. IU hit four free throws down the stretch to make the final 72–67.

Although May had 27 points and Benson 21, it was Wayne Radford's heroics that many believe saved the day for the Hoosiers. Radford had 16 points coming off the bench on 6-of-7 shooting from the field, giving the Hoosiers the lift they needed to continue their undefeated season.

2. December 10, 2011—The "Wat Shot" Beats No. 1 Kentucky

This one didn't lead to a championship or an undefeated season, but in many ways it signaled the return of Indiana University basketball from a dark period brought on by NCAA recruiting violations made by Kelvin Sampson in 2007 and 2008.

With Dick Vitale calling the game for ESPN, a national television audience watched as the Hoosiers hosted the No. 1 Kentucky Wildcats. Both teams were undefeated on the young season, but Kentucky had the lofty national ranking.

IU led at the half and actually caught fire in the second half, going up by 10. But Kentucky came roaring back. IU trailed by one and had the ball with 19 seconds to play, but Victor Oladipo turned it over, and the Hoosiers were forced to foul. Kentucky had two free throws, missing the first but making the second. It was 72–70 Kentucky with 5.6 seconds to play.

Christian Watford inbounded the ball to Verdell Jones III, who brought the ball upcourt. He began to drive the lane from the left side but, at the last possible moment, passed it out to Watford who was set up for a three-point shot on the left wing. Watford rose up and got the shot off before time expired. When it went in to give Indiana a 73–72 victory, college basketball experienced one of the craziest stormings of a court that has ever been witnessed.

The Indiana fans celebrated on the court well into the night, and Kentucky coach John Calipari later said it was because of that experience at the end of the game that he won't bring his Wildcats team back to Assembly Hall anytime soon. While Indiana fans would love for that rivalry to resume, if they had to have one final moment in the series to cherish against Kentucky, that would be it.

3. *February 14, 1993—Top Ranked IU Holds Off Fab Five Michigan*

This one was top-ranked Indiana against No. 4 Michigan, and for most of the day it was all Wolverines.

In fact, Michigan led by 13 at 27–14, and still led by nine at 70–61 with 11:32 to play. But that's when IU caught fire. The Hoosiers would go on a 28–8 run with Matt Nover and Greg Graham doing most of the damage. Michigan was the next one to make a run and cut the lead to 91–89 with 10 seconds to play. Brian Evans was fouled and hit two free throws with two seconds remaining, and a late Michigan basket made the final Indiana 93, Michigan 92.

The win would propel Indiana to the Big Ten championship over the much heralded Fab Five.

4. March 7, 1987—The Day Steve Alford Rooted for Michigan

Indiana came into the game against Ohio State needing to win the game and hope for a Purdue loss to tie for the Big Ten title. In front of 17,289 Hoosiers fans, the Buckeyes led by one at halftime. But IU rallied back on Senior Day to win 90–81 as Steve Alford led the way with 22 points, while Ricky Calloway had 20.

The game had been packed with pressure as this was the last chance for the seniors to win a Big Ten title. No Knight-coached seniors had ever gone through four years without winning at least one Big Ten championship. So the pressure was indeed on. After the game at the end of Alfords's senior speech, he would give the fans a special message.

"I am going to say something I never thought I would say," he said. "Let's go home and root for Michigan."

5. March 22, 1981—IU Wins NCAA Tournament Game in Assembly Hall to Advance to the Final Four

On March 22, 1981, IU faced St. Joseph's in the Mideast Regional Championship—in Assembly Hall.

Back when teams were permitted to host Regionals, Indiana first beat UAB 87–72 and then faced St. Joseph's in the Regional Championship Game. Landon Turner and Ray Tolbert each scored 14 points to lead Indiana to a 78–46 win and a trip to the Final Four.

Two games later, the Hoosiers would wrap up the season by beating North Carolina 63–50 to win the national championship.

6. March 2, 1980—Indiana Beats Ohio State for Winner-Take-All Big Ten Title Matchup

In the first game of the 1979–80 Big Ten season, Indiana lost to Ohio State 59–58. When the final game of the Big Ten campaign came, the two teams faced off again. This time they were tied for first in the Big Ten with 12–5 records, and the winner would win the conference title.

With eight minutes to play, Ohio State led 59–51. But Butch Carter capped a big Hoosiers rally with two free throws in the final seconds to send the game to overtime. Indiana would take it from there and win 76–73.

7. January 7, 2001—Haston's Shot Beats No. 1 Michigan State

Michigan State came to Bloomington January 7 with a lot going for it. The Spartans were the defending national champions and were ranked No. 1 in the nation with a 12–0 record.

Kirk Haston changed it all with one shot. Trailing 58–56, IU had the ball and one more shot. Kirk Haston set a screen for Kyle Hornsby and then popped out beyond the three-point line. Hornsby passed him the ball and Haston hit the shot to give IU a 59–58 win. Haston, who scored 27 points to lead IU, was hoisted in the air by Tom Coverdale as the students stormed the court.

8. February 19, 1989—Jay Edwards Does It Again with Another Last-Second Shot

Within a one-week span in February 1989, Jay Edwards provided IU fans with a pair of thrilling moments.

The first moment was on February 12, when Edwards drove to the left and pulled up from 16 feet out to knock down a jumper late in the game to push IU to a 64–62 win over rival Purdue.

A week later, it happened again—this time against Michigan. IU trailed 75–71 before Edwards made two free throws to cut the lead to two. Glen Rice missed a shot for Michigan, and Eric Anderson got the rebound in the closing seconds. Lyndon Jones would spot his former high school teammate Jay Edwards at the top of the key. A perfect pass and a super smooth shot that would touch nothing but the bottom of the net gave Indiana a 76–75 win.

9. March 4, 1993—Cheaney Gets in the Record Books

Indiana hosted Northwestern on March 4, and senior Calbert Cheaney needed six points to pass Steve Alford and become the all-time leading scorer in Indiana history. IU had won 15 games in a row.

Alford sent Cheaney a letter before the game that read, "When I broke Don Schlundt's record, he sent me a letter, and one of the things he said was that I was more than a basketball player, that he was glad a class individual was breaking his record. That's how I feel with you, Calbert. It's been a great pleasure to watch you develop as a player over the last four years. But, more than that, it's great to have somebody who is just a first-class individual and somebody who has been a part of the Indiana basketball family. I think you exemplify what it means to be an Indiana basketball player."

Cheaney scored from the baseline 10 seconds into the game. Then on a quick break, he swished a three, and in the first 40 seconds, he had tied Alford's record with 2,438 points. A Greg Graham miss and a Cheaney put-back later, and IU's record belonged to Cheaney just 1:06 into the game.

Indiana would go on to win 98–69 as Cheaney led the way with 35 points.

10. December 11, 1975—Another Close Win on the Road to Perfection

It was just three games into what would ultimately be IU's perfect 1976 national championship season. The Hoosiers were taking on Digger Phelps and the Notre Dame Fighting Irish.

Neither team played well, and both teams shot less than 40 percent from the field. Indiana took a big second-half lead and then held on for a 63–60 win over the No. 8 Fighting Irish.

Bob Knight said later that it wasn't pretty, but he would take it.

"It was a game that was kind of a struggle for both teams, and I guess we just out-struggled them," Knight said.

The Greatest Games

Now let's look at some different kinds of games. Not tied to a particular venue, here's a bucket list of the best games in IU history that you probably wish you would have attended. In some cases, if you're a ultimate IU fan, perhaps you did. Let's see how a few of these games may jog your memory a bit.

The Championship Games

1. March 29, 1976—A Perfect Game From a Perfect Team

The title game in 1976 would match Indiana against Big Ten foe Michigan. Indiana had already beaten the Wolverines 80–74 on the road and 72–67 in an overtime victory in Bloomington.

It is never easy to beat any team three times in one season, but to beat a really good team is very difficult. Indiana's quest for a perfect season and national championship seemed to hang in the balance just three minutes into the game as 6'6" standout guard Bobby Wilkerson lay on the floor, the victim of a Wayman Britt elbow to the side of his head. As Wilkerson was out cold, Coach Knight looked down possibly at the end of both a perfect season and a national title for the second year in a row.

Scott May had broken his arm the previous season in what many believe cost IU the title in 1975. Wilkerson was actually taken to the hospital and wouldn't return. IU trailed at the half 35–29.

"Perfection" (Indiana University Archives, P0028847)

In the second half with 15:55 left in the game, All-American Scott May pulled the Hoosiers even at 39–39. Later, with IU leading 63–59, May hit a remarkable field goal directly underneath the basket, letting loose a high-arcing shot that went almost straight up and then down through the hoop for two points. Eventually, the lead surged to 10 with under five minutes to play and then 14 at the 1:47 mark.

The final: Indiana 86, Michigan 68.

2. March 18, 1953—IU Beats Kansas to Claim Second National Title

Hall of Famer and team captain Bobby Leonard said of this team, "It was one of those ballclubs where everybody just fit together like a glove, everybody did. I think the thing was, there was no jealousy, no nothing, we went out with a team concept. I don't think I have ever

Indiana beats Kansas for NCAA title No. 2
(Indiana University Archives, P0043520)

been with a group of guys in my life that we were as close to each other as that ballclub. That was a great basketball team."

To get to this game, the Hoosiers had to avenge one of their three defeats on the season by beating in-state foe Notre Dame 79–66. In the semifinal contest, IU beat Bob Pettit and LSU 80–67. That set up the title game against defending national champion Kansas.

In a tightly contested game, Kansas made a late free throw to tie it. As time was running out, Bobby Leonard drove the left side of the lane and drew the foul as his shot almost went in, teasing around the rim before falling off. Leonard's first free throw hit the front of the rim, but his second was nothing but net, and IU led 69–68 with 27 seconds left. The Hoosiers would clamp down on the defensive end, forcing Kansas to pass the ball eight times before a desperation shot at the horn fell off the side of the rim, and the Hoosiers had their second NCAA championship.

First McCracken, then Leonard were hoisted up on the shoulders of the victorious team. After the game, reporters told Leonard that McCracken had said of him that he had icewater in his veins. Leonard replied, "If that was icewater, it sure felt warm running down my leg."

3. March 30, 1981—Hoosiers Beat North Carolina to Win Title No. 4

Indiana got to the title game at the Spectrum in Philadelphia with a 29–9 record, more losses than any other previous NCAA champion. It would be the second time IU and North Carolina played that season. The Tar Heels had beaten the Hoosiers 65–56 in Chapel Hill on December 20.

The big national news that day had been an assassination attempt on President Ronald Reagan, and for a while it was unclear whether the game would be postponed. However, with the news that the president had survived the shooting, they decided to play the game that night.

In the first five minutes of the second half—always important to Coach Knight—Indiana outscored the Tar Heels 12–6. Indiana's lead would grow to double digits on a Randy Wittman jumper, making it

Indiana beats North Carolina for title No. 4 (Indiana University Archives, P0035336)

45–34. From that point in time, North Carolina never got closer than eight points. With 1:21 to go, Steve Risley hit two free throws to push the lead back to 10, and North Carolina would never get closer.

The final score read: Indiana 63, North Carolina 50. Isiah Thomas threw the ball in the air in jubilation. He would be named MVP of the tourney, which seemed appropriate, since all season Indiana fans had become familiar with the Bible passage from Isaiah 11:6, "and a little child shall lead them." Isiah's brothers had gone around repeating the verse at Assembly Hall after Indiana had beaten St. Joseph's to punch their ticket to the Final Four.

And there in Philadelphia, Knight's title No. 2 and Indiana's No. 4 had become a reality. Coauthor Bill Murphy also had a bucket list item crossed off on that night as he sat next to former Indiana coach Everett Dean.

4. March 30, 1940—Indiana Beats Kansas to Claim First National Title

When the Hoosiers arrived in Kansas City, they were escorted to a huge, wonderful hotel. The expectation of everyone was that Kansas, who had become a basketball power, would win the tourney.

On the afternoon of the championship game, some of the players wanted to go to the movies and see *Gone with the Wind*. McCracken would have none of it, and he did not want his players to spend five hours in a movie house before the big game. However, Branch had to go to a coaches meeting, so Mary Jo, Branch's wife, took the boys to the show. During intermission (yes, the movie was that long), Mary Jo made the boys run around the block and stretch their legs. When they got back, McCracken was furious and insisted the team run some more.

When the Hoosiers arrived at the auditorium where the game would be played, coach Phog Allen and his Kansas team were being showered with gifts—much to the chagrin of the Indiana players. In fact, Curly Armstrong turned to Herman Schaefer and Bob Dro and said,

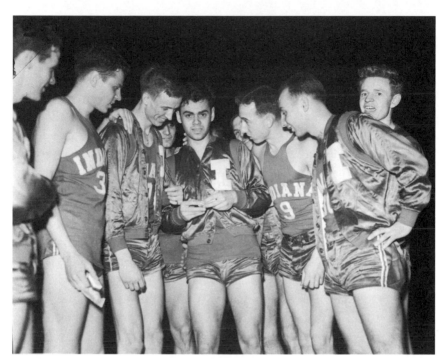

Indiana beats Kansas to claim its first NCAA title (Indiana University Archives, P0028849)

"Now, isn't that something? Let's go out there and whip them before all of their fans."

Of the game, one newspaper reporter described Indiana as showing more spark and drive than a Kentucky thoroughbred. On hand at the game was Branch's old coach, Everett Dean, to watch his former team play for the national title. The game itself started off slow with neither team able to score. Then Armstrong, Schaefer, and Dro started running, and Indiana started to take off. During the action, Armstrong gave Bob Allen, the Kansas coach's son, a fake that caused him to be out of position and take an accidental shot to the chin, knocking him to the ground.

Armstrong then looked down on poor Allen and, pointing to the Kansas bench, suggested that maybe he should go over there and "sit by Daddy." Thirteen minutes into the game, Indiana held a slim 17–14 lead, but a 15–5 run put the Hoosiers up 32–19 at the halfway mark. Indiana, under the direction of court general Marv Huffman, kept running and would race to a 60–42 championship game win. After the game, USC coach Sam Barry said of the Hoosiers, "I knew Indiana was fast, but not that fast." Marv Huffman and Jay McCreary led the Hoosiers with 12 points apiece, followed by Armstrong's 10, Schaefer's nine, Dro's seven, and five each from Bill Menke and Andy Zimmer. McCreary, Menke, and Huffman were named to the all-tourney team, with Huffman being named the Most Outstanding Player.

Indiana returned home the next afternoon to a string of cars a mile long. McCracken and the team were hoisted onto the fire truck as the parade moved down 10th Street and out to Seventh Street and the men's gymnasium, where nearly 3,000 people and a band playing "Indiana, Our Indiana" were waiting. Each player spoke to the crowd, then captain Marv Huffman held up the beautiful, four-foot-tall trophy. After the championship game, a middle-aged man approached McCracken. "I want to shake your hand," he said. "My name's Naismith."

"Are you any relation to the fellow who invented basketball?" asked McCracken.

"He was my father," the stranger replied, "and I wish he could have been here to see this game tonight. This is the greatest basketball team I have ever seen."

5. March 30, 1987—Smart Hits "The Shot" to Beat Syracuse for the Fifth Title

Of all of Indiana's five national titles, the 1987 championship was probably the most improbable. Indiana had surprised and upset No. 1–ranked UNLV to advance to the title game. Coach Knight employed an uptempo game, catching everyone by surprise, because this type of game plan fit right into the tempo UNLV liked to play. Coach Knight later explained that he thought that IU could run with the Running

"The Shot" (Indiana University Archives, P0056252)

Rebels, but if Indiana tried to slow the tempo down, UNLV would win by more than 30.

After getting past UNLV, the national title game versus Syracuse was back and forth for much of the way before the Orangemen went up 70–68 with just under two minutes to play. Keith Smart scored to tie the game, and then Syracuse hit a free throw to go up by one. With 28 seconds to play, Syracuse freshman Derrick Coleman was fouled, sending him to the line for a one-and-one.

Knight, in an effort to freeze the freshman, would call a timeout. As Indiana approached the lane lines, Keith Smart would wink at his teammates as if he knew something the 64,959 in attendance did not know. Coleman's left-handed free throw would come up short, just grazing the rim. With Syracuse deciding not to put anyone on the lines, Indiana's Daryl Thomas would easily get the rebound and pass the ball to Joe Hillman to bring the ball upcourt.

CBS broadcaster Brent Musburger said, "Indiana can win it." Knight, as was his practice, did not call timeout but let everthing play out. Hillman passed to Smart on the left side. Smart kicked the ball into Thomas, who faked a shot, only to throw the ball back out to Smart, who floated in the air toward the baseline and let fly a shot that would hit only the bottom of the net. Smart made his shot with five seconds left, and a shocked Syracuse let four seconds run off the clock before calling a timeout. Syracuse threw a full-court football pass only to have it picked off by, who else, Keith Smart. Indiana won its fifth national championship, its third under Knight.

6. March 21, 1979—Indiana Beats Purdue to Win the NIT

Instead of the usual locale—Mackey Arena or Assembly Hall—Indiana and Purdue squared off in New York City's Madison Square Garden for the title game of the 1979 NIT.

Each team had won one game against the other that year on its home court. For the 42nd annual National Invitational Tournament, Purdue wore the home whites, while Indiana wore their red road uniforms. Indiana's game plan consisted of holding down Purdue's center Joe Barry Carroll.

Purdue led by four at halftime, 29–25. They still led, by one point, 52–51, with 21 seconds left to play, when Carroll came to the free-throw line after being fouled by Butch Carter. He missed the front end of a one-and-one, and Ray Tolbert got the rebound for IU. The Boilermakers had a foul to give and fouled Mike Woodson with 16 seconds to play.

Bob Knight called three consecutive timeouts to set up the last-second play. Randy Wittman threw the ball into Carter, who returned the ball to Wittman. Wittman passed into the lane to Woodson, who threw the ball out to Carter. Carter faked a shot and then, with six seconds left, let fly a contested shot from the top of the key. The shot found its mark, and Purdue was down by one with just four seconds left.

Purdue threw the ball to halfcourt and called another timeout. The final play saw Purdue shoot from the left corner, but the shot bounced hard off the rim. Indiana had won its first NIT championship.

Coach Knight, who was a big fan of the NIT, having led his Army teams to three semifinal games, said after the game, "I've never had a bigger ambition than to win the NIT. This is as satisfying as the NCAA title." This game marked Indiana earning the second of the big two championships in college basketball.

7. March 18, 1974—Indiana Beats USC in the CCA Tournament Title Game

The conference commissioners had set up a new tournament called the Collegiate Commissioners Association (CCA) Tournament. This tournament would be for the second-place teams in the various conferences. Indiana had tied Michigan for the Big Ten championship and so met in Champaign, Illinois, to decide the winner. Indiana came out on the short end of the 75–67 score, sending Indiana to the CCA.

IU was very disappointed not to go to the NCAA Tournament, but Knight decided that, if they had to go to the CCA, they would go to win and use the games as a springboard to the next year. Indiana defeated Tennessee and Toledo to advance to the championship game against USC. Both Indiana and USC had had to win in overtime to make it to the final game. Knight informed the squad that John Laskowski, whose nickname was the "Super Sub," would start in the title game.

The game was played before a crowd of 4,721, if that can be called a crowd. Steve Green said that he could hear his mom talking—not yelling, but *talking*—in the crowd, so few people were there. USC was ahead 23–20 with nine minutes to go in the first half, when Trojans center Mike Westra committed what Bob Knight thought was palming, a violation still called in 1974. Coach Knight argued the no call enough to get his first technical. Upon receiving his first T, Knight stormed after the official and was issued technical Nos. 2 and 3 and was ejected from the game. The result, after all the technicals were taken care of, was a 28–20 lead for USC. In the next 90 seconds, freshman Kent Benson scored seven straight points to bring Indiana back into the game. Indiana held a 40–37 halftime lead.

IU outscored USC 45–23 in the second half to win 85–60. From the time Knight was ejected from the game, the Hoosiers outscored the Trojans 65–32. Steve Green led Indiana in scoring with 22, and freshman sensation Kent Benson, who would be the tourney MVP, backed Green up with 17. The Hoosiers finished the season 23–5.

The 10 Greatest Last-Second, Game-Winning Shots

In this list we've tried to focus on buzzer-beaters and winning shots that came within the last 30 seconds of the game. As many of these have been described elsewhere, we won't go into great detail.

1. The Shot

Keith Smart hit a baseline jumper to beat Syracuse in the 1987 title game.

2. Leonard's Free Throw in the 1953 Title Game

Bobby Leonard made the second of two free throws to lift IU over Kansas for the national title in 1953.

3. "Watford for the win...It went in! It went in!"

That was Don Fischer's call when Indiana knocked off No. 1 Kentucky in 2011, a win that ushered in the return of Indiana University basketball. Christian Watford hit a three from the left wing at the buzzer.

4. Calloway's Buzzer Beater Keeps 1987 Title Hopes Alive

Indiana trailed LSU by nine points with under five minutes to play in a 1987 NCAA Tournament game in Cincinnati, Ohio, before the Hoosiers got some last-second heroics. With IU trailing by one, Daryl Thomas' 10-foot shot was short in the closing seconds, but Ricky Calloway was there to grab the rebound and bank it into the basket as time expired, giving IU a 77–76 win.

5. Butch Carter Hits the Shot to Beat Purdue in the NIT Final

In the 1979 NIT final in Madison Square Garden against rival Purdue, Butch Carter hit the shot to give IU its first NIT title.

6. Alford's 10-Footer at the Buzzer Beats Michigan

Michigan led by one with eight seconds to play. Off a missed free throw, Daryl Thomas got the rebound and kicked the ball out to Steve Alford, who drove the ball deep into the lane before pulling up for a 10-foot jump shot that would bounce around and go into the basket at the buzzer for an 85–84 Indiana win.

7. Haston's Buzzer-Beater Topples No. 1 Michigan State

Trailing 58–56 to the defending national champion and No. 1–ranked Spartans, Kirk Haston hit a three-pointer to lift the Hoosiers to the 59–58 win.

8. Jimmy Rayl's Halfcourt Heave Beats Minnesota 105–104

In one of two 56-point games in Jimmy Rayl's IU career, he took an inbounds pass, dribbled to halfcourt, and let fly at the buzzer. His shot went in, and Indiana had a 105–104 win over Minnesota.

9. Cody Zeller Helps IU Capture Outright Title at Michigan

With a Big Ten title on the line, Cody Zeller scored six points in a row, the last coming with 13 seconds to play, and Indiana beat Michigan 72–71 at Crisler Arena to win the 2013 Big Ten title.

10. Pick Your Jay Edwards Buzzer-Beater

Jay Edwards hit two last-second shots in the span of a week in 1989, part of a Big Ten title team. The first was a 16-footer at the buzzer to beat Purdue 64–62, and the second was a three-pointer from the top of the key that knocked off Michigan 76–75.

The Greatest Individual Performances

As with last-second shots, there are lots of candidates for the top individual performances of all-time. Fans will debate over which feats should rank where—just as the coauthors argued about the placement of Jimmy Rayl's two 56-point games versus Steve Downing's triple-double.

Fans will argue what the best of the best should be. There's even a disagreement between the two co-authors in this case. Bill Murphy thinks that Jimmy Rayl's two big individual games belong No. 1 and No. 2 in Indiana history. Terry Hutchens thinks the list has to begin with Steve Downing doing something that had never been done before as of this writing of this book hasn't been accomplished in the 45 years since.

We'll put all three of those efforts at the top of this list.

1. Steve Downing with the Triple-Double

In Indiana basketball history, there has only ever been one triple-double. That's a staggering thought when you think of the great players that have worn the cream and crimson. But it happened in 1971 against Michigan, when Steve Downing scored 28 points, grabbed 17 rebounds, and blocked 10 shots to help beat Michigan 88–79.

2. Jimmy Rayl Scores 56 Points—Twice

The first game was on January 27, 1962, in Bloomington. Nineteen days after scoring 32 against Minnesota, Jimmy "The Splendid Splinter" Rayl scored a school-record 56 points against the Golden

Gophers in a 105–104 overtime win, going 20-of-39 from the field and 16-of-20 from the free-throw line. And this was before the three-point line.

The next year Rayl did it again. On February 23, 1963, this time against Michigan State, Rayl went 23-of-48 from the field, his field goals made and attempted both conference records. Unlike the overtime game from a year before, he had 56 points in regulation, and in fact came out of the game with more than three minutes left to play.

3. Van Arsdales Combine to Score 76 Points

In a game at Fort Wayne on December 4, 1963, the Van Arsdale twins had an incredible game against Notre Dame. Dick Van Arsdale scored a career-high 42, including 25 points in the second half. Tom Van Arsdale also scored a career-high 34, with 20 of those coming in the second half. IU rallied from a 47–40 halftime deficit to win 108–102.

4. Bellamy Saves the Best for Last

Walt Bellamy's final game at Indiana in the 1960–61 season was one for the ages. He scored 28 points and pulled down an Indiana and Big Ten single-game record 33 rebounds.

5. Woodson's Return from Back Injury Is Epic

On Valentine's Day 1980, Mike Woodson returned to the court after missing two months because of back surgery. He played in just the final six Big Ten games and still earned Big Ten Most Valuable Player honors, quite an accomplishment. It started with that first game back, as IU was at Iowa. Woodson hit his first shot coming off a screen. He went on to hit his first three shots and scored 18 points in the game to lead the Hoosiers to a 66–55 win over the Hawkeyes. It wasn't a high-scoring game for Woodson, but the circumstances dictate its inclusion in this list.

6. Bill Garrett Is First African American Starter in Big Ten

The greatest individual performances of all-time has to include Bill Garrett becoming the first African American player to start a game in Big Ten history. It happened in 1948 against DePauw. He only scored eight points, but the significance of the moment was much greater than any individual statistics.

7. Downing Goes Off against Kentucky

The date was December 11, 1971, and Steve Downing almost single-handedly led Indiana to a 90–89 win over Kentucky in Freedom Hall. In the double-overtime game, Downing played all 50 minutes, scoring 47 points and grabbing 25 rebounds.

8. Schlundt Has Memorable Final Game of IU Career

Three-time Indiana All-American Don Schlundt's final game of his IU career came against Ohio State. The Buckeyes led for most of the first 30 minutes until Schlundt got red hot. He scored 17 points in the final 10 minutes alone and for the game had 47 points on 11 baskets and 25 free throws. Hack-a-Schlundt? Not this guy.

9. Kitchel Scores 18 from the Free-Throw Line in Upset of Illinois

On January 10, 1981, IU played host to No. 12 Illinois, and Ted Kitchel had one of the most memorable performances an IU player has ever had. He took a total of 31 shots in the game—13 from the field and 18 from the free-throw line. And he made 29 of the 31 shots. Kitchel was 11-of-13 from the field and made all 18 of his foul shots to score 40 points in a 78–61 upset of the Illini.

10. Dan Dakich Shuts Down Michael Jordan

It's easy to look at great offensive performances when you make a list like this, but we would be doing the Hoosiers a disservice if we didn't mention a defensive gem as well.

Dan Dakich has one that stands out among the rest. It was March 22, 1984, and Indiana was about to face No. 1 North Carolina and a star-studded lineup that included Michael Jordan. Early in the day, Bob Knight informed Dakich that his defensive assignment was to try to contain Jordan.

Dakich said that, after Knight informed him of his task for the night, he went back to his hotel room and threw up. He also said that, when Knight told him of the assignment, the veteran coach gave him a little advice. He said, "Try not to go out there and embarrass both of us tonight."

In the first few minutes, Jordan scored two baskets. But at the same time, Dakich was setting a tone, too. He was fighting through screens set for Jordan by going over the top of them, making a statement to all there that day that he was going to stay in front of Jordan, denying him a clean drive to the basket, even though he knew Jordan was much quicker. Dakich hoped to use position defense and great fundamental basketball to counter Jordan's athleticism.

Jordan didn't score again in the first half. IU pushed the lead to six with the first basket in the second half. Jordan scored his sixth point of the game. Shortly after that, Dakich got his third and fourth fouls in very quick fashion. Coach Knight, playing a hunch, kept Dakich in the game despite the four fouls.

Then Dakich, still carrying his fourth foul, blocked Jordan off the boards, causing Jordan to go over Dakich's back to pick up his third foul. With four minutes to go, Dakich fouled out after holding Jordan to eight points and one rebound. Dakich left the court with four points, three assists, and three rebounds, but the real story was the job he had done defensively on the great Michael Jordan.

Indiana shocked the nation that day by knocking off No. 1 North Carolina 72–68. And while Steve Alford connected for 27 points, the game will always be remembered as the day Dan Dakich stopped Michael Jordan.

TRADITIONS

One of the things that makes Indiana basketball special for Hoosier Nation is the number of traditions that belong to the Hoosiers. Some of them are unique to Indiana basketball, but they all hold a special place in the hearts of IU fans everywhere.

Here are nine of those traditions that Indiana basketball fans everywhere will be able to quickly relate to.

Candy-Striped Warm-up Pants

Any conversation about IU basketball traditions will always start with the candy stripes. Many outside of Hoosier Nation think they look ridiculous. Some say it's a look from a time gone by. Others act as if the circus has come to town when the Hoosiers take the court.

But for the Indiana fan, the candy stripes are simply something that makes IU basketball different than any other school around. It's a unique look that was started by Bob Knight his first season at Indiana in 1971–72, and it's something that has been a part of IU basketball for five decades.

So just how did the candy-striped warm-ups come about?

Chuck Crabb, somewhat of an IU historian, has served in his current capacity as the Indiana public address announcer since the fall of 1976. In his day job, he serves as IU's assistant athletic director for facilities. Crabb said that Knight got the idea about the candy stripes from his good friends Doc Counsilman and Hobie Billingsley of IU swimming and diving fame.

"Doc Counsilman started something similar in the 1960s with robes that they wore on the deck," Crabb said. "And Bob Knight coming in, in 1971, became close friends with Doc and Hobie. He saw those and he liked them. Indiana's warm-ups under Branch McCracken had a satin look to them, and so the cream and crimson candy-striped warm-ups got added to that, and out they came on that November day of 1971 when Indiana first played in the Assembly Hall."

That 1971–72 season would be an interesting one on several fronts for IU basketball: it was the first of 29 seasons in a row with Bob Knight at the helm; it was the unveiling of Assembly Hall as the new basketball arena; it was the first time that the national championship banners hung in the south end of the arena; and it was the first year for candy-striped warm-up pants.

Since Knight left the program in September 2000, the coaches who have followed him have had varying levels of allegiance to the IU basketball traditions. But no one has dared to remove the candy-striped warm-ups from their special place in IU history.

One coach in particular, Tom Crean, embraced all the IU traditions from his very first press conference at Indiana in April 2008. "In his first press conference that day, Tom kept saying the same two words over and over, 'It's Indiana, it's Indiana,'" Crabb said. "He talked about the candy stripes and the pride in wearing them. With Coach Crean you knew you had a coach who embraced all of the traditions that were Indiana basketball, and candy stripes were big in that vein."

During that first press conference back on April 2, 2008, Crean was asked about what he would be looking for when trying to find the right players to play at Indiana. He quickly referenced the candy stripes again. "I am looking for people who are going to understand why we wear the candy-striped pants," Crean said. "I am going to look for people who understand what that uniform stands for, why it says 'Indiana' on the front."

In the years that followed Crean taking the Indiana job, he instilled a new tradition with the annual Hoosier Hysteria workout (once called Midnight Madness), where the team kicks off the new season on one of the first official practice days by holding a workout/slam dunk contest/three-point shooting contest/Hoosier Lovefest before crowds in excess of 10,000 fans at Assembly Hall.

In 2014 Crean began a new tradition in which former IU players come back and present the candy-striped warm-up pants to the incoming freshmen players. It's sort of a rite of passage. "I can't take credit for that," Crean said the night the new tradition was unveiled. "It was an idea that was brought to me. I think it's fantastic and it will really take off as a tradition. This really is about the tradition of the program and the fans. To have the former players intertwined with the new players, this makes them understand how big of a deal this is."

To truly understand what the candy stripes mean to current and former players alike, one only has to hear the story of the June 2015 wedding day of former IU basketball standout Jordan Hulls. The wedding reception, which was held in the Henke Hall of Champions at IU, included a scene where Hulls' best friends, including several former players like Cody Zeller, Victor Oladipo, Christian Watford, Will Sheehey, and Derek Elston, all posed for a picture wearing their black tuxedos from the waist up and their cream and crimson candy-striped warm-ups from the waist down.

"If that doesn't tell you everything you need to know, nothing will," Hulls said. "All of the IU basketball traditions are important to us, but the candy stripes are something that will always hold a special place in the hearts of anyone who has played at IU."

The National Championship Banners

In the book *Missing Banners* by Tom Brew and Terry Hutchens, there is a chapter that talks about what the national championship banners that hang at Assembly Hall mean not only to Indiana basketball fans but to the players themselves, and what it's like when you first see them:

> The first time you walk into Assembly Hall, your eyes are quickly directed to the south end of the arena.

Perhaps you give a quick glance at the state of Indiana logo emblazoned on the floor at center court or you look up to see the steep architecture and unusual physical shape of the building.

But within seconds your eyes are transfixed on the five 10 x 20 red and white banners that hang in the south end and mark the five national championship years in Indiana University basketball history.

Like ghosts from the past, the years 1940, 1953, 1976, 1981, and 1987 are permanently etched in the memory of Indiana basketball players, coaches, and fans.

It doesn't matter if you've just walked into the arena on game day and the teams are warming up and the pep band is playing, or if you're the first one to walk into a cold gym in the morning for practice. The lights in the arena don't even have to be on.

It's as if the banners are there tapping you on the shoulder and saying, "Hey, look at me. Look at what is truly important when it comes to Indiana basketball."

Jordan Hulls definitely had that kind of experience when he was being recruited by Indiana. Hulls was an Indiana boy, had grown up in Bloomington, and played basketball at Bloomington South. But he will never forget the night that Tom Crean called him around 10:00 PM and asked if he could meet him at Assembly Hall.

The backdrop of the story was that Hulls was scheduled to visit Purdue the next day on a recruiting trip, and Crean had heard about it and wasn't about to have Hulls' first in-state offer come from the school to the north in West Lafayette. So he called Hulls and invited him to come down to Assembly Hall. Hulls hopped in his dad's truck, and the two of them headed to the arena.

In the foreword for the book *Hoosiers Through and Through* by Terry Hutchens, Hulls recounted what he found when he arrived at Assembly Hall: "When we walked in, there was a scene right out of a movie in front of us," Hulls wrote. "As we walked in the arena, there was nothing but spotlights on the banners and dim lights on the court, just enough to make the spotlights really stand out. We gathered and talked down at center court on the state of Indiana logo, and we just admired the banners."

Matt Roth wasn't an Indiana kid and didn't have the same sense about the banners before he committed to IU, but he remembered a similar experience on his recruiting visit. "When I got recruited coming out of high school and walking into Assembly Hall that first time, that's the first thing you see," said Roth, who grew up in Washington, Illinois. "I don't even remember what the coaches were talking to me about when we walked into the door. But when you walk on that court, they're right there, and they're in your face. It was one of the reasons, if not the biggest reason, why I chose Indiana. As a player, you always know that with Indiana people, there is always the expectation of winning a national championship."

Dane Fife knows exactly what Roth is talking about. He grew up in Michigan, but his earliest memories of the recruiting process at Indiana involve walking into Assembly Hall and being in the presence of those banners. And like Roth, Fife said those banners carry with them a sense of expectation. "There's a lot of pride in earning a banner at Indiana, and with that comes a great deal of pressure, too," said Fife, a member of the 2002 IU basketball team that is remembered as the only Indiana basketball team to play for a national championship and not close the deal. "National championships are part of the expectation at Indiana," Fife said. "It doesn't matter now that it hasn't happened since 1987. That just makes people that much hungrier. Every year you open the season with that goal in mind, and every year that you don't achieve it, it's just a little bit disappointing."

Fife said that every time an iconic Indiana basketball figure came back to talk with his team when he was a player at IU from 1999 to 2002, he was reminded not only of the expectations that those banners provided but something more: a responsibility. "When Scott May walks into the building, or Quinn Buckner or Isiah Thomas, you feel a sense of pride at the things that they were able to accomplish at Indiana," Fife said. "But you also get the feeling of responsibility to them to put up that sixth national championship banner."

Roth said there wasn't a practice he participated in at Indiana in which he didn't gaze up at the banners at least once. "When you're in a tough conditioning drill or a tough practice, all the incentive you need is to look up there and know that in our case there are five teams that expect a great deal out of the players who are there," Roth said. "I think there are a lot of teams that probably felt cheated that they didn't get that title, but at the same time it's all about the opportunity."

Indiana basketball is all about tradition. Whether it's the candy-striped warm-up pants, no names on the backs of the jerseys, or the fact that no number has ever been retired in the program, there is a feeling of reverence for IU basketball within those close to the program.

The national championship banners, as well as the other banners on the north end of the arena, just add to that tradition. It also adds to that feeling you get when you walk into the arena each and every time.

"The mystique is still there," said Indianapolis radio personality Greg Rakestraw. "You've got a wall reserved only for national titles. That says a lot. Look at the new Big Ten ad this year that shows the coast-to-coast spread of the league. What pops up to represent IU? Five banners. That tells you what you need to know."

Don Fischer, the radio play-by-play voice of Indiana basketball, said for 30 years and counting that one end of Assembly Hall has never changed. He said the other end changes from time to time with things that he said "are not nearly as important."

"But the banners are what Indiana basketball is all about," Fischer said. "To me there is absolutely no question that the banners are the single biggest factor in the IU basketball tradition."

Scott Dolson, IU's deputy athletic director, was the student manager for the 1987 IU national championship team. And while he admits it has been 30 years since Indiana has raised a national championship banner, he said they still represent a tradition like no other.

"Some people try to say that it doesn't matter as much to the kids today because they weren't born when Indiana last had a national champion, but I don't agree," Dolson said. "I remember the first time I looked up at those banners, and I wondered about the 1940 team and then the '53 team, too. Those teams always will hold a special place in IU history, just like the ones that came later. I think every year when March Madness comes around, the kids of today realize just how special those five banners hanging in Assembly Hall continue to be."

Jeremy Gray, IU's associate athletic director for strategic communications and fan experience, believes there is strong evidence that the banners mean as much as ever.

"I help oversee our social media efforts here at IU Athletics," Gray said. "About half the Facebook and Twitter profile pictures of IU fans that I see are of themselves standing in front of the banners. The banners are everywhere. Their mystique is as strong as ever."

IU historians believe the banners first came into being when the new Assembly Hall opened its doors in December 1971. That coincided with the arrival of Indiana basketball coach Bob Knight. The banners were Knight's idea to initially honor those IU teams that had exceled in national competition.

Chuck Crabb was in his final two years of undergraduate study at IU and working in athletic publicity as a student aide when Assembly Hall opened. He said he believed that Knight was the banner idea promoter. "Coach talked about banners saluting championships won in national competition because a Big Ten championship was expected each year for Indiana University basketball," Crabb said. "That's why the many conference titles during his 29 years were not celebrated with individual banners."

Crabb said that Knight likely worked through athletic director Bill Orwig's lead lieutenant, assistant athletic director Bob Dro for the 1940 and 1953 national championship banners. Evidence of those banners hanging in Assembly Hall can be found in a 1973 game photograph.

No one can remember the existence of any banners commemorating IU's first two national champions before the current Assembly Hall opened its doors in 1971. Longtime *Bloomington Herald-Times* sports editor Bob Hammel said there may been some sort of display in the lobby of the Seventh Street Fieldhouse that housed IU basketball from 1928 to 1960. But he never remembered any banners.

Kit Klingelhoffer, a former associate athletic director, said unequivocally that banners did not exist in the New Fieldhouse that was the predecessor to Assembly Hall. That building hosted Indiana basketball from 1960 to 1971 and is now known as the Gladstein Fieldhouse. It was resurfaced and holds indoor events for the IU track and field teams.

After Knight had the two national champion banners hung in Assembly Hall, he had a few more added as his tenure at Indiana continued. Knight had a banner raised for IU's Final Four appearance in 1973, then the CCA banner in 1974 and the 1975 undefeated regular season and UPI national championship banner that saluted the '75 team. Knight then added banners for the three national championships he was able to win during his IU tenure.

Knight did make an exception regarding his feelings toward Big Ten individual season banners on Senior Night in 1983, when, according to Crabb, he announced just before the seniors spoke that a banner that would be known as the "People's Banner" would recognize the great fan support that helped the Hoosiers to a Big Ten title.

"Indiana needed to win its final three games—all at home—against conference contenders Purdue, Illinois, and Ohio State," Crabb said. "Coach spoke about needing fan support, and it came in the form of some of the loudest crowds during Assembly Hall's 40-plus years."

The banner policy changed after Knight left the school in September 2000. In 2001 Big Ten championship banners were created on the north end for both the men's and women's teams. But, instead of individual banners, there is a primary banner for each program that includes each year the teams won the Big Ten. In addition, a Final Four participation banner was also put in place that marks in one place every season when the Hoosiers played in the Final Four.

Tom Crean applied the same philosophy that Knight did in 1983 when he announced in 2013 that a banner would be raised for that team's outright Big Ten title as it honored players who had been through all of the difficult times that came about at the end of the Kelvin Sampson era of IU hoops.

Derek Elston said, when you walk into Assembly Hall, your eyes look in one of two directions—either at the national title banners or at the other banners in the north end of the arena. He said the 2013 banner, for obvious reasons, is the first place he looks. It is among the banners in the north end of the arena.

"What our group of guys had to endure over a four-year span, and for some a three-year span, is something that not a lot of college athletes will ever have to go through," Elston said. "So when I look over and see that 2013 Big Ten championship banner, I picture a group of guys who fought and battled for not just each other but for the fans who were there in the stands cheering us on every game when they had nothing to cheer for."

According to Crabb, the banners originally came from Annin Flagmakers Company in Verona, New Jersey, the nation's largest flag manufacturing company. During Crabb's years in sports promotions, he changed to Flag and Banner Company in Indianapolis. "They maintained the same type font line as Annin and were local, permitting us to be involved in every step of the process," Crabb said.

Crabb said the last complete set of five NCAA banners came in 1987. Flag and Banner remade the north end basic banners in 2001, remade the 1983 banner in 2010, the 2013 banner before the 2013–14 season, and the AIAW Final Four banner in 2014.

The banners are lowered before each spring commencement conducted in Assembly Hall, which permits members of IATSE Local 618 stagehand members to use a lint/fabric brush like you'd use on your good suits or dress pants to brush off the top and bottom sleeved areas and check each banner. According to Crabb, they attract dust but don't really get dirty hanging over the court.

So many former players talked about what the banners meant to them in the recruiting process. Jared Jeffries, like Hulls several years later, was an Indiana Mr. Basketball. But he said the belief that he could be part of a banner-hanging team was why he ultimately chose the Hoosiers over Duke.

"Coach Knight made me believe that I had a chance to hang a banner up there," Jeffries said. "Coach told me that he had never coached a player like me at Indiana, and that always meant a lot because there had been a lot of great players come through there. That's one of the most disappointing things about never getting the chance to play for him. But there's no doubt that thinking that I had a chance to hang another banner there and believing what Coach Knight said had a big role in my decision to go to Indiana."

Martha the Mop Lady

For the current generation of Indiana basketball fans, the video clip of Martha the Mop Lady roaming the back hallway of Assembly Hall in the after hours of an IU basketball game and singing the IU Fight Song is something they see before every game on the video screen.

For the more diehard fans, however, this is a tradition that goes back to the 1970s when Martha was part of an ad campaign created by Farm Bureau Insurance. In both cases, Martha is one of the more recognizable figures in IU basketball lore.

How Martha came to be such an iconic figure with the Hoosiers is an interesting story. Chuck Crabb explained that, at the time, WTTV had the television rights to both IU and Purdue basketball, and Cranfill Advertising represented Farm Bureau Insurance. Farm Bureau was a title sponsor on those broadcasts. This was long before the Big Ten conference assumed all the live television game rights. "Cranfill Advertising wanted something novel," Crabb said, "and so they came up with for Purdue the attic look where the guy found the old tuba and plays 'Hail Purdue,' and for Indiana, not having a mascot or something along those lines, the thought was to try something a little different."

Crabb said the idea was born from the NBC comedy *Hazel*, in which Shirley Booth played Hazel, the maid for the Baxter Family. So Cranfill used that as a model, and they went to a talent agency in Chicago and got a Lyric Opera singer to come to Assembly Hall on a Saturday morning.

"They set the lighting simply by using the night security lighting in the east court level hallway to show a custodial-type person coming down a hallway pushing a broom and humming the IU Fight Song," Crabb said. "[When] the lady came [closer] to the camera, she would start singing the words to the fight song, and the intention was, at the end of the opening, she was going to run out onto the floor to, if you will, an imaginary crowd, and the roar of the crowd and the lights would come up."

After filming the spot, however, the editors went a different route when they got back to the editing room.

"When they sat down to edit the tape, they saw what they had with Martha Webster. When this Lyric Opera singer got to the end of it and sang, 'Oh Indiana, our Indiana, Indiana, we're all for you,' she had a big wave, a giggle, a laugh, and kind of waved her hand and then just pushed off camera," Crabb said. "They saw they had a gold mine. So Martha in a studio recorded the sound, and they cut it, and that was the opening for Indiana basketball beginning in 1978 for many, many years. It became a huge hit. It became absolutely a monster celebration of Indiana basketball."

Crabb said that IU had two occasions in the late 1980s when IU brought Martha Webster back to Assembly Hall, and she reprised the role live at an IU game for an opening. He said both times they had issues with wireless microphones.

"But Martha, being the trooper that she was, pantomimed and did all the singing on the court, and the crowd did the words," Crabb said. "They all sang 'Indiana, our Indiana.'"

Toward the end of the Bob Knight era of IU basketball, Indiana brought in local Bloomington radio personality and 1987 Miss Indiana, Sheila Stephen, and she played Martha for either a Hoosier Hysteria or a pregame appearance. There was also a student one year that handled the role, a jazz major in the Jacobs School of Music.

Martha Webster is now deceased. She lived into her eighties and in fact had her own IU Cleaning Lady Facebook page. At one point, around 2012, she wrote the following on her page to IU fans:

> To all the loyal and loving fans who take the time to send their thoughts, I want to say: You make me so very happy and proud that the efforts to make a "nice little commercial" have blossomed over the years. Looking back over more than 75 years of performing (I am now 80—a big surprise to me), I have to say that being the IU Cleaning Lady, or Mop Lady, is among my most treasured memories. I am writing a book about some of my many musical "adventures" and you all are to be highlighted among my blessings. Thank you from the bottom of my heart.

Crabb said that, long after Webster had stopped returning to IU to perform the role, he exchanged letters with her at the beginning of every season. He would send her a media guide and a poster, and they kept in touch that way.

Crabb also remembered an interesting meeting some folks within the IU administration had with Webster late in her life. "Martha had a great love for Indiana basketball," Crabb said. "Martha had a day job where she worked as a telemarketer for the Chicago Blackhawks. When the Big Ten began the postseason Big Ten Basketball Tournament, our ticket office people went to the United Center [in Chicago] for a meeting one day. They were pulled over by the United Center staff, and they said that they wanted the IU people to visit with one of their telemarketers because, 'She maintains that she's a great part of Indiana basketball. Her name is Martha.' The late Bill King and Mike Roberts were our staff up there, and they walked back and instantly recognized Martha Webster at this desk. And they started saying to the United Center Staff, 'You don't realize how big of a personality she is in Bloomington and the state of Indiana.'"

In 2010, two years after Tom Crean took over the IU basketball program, Indiana brought the old Martha Webster Mop Lady video back into the fold and now plays it before every home game on the big screen above center court.

Beginning in November 2010, IU Athletics and Indiana Farm Bureau Insurance announced that after a 20-year hiatus, the original commercial spot would be making a comeback at IU basketball games. It aired for the November 16 game against Mississippi Valley State and was shown right after the national anthem and right before tipoff.

"'Martha' is one of the most iconic advertisements in the 76-year history of Indiana Farm Bureau Insurance," said Thomas J. Faulconer, senior vice president and chief marketing officer of Indiana Farm Bureau Insurance in a press release at the time. "Not a day goes by we don't hear questions about the spot, and interestingly, people think we still use it. The nostalgic connection with the ad goes far beyond company branding and into the hearts of Hoosiers we serve. We're eager to bring 'Martha' back as our gift to Indiana University."

IU athletic director Fred Glass said bringing the Martha video back to its rightful place in Hoosier basketball history was a win-win for IU fans. "We were all just as thrilled to hear the vintage Martha spot was returning and appreciate Indiana Farm Bureau Insurance for recognizing what a special, unique affiliation she had to our Hoosier fans all those years," Glass said. "Martha's obvious passion for IU basketball was infectious and led to a following that was like none other. No doubt our fans will be excited to know she's coming back."

Crabb said it's one of those traditions that is unique to Indiana basketball and truly like no other. "The fans love it," he said. "There's no question that they love it, and it's wonderful to have it back in a prominent place in our basketball tradition."

The William Tell Overture

Another iconic in-game Indiana basketball tradition is the playing of the *William Tell* Overture at the under-eight-minute timeout at IU home games in Assembly Hall.

It's a tradition that involves the pep band, the cheer and dance squads, and even invites audience participation as the flags come out that spell I-N-D-I-A-N-A and H-O-O-S-I-E-R-S. Fans inside the Simon Skjodt Assembly Hall are on their feet and clapping their hands as the pep band plays the *William Tell* Overture. As the song itself comes to a close, the band transitions from that into the Indiana Fight Song. The flags then form a circle, and the fight song comes to a close just as the timeout horn goes off and the crowd yells, "I-U!" in unison.

Chuck Crabb said it's a tradition that came about in the early 1980s. "The band always had the *William Tell* Overture in its repertoire, and it kind of jumped around at various points in the game," Crabb recalled. "So Ray Cramer and some others engaged myself and some others in athletics and said, 'How do we capitalize on something like this?' And so as television started declaring natural breaks for timeouts and 16, 12, eight, and four was the adopted standard, we started using that next-to-last timeout as a rally point. So the *William Tell* became as much a rallying charge as it did maybe the lead that we had at that particular moment over an opponent."

Crabb said he had a conversation with the IU cheerleaders on the way back from a road trip to Ohio State in 1981, and they wanted to know how they could get the *William Tell* Overture more involved and dress it up a little bit. "That's where the concentric circles of the then pom squad and the cheerleaders grew, and putting a guy up in a pyramid with the 'Go Big Red' flag, and that was the start of that," Crabb said. "When Julie Horine became a cheerleader in 1985 and then the cheerleading coach in 1989, she was the one that then grew the flags with Indiana and the Hoosiers spelled out."

Interestingly, Crabb told a story of how something that Kentucky was doing at the same time ended up resulting in the under-eight-minute timeout becoming an even "larger" celebration. "Kentucky had a big blue flag, so we had to have a big crimson flag," Crabb said. "So Mark McAlister of Big Red Liquor's fame—his son, Leaf, was a cheerleader for us—and Mark came forward and said, 'I want a flag that's one foot bigger than Kentucky has. We can't let them have a bigger flag than us.' And so that came about. And then when Kentucky came out with a big blue flag on pole vault poles, then naturally Mark was on the phone with me saying he wanted a big flag like Kentucky's but one foot bigger. 'Can you get that made?' It's nice to have alumni who are supportive of that nature."

And so the tradition has grown from the song being a rallying cry in 1981 to adding the flags eight years later, and now it's a moment in the game when IU fans rise to their feet as the crimson IU flag is waved in their area.

Crabb said the *William Tell* Overture actually earned IU a technical foul one time in the 1980s, too. "We had a game with Purdue where we got late into the *William Tell* play," Crabb said. "And then you didn't have the commercial-length timeouts that you have now. And so the band is playing away, and the cheerleaders are out there celebrating with the flag, and we fortunately, in that particular game with Purdue, were destroying the Boilermakers. Jim Bain was the lead official on the game, and the horn sounded to start play. We were still in the throws of the *William Tell* Overture, and the cheerleaders were in the center of the floor with no appearance of clearing. So Jim blew the whistle, walked over to the scorer's bench, leaned down to the scorekeeper, who was next to me, and said, 'I have a technical foul on the Indiana cheerleaders for delaying resumption of play. Will you make that announcement, Mr. Announcer?' So I said that and looked to my left, and Coach Knight kind of looked over at me out of the corner of his eye and said, 'What did you just say?'"

As the story goes, Bain walked over to Knight and said "Bob, I just called a technical on your cheerleaders because they were on the floor too long and delayed resumption of play."

"So Coach Knight kind of looked up at the sky and shook his head," Crabb said. "Then he turned on his heels and walked across the court, pulled the cheerleaders together at the middle of the floor, and said, 'We love your support, but by God get off the court when the horn sounds because we want to get back to playing basketball.' So that was a greater way that the *William Tell* Overture became a part of Indiana lore."

Another recent development in the tradition has had to do with students dressing up in costume and many of them getting chosen to be one of the flag holders who race on to the court, spelling out Indiana and Hoosiers. There has been the IU Gorilla, Gumby, a guy in a hot dog outfit, just to name a few.

"There is a guy who has made it a legacy of wearing the Gorilla outfit," Crabb said. "You never see the hands and you never see the face, but it's like a clown in Ringling Brothers that you never see out of makeup. People just started wearing those different kinds of costumes. Gumby's and an assortment of DC Comics superheroes. Just a whole line of different characters that have now became a part of the game. Certainly our marketing people often look up into the stands to see who is the zaniest fan up there, because they often get brought down and are made a part of the *William Tell* Overture, carrying one of two spell-out flags when the cheerleaders are on the court."

Big Heads Behind the Basket

One thing you can't help but notice when watching Indiana basketball on television is the fans waving big heads when opponents are shooting free throws. The collection of big heads is an impressive one, with hundreds of different faces in all shapes and sizes.

The big heads are a recent IU basketball tradition that head coach Tom Crean brought with him from Marquette. "It was very successful at Marquette," Chuck Crabb said, "and our marketing people sat down with the basketball operations folks years ago and reviewed with Coach Crean exactly what he wanted to do from a marketing stand-point. They asked him what he would like to do in terms of in-game promotions and what traditions he would like to bring with him from Marquette. We asked him, what were the things that he would like to capture and have us integrate into the things we did on game day in the Assembly Hall? The Crean family willingly shared what they had seen in Milwaukee, and that's how the big heads at Indiana came about."

There are hundreds of big heads that have made appearances at games over the past several years. Some of them are filed away in a room in the athletic department and others are part of the current library of big heads that are passed out at IU home games for a unique form of fan participation. According to the IU athletic department, the big heads are produced for $70 each, and following a game, there are interns throughout the arena who make sure that no one slips out the door with their favorite big head under their arm.

What started with a few faces has grown into a Hoosiers tradition. And now fans are constantly wondering, as each new season begins, which big heads will appear for the new season?

In recent years, there has been a large assortment of faces that have become the backdrop for opponents shooting free throws. Some of them are personalities that range from Bob Knight to President Barack Obama. Some of the others seen in recent years include Hulk Hogan, Will Ferrell, Muhammad Ali, Harry Caray, Stewie from *Family Guy*, Sylvester Stallone, Dick Vitale, Richard Simmons, Gene Simmons, Marilyn Monroe, Abraham Lincoln, John F. Kennedy, and Tony Dungy.

Ben Higgins, an IU alum who starred on *The Bachelor*, has a bighead. So does Betty White and Beyoncé, not to mention a Crying Michael Jordan. At the Indiana–North Carolina game in Assembly Hall in 2016, former IU standout Isiah Thomas was on hand on a night when they honored the 1981 IU national championship team. At one point, Thomas was in the end where the big heads were located, and he was seen holding the Crying Michael Jordan big head. There's plenty of irony there, for sure.

Dustin from the popular Netflix show *Stranger Things* has a bighead. Joe Buck, another IU alum, has one. So does Kanye West, Kevin Hart, Kevin Spacey, and Kris Kardashian. Leonardo DiCaprio, Margot Robbie, and Mark Cuban have big heads, as does Amy Poehler's character Leslie Knope from *Parks and Recreation*. Swimmer Michael Phelps has a bighead. So does Peyton Manning and IU alum Sage Steele.

Many are former IU basketball players or high profile athletes who made a name at IU and now are doing well in the professional ranks. For example, there's a Yogi Ferrell big head and one for Troy Williams, too. Cody Zeller has a big head and so does Victor Oladipo. Former IU baseball standout Kyle Schwarber, who won the World Series with the Chicago Cubs in 2016 has a big head. So does Jordan Howard, who starred for IU in football and was drafted by the Chicago Bears. Tevin Coleman has a big head.

There are characters, too. Waldo has made an appearance, as has the Cookie Monster, the Geico gecko, and Woody from *Toy Story*. Harry Potter and the Grinch have been there, too, as has Super Mario. The Showalter Fountain fish have a bighead. Martha the Mop Lady has a bighead, too. And don't forget Olaf from the Disney movie *Frozen*.

Some are color, some are black and white. Some are more recognizable if you're an Indiana fan. For example, not a lot of people in the general public would be able to pick out Don Fischer, Kit Klingelhoffer, Fred Glass, or Chuck Crabb from the crowd if you didn't have ties in some way to Indiana. But all of those personalities have made an appearance in the lineup.

Crabb tells how his two youngest nephews were at a game and found Uncle Chuck's big head and made sure they got their picture taken with it.

"So it's a Facebook page divider for me," Crabb said.

No Names on the Backs of Jerseys

Indiana basketball is all about tradition, that much has been established. It certainly feels that way when you walk into Assembly Hall and see the banners hanging from the ceiling, see limited advertising done in a tasteful manner, and when you watch IU players take the floor wearing their candy-striped warm-up pants.

But it's also what the Hoosiers have under their warm-ups that screams the Indiana tradition. One constant with the Indiana uniform since it was first unveiled at the turn of the 20th century is that it is as basic as can be. The white home jerseys have the name "Indiana" across the chest in red with a block red number. On the back is only the number.

The message with Indiana basketball is a simple one: you play for the name on the front, not for the name on the back.

"It's one of the great traditions of Indiana basketball," said former IU guard Jordan Hulls. "Our players take a lot of pride in our traditions. And no names is a big one. We're playing for Indiana. That's all that really needs to be on those jerseys."

Some have said that the decision not to have names on the backs of jerseys has lost IU a recruit or two over the years. Young kids want all the bells and whistles. They want the bright new arena, they want the lights to go down low for the starting lineups, they want their name on the back of their jersey, and they want to be treated like royalty by the fan base.

At Indiana, they would get two-and-a-half of the four. IU's pregame—in which the lights go low and the video board shows a short history of Indiana basketball—is impressive. And there's no doubt that, when you play basketball at Indiana, you are treated like kings. It's a big deal to don the cream and crimson and play for the Hoosiers. Dozens of players over the years have talked about how many doors it can open in the state of Indiana with job possibilities just by having on your résumé that you played basketball at IU. You're a known commodity. You can't put a price on that.

The half would be the new Simon Skjodt Assembly Hall, which was renovated and dedicated in the fall of 2016. Thanks to a $40 million gift from alumna Cyndy Simon Skjodt and $5 million from alumnus Mark Cuban, Indiana was able to give the then 46-year-old building a much needed facelift. The south lobby was pretty much demolished and rebuilt, which included adding suites, escalators, and getting rid of the zig-zag ramps that had transported fans to the upper concourse since the building debuted in the 1971–72 season.

But the one thing Indiana can't promise a recruit is having his name on the back of his jersey. And frankly, if that was of such importance, the Hoosiers might not want him anyway. Coaches over the years at IU have sold Indiana players on how important those traditions are.

The no-name tradition was put to the test in the 2001–2002 season when Indiana entered the NCAA Tournament as a No. 5 seed in the

West. Before the tournament even began, Indiana coach Mike Davis told his team that, if they won the national championship and hung that elusive sixth banner, he would let them put names on the backs of their jerseys the next season.

The Hoosier Nation still talks about what would have happened had that occurred—and it almost did. Davis probably felt comfortable saying it since he knew IU would have to get past the No. 1 team in the nation, Duke, in the Sweet Sixteen. But the Hoosiers did just that, winning 74–73 in Lexington's Rupp Arena. Two days later, IU beat Kent State 81–69 to advance to the Final Four in Atlanta.

Now just two victories separated IU from a national title that would have meant names on the backs of jerseys. Indiana was a big underdog in the national semifinal against Kelvin Sampson and Oklahoma, but the Hoosiers found a way to win 73–64 and advance to the national title game against Maryland.

There, the dream ended with a 64–52 loss to the Terrapins. And Davis's ultimate gesture of bucking the system was avoided. It would have been interesting, though, to see if winning that elusive national title would have given Davis enough clout with IU fans to not go crazy when he unveiled those uniforms.

Most think that would be doubtful.

Some schools have shoe and uniform contracts that allow them to have multiple uniforms. The Adidas contract for IU calls for the "possibility" of one alternate uniform per season for the Hoosiers. IU has worn a different style uniform in the Big Ten Tournament or NCAA Tournament in the past, but the changes were subtle.

And there were definitely no names on the backs of jerseys.

They Don't Retire Numbers at Indiana

You can go to some arenas and look in the rafters and see one retired jersey number after another. And if you think about the great basketball history at IU, had they ever started doing that, there might have been a shortage of numbers.

Consider this: would a player like Yogi Ferrell or Dane Fife have ever had the chance to wear No. 11 at Indiana if they had retired it after Isiah Thomas wore it and led the Hoosiers to the 1981 national championship?

What about guys like Verdell Jones III, who threw the pass to Christian Watford that ended up being the three-pointer that beat Kentucky in 2011, and Luke Jimenez, who both wore No. 12? Would they have ever had the chance if IU had retired it after Steve Alford led the Hoosiers to the 1987 national title?

What number would Damon Bailey or Dean Garrett or Jimmy Rayl have worn at Indiana had the university opted to retire it after the late Archie Dees became the first IU player in history to win back-to-back Big Ten MVP trophies?

Think of Cody Zeller, and you think of the No. 40 at Indiana. But what number would he have worn if Indiana had retired the number after Calbert Cheaney left the school as its all-time leading scorer and the top scorer in Big Ten history as well?

The list just goes on and on.

But it's another long-lasting Indiana basketball tradition that you don't retire jersey numbers. For many years, players would see in their lockers placards that would tell them all of the players at IU who had worn the number they were now wearing.

It was another tradition that was being handed down from players of one team to players of another. Much like the candy-striped warm-ups are passed on at Hoosier Hysteria every season, those jersey numbers are passed along as well.

Many people think of No. 42 when they think of Mike Woodson, who played for the Hoosiers in the late 1970s and early 1980s. But Woodson would have never worn that number if they had retired it for the College Player of the Year on the perfect 1976 national championship team, Scott May.

How about this list of players who have worn No. 20 at Indiana: Ricky Calloway, Greg Graham, A.J. Ratliff, Jim Thomas, Bobby Wilkerson, and Sherron Wilkerson.

Or how about No. 21: Hallie Bryant, Quinn Buckner, Bobby "Slick" Leonard, and Chris Reynolds.

And here's one more, No. 23, worn by: Delray Brooks, Eric Gordon, and Keith Smart, to name a few.

The bottom line is that some traditions are simply more important at Indiana than doing things for all the wrong reasons. For example, if IU caved into the pressure of retiring numbers because that's what everyone else does, a good majority of Hoosier Nation would be disappointed.

But that's not the Indiana way, and it's not going to change any time soon.

No Mascot Either

O ne of the things that makes Indiana University unique from most other universities is that IU does not have a mascot. Simply put, it is difficult to properly portray what it means to be a Hoosier.

"How do you show what a Hoosier really is?" Crabb said. "It's just not an easy concept."

This isn't to say that Indiana students over the years haven't tried to come up with something that would work, but nothing has ever stuck for more than a short period of time.

In 1923 the *Indiana Daily Student* posted an article trying to drum up support to install a goat as the IU mascot. After a lot of back-and-forth discussion, the idea kind of fizzled out and wasn't broached again for more than a decade.

In 1935 the Blue Keys, an honorary society on campus, tried to get the university to make a collie its mascot. But it wasn't able to raise enough money to get the animal, and that idea faded away, too.

In 1951, deciding that perhaps a human mascot would be a better idea than an animal, the Hoosiers debuted a person called the "Hoosier Schoolmaster." The idea was that the schoolmaster would represent some of the folklore as to how the name "Hoosiers" had come about. The mascot was dressed in 19th-century attire. He had a cane and a wig. He was more of a yell leader than anything else, and like his predecessors in the IU mascot world, the Hoosier Schoolmaster never really caught on, either. At the end of the 1952 school year, the mascot was retired.

The next attempt was made in 1956 when Sigma Delta Chi came up with the "Crimson Bull" and had T-shirts and signs and other Crimson Bull likenesses made. But it never caught on.

A few years later, members of Theta Chi had an English bulldog named Ox that caught on for a short time. Ox went to football practice wearing an IU sweater and routinely posed for pictures. Once again, the idea simply never gained steam. "Ox was on the sideline for football games because a lot of football players were members of Theta Chi fraternity," Chuck Crabb said.

The first official mascot for IU was the Bison in the fall of 1965. The Bison made sense because the animal was pictured on the state seal for Indiana and once had been common in the area south of Bloomington. The problem became whether or not to use a live bison or a human version dressed up in costume. The live bison idea had too many issues, from where to keep it and who to train it to the liability standpoint of having a bison at football and basketball games.

The costume of the Bison started in its most basic form—a mask and a furry costume. A few years later, the Bison costume evolved into something a little bigger, but this had problems, too. The person wearing the costume had trouble seeing and needed to be guided around the stadium by another person. Ultimately, the limitations brought on by the Bison suit caused everyone to rethink the decision to have that as the mascot, too.

The Bison mascot continued for a few years, and in fact, when Indiana football went to the Rose Bowl in 1967, a Bison mascot with a new head and worn by a cheerleader appeared on the sideline. But there was more anti-Bison comments than support. Within a few years, the Bison idea had come to an end.

"We tried a buffalo costume," Chuck Crabb said. "There was a retired Bloomington attorney who was very involved with that activity in 1967. We had one person that wore this buffalo outfit, and it had a big head on it. And inside of it was a big bar that the guy had to hold because it was top heavy. So the guy steered the head around."

A side note, though, is that in the 2010s, the Bison came back as part of a video board element in the pregame and showed a cartoon bison rushing through the streets of Bloomington near campus and heading to Memorial Stadium. Just as it would enter the stadium, the Indiana football team would take the field.

"We've always had something with the buffalo," Crabb said. "When you look at the seal of the university or the seal of the great state of Indiana, there's a woodsman with a setting sun and a buffalo. And

The Bison mascot (Indiana University Archives, P0044553)

so the buffalo character gets displayed in that fashion, and with the sound system we have now with the woofers and the tweeters and the full range sound that we're able to project, you can crank up the bass a little bit and have quite a sound of a herd of buffalo entering the stadium."

Crabb said that Dick Barnes of Nick's English Hut and some of his buddies came up with using a Minotaur. In Greek mythology, the Minotaur was a creature with the head of a bull and the body of a man. "That's still on the coasters at Nick's English Hut," Crabb said. "It's that Minotaur look. Now, of course, they put it in an 'I' sweater with crimson colors and that was used. But again, nothing every really caught on for any length of time."

And then there was the Hoosier Hick that roamed the sidelines for IU games beginning in 1979. The official name wasn't the Hoosier Hick, but it probably should have been. Instead it was called "Mr. Hoosier Pride." It wore a cowboy hat and had a big grin on its face. Kids loved it, but everyone else was embarrassed by the image. With more people not liking it than supporting it, Mr. Hoosier Pride didn't last long either.

Crabb was also involved in the creation of Mr. Hoosier Pride. "We had a costume made, and it was very similar to how mascot heads looked back then, very stern and forceful looking," Crabb said. "And everyone said, 'You remade the Nebraska Cornhusker,' and they were right. There were a lot of similarities. Some thought it looked like the Pistol Pete of Oklahoma State. Ultimately, though, it just never caught on. And we had a basketball coach [Bob Knight] who really didn't like that character, so let's just say it never made it out of football. I guarantee you that."

Crabb said that a lot of things have been tried, but there hasn't been any consistent mascot for any length of time in IU history.

"Nothing ever really caught on," Crabb said. "It just kept coming back to the very basic question, 'What's a Hoosier?' I'm a Hoosier. You're a Hoosier, and anyone who comes to Indiana University is a Hoosier. So we all have our different definitions, and we can't come to any single conclusion."

Hoosier Hysteria ("Midnight Madness")

There are few traditions anywhere that compare to Hoosier Hysteria, particularly in its vintage form, with Indiana basketball.

When it first began, it was truly an event.

Fans would line up early and sometimes even camp overnight to have a shot at being one of the first ones in Assembly Hall for Midnight Madness, the first official day of college basketball season.

But it was more than just being the official first day. It was more like the official first moment of college basketball.

When the clock hit midnight on that Friday night prior to the official start of the season, the fans would do a loud countdown as if it was New Year's Eve in October. When midnight arrived, the Indiana University basketball team would make its way onto to the court, and the fans by then would be worked into a frenzy.

It would begin with a simple layup line as the players got warmed up, and then it would build to much, much more. The head coach, Bob Knight in the early days, but Mike Davis, Kelvin Sampson, and Tom Crean later, would address the crowd, talk a little about the current team, and then the festivities would get underway.

But let's talk a little bit more about what would lead up to the event. First of all, there was a hidden cost to the event that made it even a little more special. Technically, Hoosier Hysteria/Midnight Madness has free admission, and there is no actual ticket for the event. The hidden cost, however, is that fans are encouraged to bring a few cans of a non-perishable food item to the event that will be donated to a local food bank. In recent years that has been the Hoosier Hills Food Bank. According to the group's annual report, Hoosier Hysteria is one of its best fundraising efforts every year. In 2014, for example, Indiana basketball fans donated 6,781 pounds of food in that one event alone. Needless to say, it's a great cause and helps feed the hungry in Monroe County and beyond.

So that's one unique part of the event. The other is simply the number of people who show up. In its heyday, there were years when Midnight Madness would come close to capacity in the arena that holds more than 17,000 fans. Conventional wisdom is that if you fill the lower area (not including the balcony), there are approximately 14,000 fans in the building. There were many years when that was the case. In some years, fans would even sprinkle into the balcony, too.

Depending on the year, the doors would open sometime between 6:00 and 8:00 PM, and fans would pour into the arena and get ready to usher in a new season of Indiana basketball. It would be a big recruiting night, too. Sometimes high school standouts from Indiana schools play Friday night football and then make their way to Bloomington for Midnight Madness.

If an educated IU fan base knew there was a hot recruit in the house, they would often times take it from there and find ways to chant that person's name and make them feel welcome. NCAA rules prohibited the school itself from orchestrating such a reaction, but if fans did it on their own, that was safe. In addition, media would not be permitted to interview recruits while they were inside Assembly Hall. At the 2006 event, when highly touted recruit Eric Gordon was in the building, media was hoping to interview him but had to wait until nearly 2:00 AM when it was over to talk to him next to his family's vehicle in the parking lot at Assembly Hall, while his family waited patiently for him.

As the final few hours would count down inside the arena, the fans would do cheers and get ready to meet that season's Indiana basketball team. The pep band would play, and it would be a very festive atmosphere. In later years, after the video boards over center court at Assembly Hall got bigger and better, fans would be treated to highlights and other video presentations there, too. Finally, when the moment arrived and the team would take the court to thundering applause, the evening would begin.

Depending on the coach, the agenda might be a little different. There has usually been a slam dunk contest, either a three-point shooting contest or a spot shot competition, and then some sort of scrimmage where the Indiana players would work out against each other. While, technically, this was their first practice of the season, it wouldn't really be a practice. It was more of a chance to introduce a new team to a fan base.

As the years went on, it became more of a show. In 2011, for example, Victor Oladipo performed the song "U Got It Bad" by Usher to the delight of the Indiana fan base. There have also been a few choreographed dance numbers over recent years featuring the Indiana team. The ones without rhythm are always particularly entertaining.

In 2001 Andre Owens, a freshman from Perry Meridian, took the slam dunk contest to a new level (in fact, almost ended it for good) when, in an attempt to get the fans fired up before his final dunk, he took off his jersey and began waiving it around. IU coach Mike Davis wasn't amused and made sure that didn't happen in the future.

Tom Crean once joked that his first year at Indiana, when IU was forced to put together its entire class of recruits after April 1 because all but two players left after the Kelvin Sampson recruiting violations had surfaced, IU almost didn't have a slam dunk contest because few of his players could actually dunk. He said jokingly that a layup contest would have been a better solution.

In the early 2000s, Indiana changed the name of Midnight Madness to Hoosier Hysteria. Midnight Madness had become a trademarked term, and IU and other schools that did the same thing had to change the name, and Hoosier Hysteria certainly fit.

The event changed in other ways around 2010 when the NCAA loosened its rules and allowed Hoosier Hysteria/the first official practice to begin at 5:00 PM so that fans didn't have to be out so late. It changed again in 2013, when the NCAA actually allowed programs to move practice up a full two weeks from where it had once been, which was the closest Friday to October 15. The new rule stated that teams could hold 30 days of practice in the six weeks before their first regular-season game.

At Indiana, Hoosier Hysteria remained, but it had a different feel. It wasn't the countdown-to-midnight spectacle it had once been but moved to a late afternoon or evening event, often on a Saturday a week or two into the season. IU also would bring in a celebrity master of ceremonies for the event. One year IU alum Sage Steele of ESPN fame was the master of ceremonies.

In 2011 Indiana coach Tom Crean explained why he liked having the event better at a more manageable time of the day. He said he hoped it would allow more fans to visit Assembly Hall and Cook Hall, IU's practice facility, for the first time.

"One of the things that I enjoy most, is to meet families who come to a game or this event with their children and expose them to IU basketball for the first time," Crean said. "Our hope is that we will have a lot of first-time visitors who, when they experience this event with all of the longtime loyal students and fans, become Hoosier fans for life."

Perhaps, but there are a lot of old-time Hoosiers fans who have fond memories of Midnight Madness and that New Year's Eve–like countdown feel to the beginning of a new season of Indiana basketball.

Senior Night

Senior Night has always held a special place in the hearts of Indiana fans as they looked forward to the speeches given by the players. It has always been a kind of rite of passage. The tradition began under coach Bob Knight in 1973, when in his second season at IU, he brought his senior class back out on the floor after their final home game to give a speech to the fans.

Over the years, IU's players would often joke, after playing for Knight for four years, that "making it to the microphone" was a big accomplishment because it meant they had survived their career with a very demanding coach.

Unlike the ceremonies adopted by many other schools that are often done an hour or so before a game, Indiana has always held it after the game. One advantage to doing it before would be you would be guaranteed that everyone would be in a good mood because the game hadn't been played and you wouldn't take the chance of it being an unfavorable outcome.

But again, IU tends to stick to its traditions. And the tradition has always been to hold the Senior Night speeches after the game, and so that's what IU does. In recent years, players have been presented with a framed IU basketball jersey to commemorate their careers at IU. Their parents and siblings will often join them at the baseline where, one by one, they're called to the microphone after the coach has said some words for them.

Some keep it brief, but often times it's more like an Academy Award acceptance speech, where the winner ignores the teleprompter message that says they need to go to a commercial break and continues to thank everyone under the sun. The players thank their teammates, their coaches, the trainers and strength and conditioning people, the secretaries in the basketball office, the team doctors, their academic advisors, and the list goes on and on.

Todd Leary, who played at Indiana from 1989 to 1994, is often credited with having the longest Senior Night speech in IU history. It's estimated that Leary's speech lasted 30 minutes.

On the other end of the spectrum, people remember quiet and soft-spoken Mike White, who quickly got to the microphone for his Senior Speech in 2008. White had only been at IU two years because he was a junior-college transfer, but still his is remembered by many as being the quickest Senior Night speech of all time. White thanked about three people, and the speech lasted less than 30 seconds.

Jarrad Odle, who played for the Hoosiers from 1999 to 2002, may have said it best when he got to the microphone for his speech in 2002. "I put four years in for you guys," he said. "You can give me 20 minutes."

The 2002 Senior Night was also a much anticipated night for Odle's teammate, Dane Fife. There was a lot of talk going around the team and with Fife's brothers that night that Dane was going to propose to his longtime girlfriend at the microphone. His brothers were making book on it. As it turned out, he didn't. It was probably a good thing because the couple broke up within about six months, and less than a year later she had married someone else.

Fife came back and spent two seasons on Mike Davis' staff at IU through the end of the 2005 season. Errek Suhr was a walk-on for the Hoosiers who graduated in 2007. Suhr was the next player to wear Fife's No. 11 jersey, and when he got to the microphone on Senior Night, he told a story about Fife. Suhr recalled one of the first times he met Fife, a player he had looked up to when growing up in the Bloomington area. Suhr wanted to be like Fife if he ever played basketball for IU. For some reason, Fife always called him Chris, even though his name was Errek. Fife said he wasn't sure why he did it, but when he looked at Suhr, he always thought of him as Chris.

"I said, 'You know what, my name's Errek,'" Suhr recalled during his Senior Night speech. "And [Fife] said, 'I don't give a [crap]. Play some defense.' A lot of guys wouldn't like that, but I was like, 'That's pretty awesome. Dane Fife is cussing me out.'"

Some players have gotten emotional, too. A.J. Moye, who graduated in 2004, broke into tears when he reached the microphone and the fans were chanting, "A.J. Mo-ye, A.J. Mo-ye."

Even Bob Knight got emotional on Senior Night in 1995 when his son, Pat Knight, was a senior about to give his Senior Night speech. As Knight made comments before each player stepped to the microphone, he paused when it was time to talk about his son. "Patrick Knight is my all-time favorite Indiana player," Knight said as he stepped away and gave his son a warm embrace.

And some have tried to be creative, too. Kory Barnett, a little-used walk-on who was known more for his antics as a member of the bench mob supporting his teammates, was also remembered for his Senior Night speech in 2012. He wrote a poem:

> As I ran out through the tunnel and onto the court,
> My last game in the greatest venue of all sports,
> I reminisce of all the blood, sweat, and tears
> And beating the No. 1 Wildcats amongst all the cheers.
> As a senior, the wins over Kentucky and Purdue definitely top off the list.
> What's even better is that a national championship banner in West Lafayette just doesn't exist.
> Although I passed up many opportunities to leave early for the NBA,
> It was worth it just to be a Bench Mob player each and every day.
> Some of you may ask yourself, Just what is the bench mob?
> It's hard to explain, it's hard to describe. But it's my job.
> Bench mob is voice-losing, arm-waving, 3D goggle–wearing, total chaos,
> It's holding each other back after Jordie lays down some hot sauce.
> Bench mob is a way of life, and I'm blessed to have been a part of it.
> But the foundation has been set, the torch will be passed, and it will be time for me to sit.

As a senior I've seen many nicknames come my way,
From A to Zero to Human Victory Cigar, it changes day to day.
But alas I have talked to the doctor, and he has informed me that it is
the best time for the Human Victory Cigar to retire.
For all the smoke, for the victories and banners to come will surely set
your lungs on fire.
I may go out to the real world and be a coach, a writer, or a producer.
But I can tell you this, no matter where I go, no matter what I do, I'll
always be a Hoosier.
Thank you.

The Cream and Crimson

The one thing you find out pretty quickly about Indiana basketball fans is that they represent.

This can show up in many ways. For one, everywhere Indiana plays, IU fans turn out in great numbers. It doesn't matter if it's Hawaii or Alaska, you're going to have Hoosiers fans there in droves. Go to a Northwestern-IU game on the road sometime and see what a home-away-from-home crowd looks like. Walk through the concourse area for an IU–Penn State basketball game at the Bryce Jordan Center, and you'll see IU fans everywhere. And that's just a typical road game. It's like that everywhere Indiana plays.

Make no mistake, Indiana represents.

Showing Off the Cream and Crimson

Hoosiers fans do it in outward ways, too. People wear their IU gear proudly. Whether it's an IU ballcap, a jersey, or someone wearing candy-striped pants, you see the cream and crimson proudly displayed at every turn. Sure, you see it on game days, but you also see it in shopping malls, downtown venues, and eating establishments all across the state of Indiana and beyond.

So what are the top apparel preferences for most Indiana fans?

We went to the source of such information and asked Amy Coble, the manager of the IU Varsity Shop, just inside the doors at the west entrance of the Simon Skjodt Assembly Hall.

Here's the list from the most popular on down:

Authentic Jerseys

Jerseys are always going to be big. The challenge, when purchasing authentic jerseys from the licensed IU apparel shops, is that only a few numbers are permitted to be sold. Those numbers usually include

No. 1 and the number of the current year. So if the year were 2016, you might be able to get the No. 16. IU Licensing and Trademarks also permits the numbers 18 and 20 to be used because 1820 was the year that IU was founded, but that's it.

Now, if you act fast, you may still be able to get some other numbers, too. That's because the rules have changed, and there are still some jerseys on the IU Varsity Shop website (as of early 2017) that had a few other numbers. For example, the numbers 4, 5, 11, and 40 were still being sold on the website as of early 2017. Often times, the numbers of those are very few, though, and they get gobbled up quickly.

One way to know if an IU jersey is truly authentic is to look on the back and see if you see a player's name. That's one of Indiana's biggest traditions—no names on the back of jerseys.

Generally, the reason that only a few numbers are allowed is so that IU Licensing and Trademarks can keep a handle on everything that is going out the front door. So you see a lot of the No. 1, which is good for guys like Jordan Hulls, Jared Jeffries, Noah Vonleh, and James Blackmon Jr. They have to think that there are a lot of IU fans giving them some love, when in reality, it's one of the only numbers that's officially permitted to be sold.

That doesn't mean there aren't some knockoffs that are being sold, too.

One number you see a lot of in Assembly Hall is the No. 40. You really saw it a lot back in 2013 when Cody Zeller was wearing it his sophomore season. It used to be fun to walk up to young Indiana basketball fans, point at the No. 40, and say, "Hey, that's cool, you're wearing Calbert Cheaney's number!" To which they would always reply that it was Zeller, but that joke never got old.

Looking for an Adidas crimson or white replica jersey? In the 2016–17 basketball season, it would run you about $75 plus tax for the real thing. There are some that you can get for $10 or less that are still considered authentic, but that's usually the bottom end of the price range.

Candy Stripes

There are a lot of people who will argue that candy stripes are the No. 1 apparel item over jerseys. You definitely see both of them a lot, but with candy stripes you simply make a bolder fashion statement from time to time.

Take a look around when you walk into a game at Assembly Hall or walk around Bloomington on game day. Clearly, all of your friends are doing it. If you're an IU basketball fan, nothing is cooler than wearing candy stripes.

The best place to purchase them is either in the Varsity Shop at Assembly Hall, located just inside the west lobby, or by going online to www.iuvshop.com, the official IU athletics merchandise website. Another spot is www.indianauniversityshop.com.

If you're an adult, the real-deal Adidas candy-striped pants will run you $99.98. The pants are available in small, medium, large, and extra large. There are also candy-striped pants available for ladies. These are candy-striped leggings made by League. They run $47.98.

Looking for candy stripes for the young people in your household? They're available for purchase as well. The kids' version goes for $40 and are available in two sizes, medium (5/6) and large (7). The youth candy-striped pants go for $50 and are available in small (8), medium (10/12), large (14/16), and extra large (18/20).

If you want the famed pants, however, you're smart to get them early in the season, because the store often runs out. They normally get 1,000 pairs to start the season, and once they're sold, they're gone until the following season. A reorder on the pants takes four months to deliver.

"We have had several seasons where we've run out of them completely," said Amy Coble, manager of the IU Varsity Shop in Assembly Hall. "It often depends on the success of the team, but a lot of times we're sold out by early in the year."

So load up on candy stripes. The one thing you can be certain of when it comes to this iconic piece fashion is that it will never go out of style.

Replica Shorts

Another popular item is the IU basketball shorts. The real ones, sold at the Varsity Shop, will run around $65. You can always opt for the knockoffs, but the real thing can be found at the IU Varsity Shop, located inside the west lobby of Assembly Hall.

Basketballs

There are a couple of different basketball options. There are cream-and-crimson rubber basketballs that are sold in a couple of different sizes and there's also a nice brown basketball with white panels that makes for a good autographed ball. Both are sold in Assembly Hall.

Ballcaps

Need an IU ballcap? You're in luck. There are literally 40 or more different designs of IU caps in all colors and styles. Most have the block IU displayed in some fashion, but there are caps for every sport at IU, from wrestling to soccer to football and basketball, as well. There's a cap for rugby and lacrosse. There's a cap that has the Kelley School of Business on it.

And they are very popular items at the Varsity Shop.

Polo Shirts

Again, lots of colors, styles, and sizes, but if this is what you want, you'll find lots of options to show off your spirit and colors.

T-Shirts

Once again, like the caps, there are shirts for every sport at Indiana, and if you've seen the logo, it's 24 Sports, One Team. The prices range from about $20 to $35 for short-sleeve T's and a little more for the long-sleeved ones.

Blankets

These may be more popular during football season or the Christmas holidays, but blankets are a big seller at the IU Varsity Shop. And there is a lot of variety here, as well.

Quarter-Zips

These short-zippered sweatshirts are a popular item at the Varsity Shop. The problem tends to be inventory. These come in and they move quickly. They just don't seem to stay on the shelves very long.

Stuffed Animals

This is what they refer to in the Varsity Shop as "plush" products. The various stuffed animals, many wearing IU gear, are included on this list.

Just for Kids

What about for children? Are there lots of options for IU kids, too?

There is everything from cheerleading outfits to jerseys and candy stripes for kids, too. Need a copy of an IU basketball children's book? You can pick up a copy of *Hoo-Hoo-Hoo Hoosiers*, too. (A shameless plug indeed.)

We asked the IU Varsity Shop people to give us a feel for the top-selling children's items, and this was their list:

1. Basketballs
2. Candy stripes

3. Jerseys
4. Replica basketball shorts
5. Pom poms
6. Hair ties
7. Face paint
8. Face stickers
9. Spirit beads
10. Foam fingers

The bottom line is that if you want something with Indiana on it, you're going to find it. And every year there is new stuff hitting the shelves. A lot of IU fans like the traditional wear, but there's a segment that wants something new, too.

According to Amy Coble at the Varsity Shop, Indiana basketball fans have varied tastes. Some are looking for the "new look" in apparel each and every year, where others prefer the same, traditional feel year in and year out.

"I would say it's a mix of both," Coble said. "Most fans want tradition and simplicity along with a new feel. For example, taking the candy stripe and using it for a script Indiana [traditional] and putting it on a new T-shirt style."

Get Involved with an IU Alumni Chapter

Looking to get involved in a way where you can support Indiana athletics with friends and neighbors in an organized setting? The Indiana University Alumni Association may have something for you.

The best place to find out what's going on with the IU Alumni Association is to check out their website at www.alumni.indiana.edu.

Here's what it says on the alumni website under the "Get Together: Chapters & Groups" tab:

> With more than 160 alumni communities worldwide, the IU Alumni Association is represented in alumni groups based on geographic region, shared interests and backgrounds, and fields of study.
>
> Gather with IU alumni in your community through your local chapter.
>
> Find an international IU community.
>
> Connect with alumni who share your particular IU interests or experiences (members of the Marching Hundred, for instance, or Latino alumni) through affiliate groups.
>
> Get together with alumni from your IU school, department, or program.
>
> All who love IU are welcome. IUAA membership is not required.

If you check the website you can find the numbers and email addresses to make contact with any IU Alumni group in your area.

For example, let's say you wanted to get involved in an IU Alumni chapter in the state of Indiana. The following are the chapters that exist within the state:

- Bartholomew County
- Boone County
- Cass County
- Central Indiana Chapter
- Greater Evansville Chapter
- Henry County
- Howard / Tipton Counties Chapter
- Johnson County
- Kosciusko County Chapter
- Lakeshore Region Chapter

- Louisville/Southern Indiana
- Madison County Chapter
- Monroe County Chapter
- Northeast Indiana Chapter
- Southwest Indiana Chapter
- St. Joseph County Chapter
- Vincennes / Knox County Chapter
- West Central Indiana Chapter
- Whitewater Valley Chapter

But it's clearly not just an Indiana thing. There are alumni chapters out there for people from most states to access. If you spend the winter's in Florida, there are several very active chapters in that area. Live in and around Colorado? The Denver chapter is very active. The same can be said for so many other chapters out there.

The bottom line: If you have an interest in the IU Alumni Association, they have something for you. Just go to this website for more information: www.alumni.indiana.edu.

Indiana Man Caves

There are other ways to show off your Indiana pride, too. Some people do this through their Indiana Man Caves.

Many people have their own version of these rooms, some quite large, others very small. It may be a separate building, a basement, a spare room, a study. They vary in space and location. The one thing they have in common is that they are dedicated to Indiana University in some form or another.

So what do these look like? How can you make or have one? Where do you get the items? What do you need? What items would indeed be special?

The size of the room does not matter as far as making it look really nice. Of course, the size will limit the number of items one might

Brady Evans, who lives in Bloomington, in his man cave

choose to display, but no matter what the size, it can be both tasteful and fun.

So what do you want in your room? First, you should start with autographed memorabilia. What should you have autographed? For one, pictures—a photo of the player in action is always wonderful. Hint: have the player sign a picture of their first game or a special play, such as a winning shot. A signed photo of Keith Smart's winning shot in 1987, a picture of Christian Watford's shot against Kentucky, or Calbert Chaney's shot to set the scoring record are wonderful starts and keepsakes. So how can you get these? Well, there is eBay, but collector stores are always wonderful, as well. However, the best way is to get a picture and get it signed in person.

Autographed photographs are best displayed when they are framed and matted professionally. Although this is more expensive, framing your pictures this way, using museum glass, will preserve your autographs and make your prints more valuable. However, for the true IU fan, the value of your picture is and should be up to you, and many times depends on the memories.

Photographs should not be the only autographed items in your room. Autographed balls from a special game or championship game or team are also very special. Other autographed items for your room can be autographed books. At Assembly Hall, within the last two years, Cody Zeller and Bobby Leonard have signed their books for fans, and in the lobby of Assembly Hall, various authors are always signing their books. In 2016 members of the perfect 1976 team were busy after the game honoring them, signing all sorts of items for fans who remembered that glorious time in Hoosiers history.

If you were lucky enough to be at a special game, you could include the ticket stub with the photo, such as one fan had with a Cody Zeller signed picture of his dunk against Kentucky with the ticket enclosed in the frame. It was just a statement to people enjoying his room that, yes, he was at that game.

One fan had a signed photo of Watford's shot with a $20 bill enclosed in the frame, a reminder of the fan's winning bet against a Kentucky fan. He had also framed a signed picture of Anthony Thompson's record-setting touchdown game with the ticket included in the frame.

Again, we cannot stress enough how awesome autographs can be for your room, for it says for once and for all that these are some of the players you have met along the way. Selfies are always welcomed, as well—or, for us older people, a picture with the player. Tough autographs are ones from people who have passed away, but they can be had, just be careful that they are real; get them from a trustworthy source. An estate auction or a grandparent or someone who would have been around during that time period is best.

We gave you a few ideas earlier how to get autographs, so here are some other hints. In basketball, after a game at Assembly Hall, usually three players will come out to sign for those who are waiting in line. Also, just going down to Bloomington and waiting outside Cook Hall for players to come out of practice will work, as well. And, as we said before, places like the Collectors Den will have signings from time to time, as they did last April with both Yogi and Coach Knight appearing on different days.

Any good cave has some rare or unusual items, such as one that has a collection of mini–football helmets, one of every kind the Indiana football team has ever worn over the years. According to this cave owner, there are 43 helmets, including four different leather ones. He said you can go on the Internet to find people making these helmets. To go along with the football theme, another collector has all six pennants made for the 1967 Rose Bowl team, including one that features quarterback Harry Gonso and tailback John Isenbarger.

You can get pieces of bleachers from Memorial Stadium (1925–1982), a block taken from the original seating on the 50-yard line. A piece of a bleacher from the 17th Street Fieldhouse (1960–1970), and Assembly Hall (1971–1995), or a piece of the floor from the Old Fieldhouse (1928–1959), or a piece of the floor from Assembly Hall (1976–1995)—a floor that saw the Hoosiers go 237–36. You could add

Evans showing off another wall of his man cave

to your collection a Rose Bowl Reunion medal, complete with pictures of the stadium, a rose, block IU, and of course "the Bucket."

Another medal was from the football stadium dedication game on October 22, 1960, against Michigan State, the Brass Spittoon game. Another collector added to his cave two miniature white plastic footballs—one from 1966, sponsored by Bloomington National Bank, and one from the Rose Bowl year of 1967, from Colonial Bakery. This collector explained how as a young boy he dove for the balls when thrown into the stands at the knothole section. You can get your own Old Oaken Bucket or Brass Spittoon by going to www.rivalrytrophy. com.

In 2016 you can purchase a red plastic back of the chairs from Assembly Hall. Another collector tells of having a model of both Assembly Hall and Memorial Stadium from Danberry Mint that on occasion can be found on eBay. Or, while not as nice, they have similar ones that light up at the university bookstore, TIS (Tichenor Institutional Services). Several collectors have put in their man caves red, white, cream, and clear plastic cups that have been given out over the years at Assembly Hall. And, of course, what man (or woman) cave would be complete without the famous bobbleheads? Indiana has given out Randle El, Anthony Thompson, Tom Crean, and Kent Benson bobbleheads over the years. The Bucks had a Jon McGlocklin one, the NFL a Trent Green. Indiana also featured a Jerry Yeagly, and the Suns had a Dick Van Arsdale. Buy two Dick Van Arsdale bobbleheads and paint one with the No. 25, and you have yourself a Tom Van Arsdale bobblehead, as well. There is also a very rare Archie Dees bobblehead if you can find one.

In 1975 and 1976, 7-Up bottles featured Indiana basketball feats; these are easy to find and a great addition to your cave. Also, Coca-Cola featured a plate featuring Coach Knight and the 1976 perfect season. There are white steins celebrating the five national championships in basketball as well as the Rose Bowl and Holiday Bowl.

Then there is John Hoesman, who carves wooden figures. He has made Indiana figures such as Bob Knight, Branch McCracken, Everett Dean, Bo McMillin, John Pont, Bill Mallory, Tom Crean, Steve Alford, Tevin Coleman, and Cody Zeller, among others. You can contact John at john@carvingfool.com.

Then, of course, there are McFarland figures, which have featured Trent Green and Isiah Thomas. There are companies such as High Country Collectibles that feature custom-made figures, such as an Isiah Thomas in an Indiana uniform, as well as a Tevin Coleman figure and an Anthony Thompson figure. Since these are custom-made, other favorite players can be made, as well.

One collector has a very rare Indiana player pajama bag that was sold at Memorial Stadium in the 1960s. We wish you luck in finding it. It is very, very rare, and also very, very cool. We can say without reservation that somebody's bucket list just got a big-time check by it.

Yet another man cave featured a framed set of pins celebrating their five national titles as well as their (at the time) 21 Big Ten titles. This collector had medallions that also featured national and Big Ten championships, as well as CCA and NIT championships.

For fans of Indiana basketball from the 1960s, we found that, on Dick Van Arsdale's art website, you can buy pictures of the New Fieldhouse done by Van Arsdale, who played in that building from the 1962–63 to the 1964–65 season.

At Cracker Barrel, you can buy a red Indiana rocker to put in your man/woman cave. Posters given out through the years adorn another collector's walls, while the basketball schedule posters line another cave. Still another owner has books and programs from as far back as the 1920s, many, as we said earlier, signed by players and/or the authors.

Maybe not a must but a very cool item for a cave is a big-screen TV. One collector has such a set up with DVDs of games from as far back as 1940, a really great asset on non-game days, to be able to sit back

Brett White's man cave features three generations of Hoosier connections. Both his dad and grandfather played football at IU.

in your big red IU rocker and watch great games from the past. Which game would be on your bucket list? The first NCAA championship in 1940, a silent black-and-white film? Or the 2016 NCAA victory over Kentucky in beautiful color?

We walked into one cave and were confronted with stacks of leather-bound books that contained sports cards of former Indiana players. One book contained one card of each player, signed by that player, divided into sections of basketball, football, and baseball and other sports, including cards from the 2016 women's basketball team that won every home game that season.

Now let's look at man caves, their owners, and the history behind them. First there is Brady, a 2011 Indiana grad. We asked what made him start his man cave. "When I was about five years old, I got a pair of candy-striped pants," he said, "and that pretty much got me started. My first real purchase that started my cave was a Randle El auto-graphed 8 x 10 picture. We bought our first home, and I had a spare

White in his man cave

room that became my first man cave. Then we moved to a different city, and my man cave started with a spare room in our apartment. Now we have moved into our current house, and again our spare room has become my man cave." When asked what his favorite part of his current man cave was, he responded, "It's my section over Bob Knight and his teams at Indiana University. Even though I wasn't really around for most of it, it was such a special time for Indiana basketball. So my section over Knight and his teams holds just such a special place. I really wanted to make that section very nice. The wood carvings are also very special, and I enjoy collecting them and deciding which ones to have John make."

Brady's man cave is divided into sections: one side of the room is devoted to football, while the other is devoted to basketball. Brady has put his man cave into sections by both coaches and sports. Two walls are dedicated to basketball, with one corner devoted to Coach Knight. There is also a Tom Crean section and a Mike Davis section. His walls dedicated to football are divided into a Bucket game section

Over 125 pictures are displayed in David Murray's man cave.

and a Bowl game section. In both sections, autographed 8 x 10 photos decorate the walls from top to bottom. In looking at Brady's man cave, two items dominate: the 8 x 10s and his wood carvings, of which he now has 14. Brady, like many other collectors, has a collection that is a combination of eBay finds, paintings, and carvings, as well as IU giveaways.

We went to Bloomington to visit Chris, a 33-year-old Hoosiers fan and Indiana grad. As a lifelong Bloomington resident with family members who both went to and worked at the school, his love for IU has been a lifelong passion.

Chris has many wonderful items in his collection, which include 10 different game-worn jerseys, such as Lyndon Jones, Kirk Haston, Charlie Miller, Brian Evans, D.J. White, and a wonderfully old Jeff Stockdale jersey from the Lou Watson era of the late 1960s. He has several autographed basketballs, from the 1975 team to the 2013 team. He has a Steve Alford basketball trophy and a 1928 basketball from an Indiana-Ohio game. His collection also includes a library of Indiana books, as well as different pins and pieces of floors.

However, Chris's passion is his collection of programs, schedules, and ticket stubs. "My father got me interested in old things, he would take me antiquing with him," he said. "Then being a history teacher and loving history and wanting to preserve the history of Indiana, it just came naturally." His collection of schedules is both impressive and rare.

There is his 1914 Indiana University basketball schedule that reads like a book, and as you open each page, more of the schedule is revealed at the top, while local merchants' ads are at the bottom. It is a most fascinating schedule, and one we were very glad to have been able to see. Indiana's pocket basketball schedules go back in time, but it wasn't until 1952–53 that the faces of the players appeared on the schedule. In a true twist of fate, this was the same season Indiana would win the championship, a title no one could have predicted. Indeed, Illinois was favored to win both the Big Ten and the NCAA championship, but there were the faces of the players gracing the 1952–53 Indiana basketball schedule. Indiana would again go back to the picture-less schedule until the 1961 season, when the New Fieldhouse was featured, followed by pictures of Rayl and the Van Arsdales in later years. Pictures of Lou Watson and Bob Knight adorned future schedules.

Chris also proudly displayed programs from the first games played in the New Fieldhouse, as well as Assembly Hall. A program from Everett Dean's first game and the dedication game from the Old Fieldhouse are also a part of this treasured collection.

Chris has a card signed by coach Branch McCracken and players from the 1940 NCAA national championship team. But, of all his many wonderful treasures, his favorite is his game-used Damon Bailey jersey, framed, mounted, and proudly displayed in his family room.

Then there is the story of David in Indianapolis, a lifelong Hoosiers fan dating back to the 1950s. David's family worked and went to Indiana University, and he grew up bleeding cream and crimson. "As a young boy, I grew up loving Indiana," he said. "In fact, I don't remember life without rooting for IU. How did I start my man cave? Well, it started, you could say, as a boy cave, if there is such a thing. My grandparents lived in Bloomington and saved the newspapers for me. I had a metal bookcase that I cut out the pictures from the papers and put on the book cases. I hung the pennants from that bookcase, and the pins and buttons you could buy also went on that bookcase. I also keep all my tickets and programs from those games as well." He has many 8 x 10 photos hanging on his man cave wall and has graduated to wooden bookcases for his many artifacts, which include pins, buttons, bobble-heads, and mini–football helmets.

He displayed his collection in sections, as well. There is the Rose Bowl collection, the basketball collection from the 1950s and '60s, a Coach Knight and 1970s, '80s, and '90s section, and a section of Indiana books. On the wall, his pictures are divided into basketball players, NCAA championship games, and football players. "My first two favorite players when I was a kid were Archie Dees and Woody Moore," he explained. "So I started working the pictures around those two in the center. I just thought it was a nice touch to remember those early days."

We asked David what his favorite piece to his collection was. "I would have to say that I have this pajama bag that is the face of an Indiana football player that my grandmother got me in the early '60s when I was young. One year, I decided to have my own homecoming display at my grandparents' house. So I took the pajama bag, filled it, put it on a body I made with youth football pads, a football jersey, and pants; took a toy gun and made a little stick deer. I put a sign out saying, 'Shoot Down the Bucks.' It must have looked really awful, but I remember cars slowing down to look at it as they passed by. I was so proud at the time. I just laugh, thinking about it now, but I guess with those memories, that is my favorite piece of all—the really awesome things in my collection. Funny but true."

David's story points out what we think a true, meaningful man cave is, one that means something very special to you and may even tell a story of your life as it relates to Indiana University.

Then there is Brett's story. Brett grew up with his grandfather and father playing football at Indiana University. They didn't just play: his grandfather kicked the winning field goal against Purdue in 1940. Always special to win the bucket. And his father was a member of the 1967 Rose Bowl team. So as Brett said, "I just grew up with Indiana University as part of our family. Saturday afternoon in the fall was filled with Indiana University football come rain, sleet, or snow. We were always there, it was just part of our way of life. I think, without really knowing it, I also had a boy cave before my man cave. As a young boy, my room was decorated with IU stuff. On my 11th birthday, I got a picture made up of the 1992–93 Indiana basketball team signed by all the players and Coach Knight. [That] and a wonderful signed artwork picture of coach Jerry Yeagley are the two things that I had from my boyhood. I really started my collection in earnest after I graduated from Indiana."

As you walk into Brett's man cave, you feel as if you've walked into heaven, and no, it's not Iowa, it's Indiana. Brett has arranged his room into themes. First, you are hit with the huge big-screen TV on the far wall. To the left of the TV is his section over football trophies and family artifacts. There are two very impressive Old Oaken Buckets, simply great pieces that are made from wood, and one made of cement. The cement bucket is very heavy, please take our word for it. There is his grandfather's red letter jacket and an Indiana helmet displayed proudly on a mannequin. A picture of his grandfather, Gene White, on a poster schedule for the 1941 football season kicking the winning field goal in 1940.

Brett also has two brass spittoons, the trophy between Indiana and Michigan State in football. There are other pictures in this corner from the 1940s and the Rose Bowl team. In the opposite corner is a trophy to Bob Knight as Coach of the Year. This beautiful basketball trophy is surrounded by pictures of the 1987 NCAA championship team and the call of Don Fischer on Keith Smart's game-winning basket.

In the center of the room is a coffee table with a glass top, and underneath the glass are copies of programs, tickets, and pins from Indiana and Purdue football games. All in all, Brett has seven full-size Indiana football helmets, from the current Indiana flag helmet to the red leather Michigan-style wing helmet. As you walk along this wall to the back, there are photos from current IU basketball players and a 16 x 20 canvas picture of a young Walt Bellamy with his teammates.

You reach his two cabinets, and what treasures await you there. There are pictures, ticket stubs, stuffed IU animals, medals, pins, rings, bobbleheads, a real Indiana University sport treasure. One theme, quite naturally, is dedicated to the 1967 Rose Bowl team, with pins from the Rose Bowl year. There are mugs, pins, rings, glasses, posters, and other Indiana items like the warm-ups from Steve Green that has "Hoosiers" in script rather than the Indiana script on the back.

Brett decided one day he needed more space. So, instead of going out, he decided to go up, and when his wife upstairs asked what he was doing, he proclaimed he was tacking posters to the ceiling.

There are chairs from locker rooms and pictures of players throughout the room to the point you find yourself spinning around like a top trying to take it all in. In yet another corner, you can see the game ball from the NIT championship game, a win over Purdue. There's a game ball from the 1973 NCAA regionals and game balls from football bowl games, as well. As you walk around, you find yourself lost in a museum of Indiana University sports history that just doesn't seem to stop.

So we have highlighted man caves from Brady, Chris, Dave, and Brett. To be sure, there are many, many others out there and great bucket list items to be had. You may try to find these items, and one may become your favorite. Happy hunting.

But what about many of you who want your own man cave but also want the ease of going to a store and buying what you want without all the pain and effort of tracking down the hard-to-find items? Don't worry, we are here for you. Let's go to Bloomington and go to TIS. We will list items you could purchase to create your own man cave, so let's go shopping.

Do you want something to hang on your walls? Well, we can take care of that. Nothing says Indiana basketball like banners, and TIS has them. There is the red wool blend banner that highlights the five NCAA national championships. It is 14" x 20" and goes for $34.99. Or there's the fave red felt banner featuring the 1940, 1953, 1976, 1981, and 1987 championships, measuring 12" x 18" for $59.99. Or you can go really big with a red wool blend national championship banner that is 24" x 36" for $64.99.

Maybe you would rather go with plaques. You can go with the family to the big plaque that says, "This family is full of heart but most of all we cheer together for IU. We are a Hoosier family," for $79.99. There are also plaques that have a red and black background covered by glass. One says, "The man cave est. 1820 Indiana Hoosier fans." Another features a picture of Memorial Stadium that spells out "Indiana Hoosier Football," and one does the same thing with Assembly Hall, spelling "Indiana Hoosier Basketball." All feature a gold coin, and all cost $59.99.

There is a red wooden plaque that says, "Gone to the game," which sells for $19.99, or even a red wooden plaque that serves as a bottle opener and says, "I'll enjoy the win," for $25.99. But maybe you want to start with a picture or two. TIS can supply you with a large picture of Assembly Hall or Memorial Stadium for $24.99, or pictures of Cody Zeller or Victor Oladipo for $15.99.

Do you want to hang a flag? They have many to choose from. There is a red, black, and white IU flag, a script Indiana flag on a red background, a black IU with the words "Indiana Hoosiers" also on the flag. Of course, there is a flag that resembles the American flag with red and white stripes and a black IU where the field of stars should be. These flags all measure 3' x 5' and range in price from $24.99 to

$69.99. There is a beautiful red banner that reads "Pride, Tradition, Honor, We Are Indiana," you could hang for $39.99.

During basketball season or a cold late-season football game, you might want a blanket in your cave. You can have a royal plush blanket for $35.99, a woven tapestry throw featuring screens at IU for $34.99. You're warm, your walls are covered with your love for IU. You're ready for visitors and games. Your TV's ready and food is on, but before or after the game, what can you do? Well, we can help you there too. You can get a game of checkers with an Indiana basketball theme, complete with basketballs to crown your kings. Entirely appropriate for any Indiana basketball fan who considers the Hoosiers royalty.

You can also get a set of playing cards that feature players from the McCracken, Knight, Watson, Davis, and Crean eras. One thing we can say for sure is that man caves are as unique as their owners. So if you put one together, add your own touch and enjoy your collection and room as much as possible.

Must Reads for Indiana Basketball Fans

There have been a ton of books written over the years about Indiana basketball. Many of them have been about Bob Knight, who coached Indiana for 29 seasons and won a trio of national championships during his time in Bloomington. Others have been written about specific teams or players. There have been books written about IU's other most decorated coach, Branch McCracken, who won the school's first two national championships in 1940 and 1953.

There have been books written by players who have played for Knight, and there have been unauthorized biographies, too. The top-selling IU book of all-time is *A Season on the Brink* by John Feinstein. Feinstein spent the 1985–86 season with Indiana and was granted practically unlimited access to the Hoosiers by Bob Knight. *Sports*

Illustrated called it "one of the best sports books of all time," and it sold millions of copies.

Many of the books listed below likely sold hundreds of copies, but they're still significant because they are written about a program that has a passionate fan base and one that is interested about anything that is written about their Hoosiers. Bottom line: there are plenty of good options for your Indiana University basketball reading pleasure.

(Book descriptions courtesy of the publishers.)

1. *Branch*
by Bill Murphy

Many Indiana University fans have heard the name Branch McCracken, after whom the hallowed court at Assembly Hall is named, but how many of them know about the legendary coach himself? Before Tom Crean, before Bob Knight, IU basketball relied on this man to make the school famous for its hoops stars. And, boy, did he—with two national titles, four Big Ten titles, and numerous other accolades, McCracken defined Hoosier Hysteria for a generation. However, his greatest legacy remains the example of good character he set and the way he touched the lives of everyone around him. Fans remember him as the coach who helped IU break the color barrier in Big Ten basketball, and players remember him as a second father. If, as McCracken once wrote, "A coach is not paid in money or winning teams, but in the men his players become," he was a rich man, indeed. Branch McCracken made Indiana University basketball a force to be reckoned with, and this is his story.

2. *Rising from the Ashes: The Return of Indiana University Basketball*
by Terry Hutchens

Coach Tom Crean brought the storied Indiana Hoosiers basketball program back to national prominence by taking an unranked team at the beginning of the 2011 season all the way to the 2012 Sweet Sixteen.

Indiana University's coach since 2008, the story of Coach Crean's successful rebuilding is of interest to serious college basketball fans and coaches everywhere. The success of the 2011–12 team and a top-ranked incoming class is sure to gain the keen interest of any Hoosiers fan.

The book opens with the shot by Christian Watford that beat the Kentucky Wildcats and ended Indiana's pre-conference schedule. That victory, over then No. 1 Kentucky, was the point when Hoosiers fans knew their team was back. A history of the program from the departure of Bob Knight through the difficult years faced by coach Mike Davis and the controversial years that followed under coach Kelvin Sampson follows.

The book continues with complete coverage of the rebuilding of the program by coach Tom Crean. Readers then get to relive that entire exciting season through to its end.

3. *Hoosiers Through and Through*

by Terry Hutchens

Five hundred and eighty-three basketball players from the state of Indiana have gone on to play basketball at Indiana University in more than 110 years of competition. Among the group are 26 players who won the coveted Mr. Basketball award as high school seniors. Also included are 35 players who went on to become All-Americans at IU and 10 who were Big Ten Most Valuable Players. In 2000 Indiana released its All-Century Team of the best players at IU in the previous 100 years. Nine of the players on that team were from the state of Indiana prior to playing at IU. All 583 of these players could be considered Hoosiers through and through. They grew up shooting baskets on hoops all across the state of Indiana and dreamed about someday playing for the state school. For these athletes, that dream came true. This book acknowledges all of them while focusing on the top 50 players all-time in Indiana University lore who hailed from the Hoosier state.

4. *Indiana University Basketball Encyclopedia*

by Jason Hiner (revised by Terry Hutchens)

Few other elite college basketball programs can match the tradition of excellence that reigns at Indiana University, while the fierce devotion of IU basketball fans has been selling out arenas and inspiring generation after generation of Hoosiers fans for over a century. This revised edition of the *Indiana University Basketball Encyclopedia* captures the glory, the tradition, and the championships, from the team's inaugural games in the winter of 1901 through the 2011–12 season. The most comprehensive book ever written about IU basketball, this encyclopedia covers every season and every game the Hoosiers played through 2012, including all of the program's Big Ten Conference championships and NCAA championships. Fans will relive the most exhilarating victories and the most heart-wrenching defeats. Included within are profiles of legendary Hoosiers stars, from Don Schlundt and the Van Arsdale twins to Calbert Cheaney and Damon Bailey. The rivalries, excitement, and history of the Hoosiers are captured here with vivid detail and unparalleled statistical accuracy. *Indiana University Basketball Encyclopedia* is a must-have for the library of every devoted IU basketball fan and a fitting guide to one of the most storied traditions in all of college basketball.

5. *A Season on the Brink*

by John Feinstein

Twenty-five years after it spent 16 weeks atop the *New York Times* bestseller list, *A Season on the Brink* remains the most celebrated basketball book ever written. Granted unprecedented access to legendary coach Bob Knight and the Indiana Hoosiers during the 1985–86 season, John Feinstein saw and heard it all—practices, team meetings, strategy sessions, and midgame huddles—as the team worked to return to championship form. The result is an unforgettable chronicle that not only captures the drama and pressure of big-time college basketball but also paints a vivid portrait of a complex, brilliant coach as he walks the fine line between genius and madness.

6. Knight: My Story

by Bob Hammel

Few people in sports have had more books written about them. This is the first by Bob Knight—one of the most literate, candid, quoted, and outspoken men in American public life, telling in this first-person account of his full, rich life. Much of that life has been in basketball, most of it because of basketball, but it also has brought him forward as a coach, who has proved academic responsibility and production of championship college athletic teams not only can coexist but should. His excitement as things start anew for him at Texas Tech is matched here by his characteristic frankness and remarkable recollection of a life he clearly has enjoyed.

7. 100 Things Hoosiers Fans Should Know & Do Before They Die

by Stan Sutton

This guide to all things Hoosiers tells the history of Indiana University basketball across several decades and covers anything and everything a fan should know. It takes years of Hoosiers history and distills it to the absolute best and most compelling, identifying the personalities, events, and facts that every living and breathing fan should know without hesitation. Numbers, nicknames, memorable moments, singular achievements, and signature plays all highlight the list of 100. Stan Sutton, a longtime IU beat writer, has assembled all the information and achievements that are sure to educate and entertain new and old fans alike. In its century-plus of college basketball, Indiana University has established a winning tradition that includes five NCAA championships and 20 Big Ten conference championships, all of which is celebrated in this entertaining resource.

8. Tales from the Indiana Hoosiers Locker Room: A Collection of the Greatest Indiana Basketball Stories Ever Told

by John Laskowski and Stan Sutton

Tales from the Indiana Hoosiers Locker Room covers over a century of Indiana University basketball. Current and former Hoosiers talk of the excitement, the disappointment, and the celebration that has turned IU basketball into a statewide religion. The history of the Indiana program is revealed through the memories of the school's hundreds of lettermen. Without a doubt, this is a must-read for every March Madness and college basketball fan.

9. The Power of Negative Thinking: An Unconventional Approach to Achieving Positive Results

by Bob Knight with Bob Hammel

Norman Vincent Peale's *The Power of Positive Thinking*, a classic bestseller, has inspired an optimistic perspective for millions of Americans. Now, in an inspirational and entertaining rebuttal, the legendary basketball coach Bob Knight explains why "negative thinking" will actually produce more positive results, in sports and in daily life. Coach Knight, the second-winningest coach in NCAA history with 902 victories, explains that victory is often attained by the team that makes the fewest mistakes. His coaching philosophy was to instill discipline by "preparing to win" rather than hoping to win. That meant understanding the downside and drilling his teams to prevent the things that could go wrong. And when his teams did win, he made sure they didn't dwell on their success, but rather looked immediately to the challenges of the next game. He applies this lesson to business strategy as well.

Coach Knight has long been inspired by his grandmother's words, "If wishes were horses, beggars would ride." As the first person to teach Knight about the power of negative thinking, this book is dedicated to her pragmatic spirit.

10. Bob Knight: His Own Man
by Joan Mellen

A biography of Bob Knight written in 1997.

11. Days of Knight: How the General Changed My Life
by Kirk Haston

What happens when a 6'9" kid from Lobelville, Tennessee, is recruited by legendary basketball coach Bob Knight? Kirk Haston's life was changed forever with just a two-minute phone call. Containing previously unknown Knight stories, anecdotes, and choice quotes, fans will gain an inside look at the notoriously private man and his no-nonsense coaching style. Which past Hoosiers basketball greats returned to talk to and practice with current teams? How did Knight mentally challenge his players in practices? How did the players feel when Knight was fired? In this touching and humorous book, Haston shares these answers and more, including his own Hoosier highs shooting a famous three-point winning shot against number one ranked Michigan State and lows losing his mom in a heartbreaking tornado accident. *Days of Knight* is a book every die-hard IU basketball fan will treasure.

12. Raising Boys the Zeller Way
by Steve Zeller and Lorri Zeller

Steve and Lorri Zeller (parents of Luke, Tyler, and Cody Zeller) provide an inside look at the principles they implemented in their household, and share transparent and entertaining anecdotes about their parenting journey. Luke, Tyler, and Cody each finished at the top of their high school class, won Indiana's coveted Mr. Basketball award, played NCAA Division I basketball, and earned a contract in the NBA. The book alternates between Steve and Lorri's voice and includes comments from each of their boys throughout the manuscript. It's a one-of-a-kind read and an entertaining ride, recommended for both parents and basketball enthusiasts.

13. Jadlow: On the Rebound

by Todd Jadlow with Tom Brew

Todd Jadlow tells all about playing for Bob Knight, his professional life filled with drugs, alcohol and years in jail, and his inspiring road to recovery.

14. Getting Open: The Unknown Story of Bill Garrett and the Integration of College Basketball

by Tom Graham and Rachel Graham Cody

Bill Garrett was the Jackie Robinson of college basketball. In 1947, the same year Robinson broke the color line in major league baseball, Garrett integrated big-time college basketball. By joining the basketball program at Indiana University, he broke the gentleman's agreement that had barred black players from the Big Ten, college basketball's most important conference. While enduring taunts from opponents and pervasive segregation at home and on the road, Garrett became the best player Indiana had ever had, an all-American, and, in 1951, the third African American drafted in the NBA. In basketball, as Indiana went so went the country. Within a year of his graduation from IU, there were six African American basketball players on Big Ten teams. Soon tens, then hundreds, and finally thousands walked through the door Garrett opened to create modern college and professional basketball.

15. Landon Turner's Tales from the 1980–81 Indiana Hoosiers

by Landon Turner and Bob Hammel

In 1981 Indiana basketball fans still were exulting over the 1975–76 team's march to the NCAA championship. After all, those Hoosiers were the last to go unbeaten throughout the regular season and postseason, a record that still stands today. The '81 Hoosiers won five NCAA Tournament games with a winning margin of 23 points, evoking comparisons with Bob Knight's earlier championship team. But the '81 Hoosiers were far from invincible, losing nine games before ending the year with a 10-game winning streak. During a two-week stretch Indiana lost to Kentucky, Notre Dame and North Carolina, and during a trip to Hawaii dropped games to Clemson and Pan American. En route home from Hawaii, Coach Knight ran into North Carolina's Dean Smith in an airport and they both lamented how poorly their teams were playing. Probably neither suspected that the Hoosiers and Tar Heels would play for the national championship three months later. Turner went from a terrific physical specimen riding the bench to an offensive and defensive leader, filling a void that had cost IU dearly earlier that year. Four months after his team won the championship, Turner was paralyzed from the chest down when his car skidded off a curving Indiana highway as he was driving with three friends to an Ohio amusement park. Indiana's reversal of form and Landon's battle back from tragedy is related not only by Turner, but by the teammates who battled through his recovery at his bedside.

16. Mac's Boys: Branch McCracken and the Legendary 1953 Hurryin' Hoosiers

by Jason Hiner

This is the story of the 1953 Hoosiers, NCAA champions, coached by Branch McCracken and boldly led by star players Bobby Leonard and Don Schlundt. This legendary Indiana University team from the pre–Bob Knight era has begun to fade from memory, but Mac's Boys brings it vividly back to life.

One of the Hoosier state's most beloved basketball teams, the 1953 Hoosiers was also one of the best in the history of college hoops. It was a squad that had a great coach, a pair of star players, and teammates who accepted their roles and executed them flawlessly. With Leonard and Schlundt sharing the spotlight, there was the versatile forward Dick Farley (who would have been an All-American had he played on any other team), tenacious rebounder Charlie Kraak, and the hustling, ball-hawking guard Burke Scott. They were the heart of a team that put together one of the greatest hot streaks ever seen in Big Ten basketball, and then capped it off with a run through the NCAA tournament.

17. Playing for Knight: My Six Seasons with Coach Knight
by Steve Alford and John Garrity

An Olympic gold medalist recalls his four years on Indiana University's basketball team under the brilliant but controversial coach Bobby Knight, whose volatility and manipulative tendencies exacted a heavy toll from his players.

18. Same Knight, Different Channel: Basketball Legend Bob Knight at West Point and Today
by Jack Isenhour

Basketball legend Bob Knight is fond of saying that he has never gotten over West Point. In *Same Knight, Different Channel*, Jack Isenhour takes him at his word. A player on Knight's first West Point team, Isenhour shows how the controversial coach has changed little from his early days at the academy, temper tantrums and all. Knight made up his mind there to "win-gotta win" and follows that philosophy to this day.

Knight's sentiment was in step with the core value of "there is no substitute for victory" at West Point, where soldiers were being trained to fight and win the next war. So it came as little surprise following Knight's 18–8 record in his inaugural 1965–66 season—a season in which the twenty-five-year-old, hot-headed coach berated officials, totaled chairs, and got into his first shouting match with an athletic director—that West Point chose to keep the young Coach Knight on. What's a tantrum or two in the name of winning? With that, "Bobby T" was born. Knight's bad-boy persona—the hair-trigger temper, the acting out, and the defiance—was codified as at least tolerable, if not acceptable, behavior.

19. The Glory of Old IU
by Bob Hammel and Kit Klingelhoffer

A handsome coffee-table book, Glory of old IU is the most comprehensive book ever written about Indiana University athletics. Never-before-published details about the 100 years of IU's membership in the Big Ten Conference are captured in this one-of-a-kind book. Glory of Old IU includes vignettes about all of IU's greatest moments, including its five NCAA basketball championships. There are stories about Bob Knight, Mark Spitz, Isiah Thomas, Harry Gonso, and many others.

20. Damon: Beyond the Glory
by Damon Bailey and Wendell Trogdon

Damon, a name that needs no last for fans, lived the dream of basketball greatness in Indiana. Now that the roar of crowds now sounds for others, Damon Bailey still lives the good life as a husband, father and successful businessman. He reviews his career, is candidly critical of Bob Knight, his coach at Indiana University, and the state of basketball today.

The Ultimate Hoosiers Bucket List

Any true Indiana University basketball fan has his or her own bucket list. It may be something you wish you could do but that's not attainable. It may be something that you hope you can do one day in the future but haven't had the opportunity just yet. Or it may be a daydream of wishing you had been a part of something that happened in the past. Whatever it may be, as an IU basketball fan, it is a part of the fabric of your life. After consulting with Indiana basketball fans everywhere, we have put together an Ultimate Hoosiers Bucket List. Again, some of the things are quite possible, while others are more on the fantasy side of things. Perhaps you have done some of the things on this list or know people who have. Perhaps there are things here that you had never really thought of but will now consider doing.

Each entry includes a brief description on how you would do it, what it would cost, the difficulty factor in getting it accomplished, and how high it would rank on someone's ultimate bucket list. In determining the number of buckets, we ranked each item from one to five (with five being the most important) in terms of how essential it would be to your own version of Hoosier Hysteria. But don't misunderstand us: even things ranked as one bucket are important or we wouldn't have put them in the book. After all, all IU experiences are created equal. Here's our Ultimate Hoosiers Bucket List:

Attend a Game at Assembly Hall

- **WHERE:** 1001 East 17th Street, Bloomington, Indiana
- **COST: $$** (Ticket prices begin at $44)
- **DIFFICULTY FACTOR:** Much more difficult for conference games, much easier for most nonconference matches. Best opportunity often times is to purchase tickets for a game when IU students are out on Christmas break.
- **BUCKET RANK:** 🪣🪣🪣

This may seem like the simplest one for many IU fans, and yet for others it's the ultimate dream. Many IU fans have only had the opportunity to watch Indiana basketball on television and have never sat in the hallowed seats of Assembly Hall to see the Hoosiers play in person.

We have been lucky enough to have witnessed hundreds of games at Assembly Hall over the years. One of us saw games in the Old Fieldhouse where IU played for 11 seasons before moving into Assembly Hall in time for the 1971–72 season.

If you're an IU fan and you've never stepped inside Assembly Hall, it's a must-see—especially with the renovation of the south lobby that took place in 2016 and has transformed that area into an IU basketball mecca. The next time you happen across an IU basketball schedule, look at those games in the last week or two of December or the first few days in January and then call the IU Ticket Office at 1-866-IUSPORTS. You'll be really happy that you checked this one off your bucket list.

Buy Keith Smart or Christian Watford a Drink

- **WHERE:** Anywhere you run into them

- **COST:** $ (As much as $7–10 at your local tavern or as little as a quick reach into your cooler at a tailgate)

- **DIFFICULTY FACTOR:** It's a case of being in the right place at the right time

- **BUCKET RANK:** 🪣🪣🪣🪣

The saying goes that Keith Smart and Christian Watford are two players who will never have to buy a beer in Bloomington or in other locales around the country if they happen to run into IU fans.

Why? They hit, arguably, two of the best remembered shots in Indiana basketball history. One was with everything on the line, and the other came at a time when Indiana basketball had slipped well below the radar.

Smart's baseline jumper was the game-winner when Indiana won the 1987 national championship, beating Syracuse 74–73 in the Louisiana Superdome in New Orleans. If you haven't seen the shot on replay, you haven't been paying attention. And the reality is that any true Indiana basketball fan can remember that moment as if it were yesterday. In fact, those fans old enough to have been following IU at the time can very likely tell you exactly where they were on that Monday night in late March 1987 when Smart hit "The Shot."

Christian Watford's shot didn't have national championship importance, but many feel it signaled the return of the Indiana University basketball program to respectability. The IU basketball program had fallen on hard times in 2008 when former coach Kelvin Sampson was forced to resign after committing multiple NCAA infractions. The "Wat Shot," as it has come to be known, was a three-pointer from the left wing at the buzzer in Assembly Hall that lifted Indiana to a 73–72 win over No. 1–ranked Kentucky on December 10, 2011.

There are few things that Indiana fans enjoy more than beating Kentucky, and beating the Wildcats when they were the top-ranked team in the land was simply that much more special. And like "The Shot" that Smart hit in 1987, the "Wat Shot" has the same cult-like following. Most Indiana basketball fans can tell you where they were when Watford hit the shot that was heard 'round the college basketball world and replayed a million times on ESPN for the remainder of that season.

Both of those players will tell you today that rarely a day or two goes by when they don't run into someone who asks them to recount their shots that became such an important part of IU basketball lore.

See the Hoosiers Hang the Next National Championship Banner

- **WHERE:** Assembly Hall, 1001 East 17th Street, Bloomington, Indiana

- **COST:** Free (being in the building the night the banner is hung)

- **DIFFICULTY FACTOR:** Pretty difficult, considering it hasn't been done in Bloomington since 1987

- **BUCKET RANK:** 🪣🪣🪣🪣🪣

Ask any Indiana basketball fan if they could have one wish granted, and it would no doubt be to hang that elusive sixth national championship banner. And the year after that, they'll want No. 7. It's just the nature of Indiana basketball fans. IU fans expect their teams to play for championships and make deep runs into the NCAA Tournament. Even though it hasn't happened in over 30 years, Hoosiers fans still view Indiana basketball as one of the elite, upper-tier programs in the country.

Every year that Indiana basketball begins to have success, fans begin wondering if this could possibly be the year. It happened in both 1992 and 1993 in the Calbert Cheaney/Alan Henderson era of IU hoops. It happened in 2002 when a Cinderella IU team played in the national championship game against Maryland and led with under 10 minutes to play. It happened in 2013 when the Hoosiers were ranked No. 1 in the nation for 10 weeks before losing to Syracuse in the Sweet Sixteen. Each of those years, as Indiana crept closer to the ultimate goal, IU fans started allowing themselves to believe that this season could finally be the one.

But if and when it ever happens, you can bet that Indiana basketball fans will engage in a celebration that hasn't been experienced in Bloomington since 1987. It will be wild.

Complete the Hoosier Basketball Experience

- **WHERE:** Every Indiana basketball arena, past and present, that is still in existence

- **COST:** Free

- **DIFFICULTY FACTOR:** Not difficult, but it will take a little bit of planning on your part

- **BUCKET RANK:** 🪣🪣🪣🪣

This Bucket List wish is where you get to shoot a basket in every venue that has housed Indiana basketball over the years.

While there have been five such venues in the life of Indiana University basketball, four are still in existence today. The only casualty? The original Assembly Hall.

With that in mind, you can go to the men's gym on Seventh Street, now part of a building known as Wildermuth Intramural Center. When you walk in, walk up the staircase to the second floor and find four basketball goals that run east to west. Here you can shoot in the same gym as the Hoosiers of the late 1910s and early 1920s.

You can then walk down the stairs, staying in the same building, and find 10 courts running north and south. Here you can shoot in the same venue as Branch McCracken, Bobby "Slick" Leonard, Don Schlundt, Archie Dees, and Walt "the Bell" Bellamy.

Next you should head over to 17th Street and step onto the floor at the Simon Skjodt Assembly Hall. Call ahead and make arrangements to walk onto the hallowed hardwood of Assembly Hall and hear the echoes of such Hoosiers legends as Steve Downing, Scott May, Quinn Buckner, Kent Benson, Isiah Thomas, Steve Alford, Calbert Cheaney, and so many more. Find a ball, assume the shooting position, don't be intimidated, and let a shot fly. As the ball goes through the twine, for a moment you can experience what Indiana greats of the past have felt when they hit a shot in the famed arena.

Finally, walk into what was once called the New Fieldhouse but is now the Gladstein Fieldhouse. It's on the other side of Cook Hall near the corner of Fee Lane and 17ᵗʰ. This will be a little more challenging because technically this is BYOB (bring your own basket). The problem? The venue is now used for indoor track. But, again, you can feel the presence of all the Hoosiers greats who played in this venue from 1960 to 1972, when the floor was elevated and sawdust was on the floor at the end of the baskets to help cushion their fall.

But, if you listen, you can hear the crowd cheering for Jimmy "the Splendid Splinter" Rayl as he knocked down long-range shot after shot, well before the game of college basketball had a three-point line. Think of Tom and Dick Van Arsdale playing here, too, and Tom Bolyard. This is also the place where George McGinnis averaged more than 29 points and 17 rebounds in his lone season at Indiana.

So, if the basket is in place, step up and knock down a shot in this venue, too. Remember it will only count for two points, and know that you will have completed the Hoosier Experience.

Attend a Summer Tailgate Tour Stop

- **WHERE:** Stops around the state in places like Floyd Knobs, Evansville, Fort Wayne, and Indianapolis, to name a few

- **COST:** $ ($10–15, based on the location)

- **DIFFICULTY FACTOR:** Not difficult at all, as long as you're willing to put in the time and effort

- **BUCKET RANK:** 🪣🪣🪣

Every year several Indiana head coaches from sports like men's and women's basketball, football, baseball, and soccer will hop in an IU caravan and wander Indiana spreading goodwill and getting IU fans excited about the upcoming season.

Coaches speak to the gathered groups, often doing question-and-answer sessions afterward, and are always available for pictures and to sign autographs.

It's one of those events that has statewide appeal and gives fans the opportunity to get to know IU's coaches and support staff on a more personal basis.

Have a One-on-One Conversation with Bob Knight

• **WHERE:** Likely wherever Bob Knight would want to have the get-together

• **COST: ?** (However much it would cost you to get to where you would have to meet him)

• **DIFFICULTY FACTOR:** He would have to be willing to do it, and you'd have to know someone really well who would have the guts to ask him

• **BUCKET RANK:** 🪣🪣🪣🪣🪣

Some may say that this item should go under the fantasy heading, as the chances of getting a one-on-one interview with Coach Knight are probably slim and none. But if you had that opportunity, and Coach Knight was a willing participant, it could be a very special experience.

In many ways, Bob Knight *was* Indiana basketball for 29 years. He was the coach who put the modern-day Hoosiers on the map with a trio of national championships in 1976, 1981, and 1987. He was the often-controversial figure who threw a chair, stuffed a fan into a trash can, and caused an international incident at the Pan Am Games in Puerto Rico.

And yet he is also what many people think of the first time you mention Indiana basketball to someone outside the state of Indiana. This isn't to say the ones inside the state aren't still loyal, because many are. People continue to shell out great sums of money every year to attend Knight's dog-and-pony shows across the state, often dubbed "An Evening with Bob Knight."

Since Knight was fired in 2000, many IU basketball fans have hoped for the day when he would return to IU and be properly honored by the current administration for what he meant to the program. IU has made several attempts to bring him back, including inducting him into the university's Athletics Hall of Fame and also holding a night to honor the 1976 national champions on the 40th anniversary in 2016. But Knight has refused all offers to return.

That's what would make this event that much more special. You'd have to get Knight at the right time, in the right mood, and then make sure you ask questions that wouldn't set him off and end the conversation. The whole thing might come at a great monetary price, too. But we know a hundred IU fans who would pay a great sum of money to be able to have a one-on-one conversation with the college basketball coaching legend.

Maybe along with your bucket list, you make a second list of what questions you would ask Knight if you ever had him one-on-one. Maybe you'd ask about his final few weeks at Indiana and if he thought he could have handled IU's "zero tolerance" penalty. Maybe the topic would turn to what it is that's keeping him from returning and letting IU Nation properly honor him the way many believe he should be. Maybe you'd like to talk about grouse hunting or several other targets that the veteran coach likes to hunt. Maybe you'd just like to hear Knight talk about basketball and realize how interesting that would be, especially if it were a one-sided conversation.

Hoist a Big Head

• **WHERE:** Assembly Hall, 1001 East 17th Street, Bloomington, Indiana

• **COST: $$** (Being in the building for an IU basketball game)

• **DIFFICULTY FACTOR:** You have to convince the people passing out the posters to let you hold one

• **BUCKET RANK:** 🪣🪣🪣

Ever watch an Indiana basketball game and see the fans waving a multitude of big heads behind the basket where the opposing team shoots a free throw? Wish that was you was holding the Victor Oladipo or Cody Zeller big head? Or maybe you wish you had the Caesar big head or Abraham Lincoln?

Maybe Marilyn Monroe is more your style?

Whatever the case, imagine if you, by waving the big head during the game, were responsible for an opposing player missing a crucial free throw to help Indiana win another game at Assembly Hall.

Sit with Your Dad and Watch Indiana Win a National Title

• **WHERE:** In any one of five venues where IU has won a title, or somewhere in the future when the Hoosiers hang the next banner

• **COST: $$$** (Two tickets for a national championship game with IU playing)

- **DIFFICULTY FACTOR:** With the first five, you either did this or you didn't. With the next one, you obviously need to be in the building that night with your dad.

- **BUCKET RANK:** 🗑🗑🗑🗑🗑

Everyone wishes, and many maintain, that they were in the Spectrum in Philadelphia in 1981 or the Superdome in New Orleans in 1987 to see the Hoosiers win a national championship. It's not like the Cubs winning the World Series—nothing of that magnitude—but it has been more than 30 years since Indiana has hung a national title banner.

But what would it like to accomplish that Bucket List item and to do so with your dad sitting right next to you? Obviously, in many cases this is impossible if your father is no longer living. But what if you could do it? What would it mean to you and your dad?

When we were asking IU fans for their ultimate bucket list items, this is one that was suggested by Ryan Hart. He explained, "In 1987 I went with my dad to the Hoosier Dome to watch Indiana play in the first two rounds of the NCAA tourney against Fairfield and Auburn. We went to Louisville in 1991 to watch Indiana play Coastal Carolina and Florida State in the NCAA tourney. We watched at home together in 1987 the championship game in New Orleans, switching chairs, trying to find the right ones to give us a win. We were sitting in Little Tikes blue chairs when Keith Smart hit his shot and were sure somehow we helped."

Ryan said there was something that could even make it better, too.

"All that said, I would like to be at a title game with my dad and see us win, and if that game was in Indianapolis, that would be even better," he said.

That's not asking for too much, is it?

Attend Hoosier Hysteria

- **WHERE:** Assembly Hall, 1001 East 17th Street, Bloomington, Indiana

- **COST:** A canned food item that is donated to a local food bank.

- **DIFFICULTY FACTOR:** They usually get a crowd of more than 10,000, but rarely does it reach capacity.

- **BUCKET RANK:** 🗑️🗑️🗑️

A few years ago this event was referred to as Midnight Madness. Fans would begin filing into Assembly Hall late in the evening, and they eventually would count down the minutes to midnight when the Indiana basketball team would come out on the court for a warm-up session on the first official day of college basketball practice.

There would be shooting contests, a slam-dunk contest, and a short scrimmage. The coach might have a welcoming message for the fans, it would last an hour or so, and then IU fans would be dismissed into the night.

And you'd have a lot of sleepy people in the morning.

The event was then expanded to include the women's team, and ultimately the men's and women's teams would combine on shooting drills or team shooting competitions.

In recent years, however, Hoosier Hysteria was born and generally starts earlier in the evening so that people (and the players themselves) can get home at a reasonable time. The event is also usually on a Saturday night to try and attract the biggest crowds, and it's often held a few weeks after the official first day of practice.

A recent tradition that was started under head coach Tom Crean is for former players to come back and present the new Indiana players with their candy-striped warm-up pants. The candy stripes are an important part of the IU basketball tradition, and the ceremony just solidifies it that much more.

If you're an IU basketball fan, and you haven't been to Hoosier Hysteria, it's a must-do bucket list item. And to now be able to experience it in the newly renovated Simon Skjodt Assembly Hall just adds to the value. The new arena has all the bells and whistles of today's state-of-the-art facilities, but it's packaged inside one of the most iconic venues in all of college sports. The Hoosiers have won 84 percent of their games there in the first 46 years of the building's existence.

While Hoosier Hysteria does have a tendency to turn into a mini–Hoosier Lovefest, a good time is generally had by all.

Camp Out at Assembly Hall

• **WHERE:** Assembly Hall, 1001 East 17th Street, Bloomington, Indiana

• **COST:** $$ (Have student tickets and some time on your hands)

• **DIFFICULTY FACTOR:** Not difficult at all, as long as you're willing to put in the time and effort

• **BUCKET RANK:** 🗑🗑🗑

During the Tom Crean era in particular, Indiana fans have made it a regular occurrence to get in line and camp out with friends for multiple days leading up to a key IU basketball game.

This is because the student section at Indiana, which with 7,200 seats is the largest student section in the country, is filled on a first-come, first-served basis. So, if you're willing to put in the time, you can camp out and get the prime seat locations within the section.

On more than one occasion in recent seasons, when students were camping out in sub-freezing temperatures, athletic department officials have provided them with priority passes and encouraged them to go back to their dorms and apartments and sleep there. At other times, Tom Crean or other administrators have come around with pizza as a way of saying thank you to the students who are often lined up in a snake-like line that goes from the southeast end of Assembly Hall down past the Gladstein Fieldhouse and past Cook Hall.

Be Out with the 1976 Undefeated Indiana National Champions on the Night When the Final Unbeaten Team from That Particular Season Drops Its First Game

• **WHERE:** At an undetermined location

• **COST: ?** (However much it would cost to hang out with the champs)

• **DIFFICULTY FACTOR:** Like the Bob Knight bucket list item, you'd have to know some of these players really well

• **BUCKET RANK:** 🗑🗑🗑🗑

You never know if they really all gather together at some point and toast the last undefeated national championship team or not. But, if they did, there are Indiana basketball fans who would pay a good sum of money to be in their company.

Heck, there are IU fans who would pay big money to be a fly on the wall of that meeting. Just think about what it would be like to hang with Scott May, Quinn Buckner, Kent Benson, Bobby Wilkerson, and Tom Abernethy all these years later and talk about the old days and hear stories of the legendary 1975 and 1976 seasons. My guess is they would have a ton of stories to share about Coach Knight, as that's always a hot topic when former teams that played for him get together.

Very few people have the opportunity to ever say they were perfect at something. But that's the claim that the 1976 Indiana University basketball team can stake. Indiana finished the 1976 season a perfect 32–0 overall, 18–0 in the Big Ten (for the second year in a row), and beat St. John's, Alabama, Marquette, UCLA, and Michigan on its way to the school's third national championship. Indiana beat UCLA 65–51 and Michigan 86–68 in the final two games in Philadelphia.

There are many who believe the title of being the last undefeated national basketball champions could very well stay with the Hoosiers for a long, long time. It has now been more than 40 years since a team has gone through the entire college basketball season perfect.

Sit Behind the Home Bench at Assembly Hall

- **WHERE:** 1001 East 17th Street, Bloomington, Indiana

- **COST: $$$$** (Ticket prices begin at $44)

- **DIFFICULTY FACTOR:** This is obviously much more difficult than just getting a seat in the arena. This one generally requires either knowing someone close to the program or being willing to pay top dollar on the resale market.

- **BUCKET RANK:** 🪣🪣🪣🪣

There's something about being so close to the action, where you can truly appreciate the size of the players and also listen to some of the banter between the coaching staff and the players as the game goes on.

There's also something for the true IU fan about being in elite company. By elite, we're talking about other people who usually occupy those seats. Generally, the first five or six rows behind the bench are reserved for former IU players and their friends, IU recruits and their families, people with close ties to the program, and often times parents and relatives of current players. In another words, you're in good company.

Many IU fans never have an opportunity to sit this close to the action. If the opportunity ever presents itself, however, you should jump at the chance to experience IU greatness up close and personal.

Watch Bob Knight Roam the Sidelines at Assembly Hall

- **WHERE:** 1001 East 17th Street, Bloomington, Indiana

- **COST: $$** (Game ticket)

- **DIFFICULTY FACTOR:** Guessing that many of you had this experience

- **BUCKET RANK:** 🪣🪣🪣🪣

Bob Knight in many ways was an attraction within the attraction of attending an Indiana basketball game. There was always a sense of anticipation when it came to what Knight might do at an Indiana home game.

If a referee like Ted Valentine, Ed Hightower, or several others happened to be calling the game, you could pretty much count on extra fireworks.

If a coach like Purdue's Gene Keady was on the other bench, the drama could be even greater as Keady would put on a show, as well. Though Knight and Keady were good friends off the court, they had some classic battles on it.

And with Knight, you just never knew what he was going to do. You didn't have to worry about him throwing another chair like he did on February 23, 1985, because the university had found a way to secure the chairs in place. But there were so many other possibilities that you just never knew what might come next. Would Knight grab the public address microphone from announcer Chuck Crabb to admonish the fans for a certain negative cheer? Would he go off on an official and make clear his displeasure? Would said action result in a technical foul that could only cause the situation to escalate in terms of fan involvement? Would he bump a player, grab a jersey, or do something that would likely make national news?

The reality was that Indiana fans who attended games in Assembly Hall when Knight was the coach were indeed watching the game, but they also had a quick eye trained on Knight. If anything occurred in the game that might be the least bit controversial, your eyes quickly darted to the coach in the red sweater or plaid sportscoat.

It is our guess that a great many of you reading this book had the opportunity to see Knight coach at Assembly Hall in person, so you know exactly what we're talking about. And you can promptly put a check mark on this item to indicate this is one you were lucky enough to have accomplished.

Visit the Indiana Basketball Hall of Fame in New Castle

• **WHERE:** 408 Trojan Lane, New Castle, Indiana

• **WHEN:** Open 10:00 AM to 5:00 PM, Monday through Saturday

• **COST:** $ (Adults and teens, $5.00; children aged 5–12, $3.00. Group rates are available in advance. Parking is free. The Hall of Fame is also available for rental and is a great venue for receptions, corporate events, parties, and reunions.)

• **DIFFICULTY FACTOR:** Easy, just drive there. It is 28 miles from Richmond, 25 miles from Anderson, and less than two hours from Fort Wayne, Lafayette, Terre Haute, and Bloomington.

• **BUCKET RANK:** 🪣🪣🪣🪣🪣

As you walk into the Hall of Fame, notice the outside—the huge basketball shoe, the flag pole with state champions, and most of the state of Indiana Bricks with the manes of players, schools, and other individuals.

You need to know the history of the Hall of Fame. The Hall started out as the brainchild of Tom Carnegie and Ray Ransom Johnson in 1962, in conjunction with the Indianapolis Downtown Lions Club. It was located in a building in downtown Indianapolis on Pennsylvania Avenue.

The Hall would relocate to its New Castle home on June 30, 1990. The new building is a 14,000-square-foot museum to Indiana high school basketball. Interactive displays allow you to take the Game Winning Shot. Display your Indiana basketball knowledge on the trivia game. Become a sportscaster on You Make the Call or attempt to block the shots of Oscar Robertson and Stephanie White.

The conference room of the Indiana Basketball Hall of Fame in New Castle, adorned with pictures of IU players and team champions

For true Hoosiers fans, you must ask to go into the conference room. There on the wall are eight beautiful paintings of Indiana basketball history. Going left to right are the 1981 starting five with Jimmy Thomas. Next is a painting of the perfect 1976 team, featuring Knight, Benson, Buckner, and Wilkerson; followed by a picture of Tom Bolyard and Jimmy Rayl; a picture of Steve Alford; one of Lou Watson; Bill Garrett; George McGinnis; and, finally, one of Branch McCracken. Bring your cameras, you will want a picture of all the paintings by C.W. Mundy.

Before going downstairs, you can see Calbert Cheaney's IU and Washington (NBA) jerseys, along with his Rupp and Naismith Player of the Year trophies. There are pictures of Randy Wittman and Mike Woodson along with jerseys from Cody Zeller and Eric Gordon; Phil Buck's picture and his Rossville Sweater; and Charlie Hall's jacket and picture. You can measure your hand against George McGinnis' on a basketball. Downstairs are the stained-glass panels for Branch

McCracken and Everett Dean, a picture of Tom Van Arsdale with the Cincinnati Royals, and a picture of Michael Lewis becoming Jasper's all-time leading scorer. Paul Poff's picture and Indiana All-Star jersey. Notice there is no number on the front. A basketball from the Church Street Shootout between New Castle and Kokomo, better known as "Ray Pavy 51, Jimmy Rayl 49." Notice it is signed by both players. There is a picture and trophy for Tom and Dick Van Arsdale's 1961 *Time* Athlete of the Year award. You can compare your shoe size with Kent Benson, Steve Alford, and Tom Coverdale. There is Hallie Bryant's Globetrotter jersey and picture, Bobby Leonard's ball and picture, Tom and Dick Van Arsdale picture as teammates with Phoenix, George McGinnis warm-ups and a huge picture of big George with the Pacers. Be sure to see the Hall of Fame pictures and see how many IU players are a part of the Hall of Fame.

Hall of Fame stained glass of Branch McCracken and other IU notables

Get to See Don Schlundt Play in Person

- **WHERE:** It would have been the new fieldhouse (now called Wildermuth Intramural Center)

- **COST: ?** (Whatever tickets sold for in the early 1950s)

- **DIFFICULTY FACTOR:** Not a tough ticket if you have a time machine

- **BUCKET RANK:** 🗑️🗑️🗑️🗑️🗑️

This one is under the fantasy heading, as it's impossible unless you were lucky enough (and old enough) to have seen Don Schlundt play for the Hoosiers more than 50 years ago. But future generations of Indiana basketball fans have marveled at the things that Schlundt was able to accomplish in his four seasons at IU.

When Schlundt arrived at Indiana, the school record for scoring was 700 points. It was the early 1950s, and Indiana had one national championship to its name, the 1940 Hoosiers coached by Branch McCracken. The legendary McCracken was still the IU coach and was about to assemble another special IU basketball team led by Schlundt, a 6'7" center from South Bend.

Schlundt didn't just break the school scoring record, he shattered it. One of the reasons was that he played an extra year than he normally could have because of the Korean War exemption. Because of the war, players were allowed for one season to play varsity basketball right away because of a shortage of men back home.

So Schlundt took advantage of that. But as people would quickly find out, Schlundt was a special player in his own right. By the time Schlundt left IU, he had broken the scoring record of 700 points by a factor of three, having scored more than 2,100 points.

There were a couple of other records that Schlundt set that have never been broken. A few of them never will. He attempted 1,076 free throws in his IU career. That's 450 more than Steve Alford, the No. 2 person on the all-time list. And he made better than 70 percent of those shots, so he has 300 more made free throws than anyone in history. He was also the fastest player in IU history to score 1,000 points for his career, accomplishing the feat in 43 games.

Schlundt died young in the early 1970s of stomach cancer, but anyone who saw him play said it was a special sight to behold. If we only had a time machine, it would be fun to go back and watch Schlundt and Bobby "Slick" Leonard lead the 1953 Indiana basketball team to IU's second national championship.

Stay in the Steve Alford All-American Inn

• **WHERE:** 21 East Executive Drive, New Castle, Indiana

• **COST: $$$** ($60–110 per night)

• **DIFFICULTY FACTOR:** Not difficult at all. Just make a reservation at (765) 593-1212.

• **BUCKET RANK:** 🪣🪣🪣

When visiting New Castle and the Basketball Hall of Fame, you need to stop by the Steve Alford Inn. The Inn was opened on October 25, 1997. Located outside are two basketball goals (of course) and a big basketball shoe. As you walk inside, you will see Steve Alford's jerseys from Golden State, Dallas, the USA Olympic Team, and Indiana. At the desk is Steve's Big Ten Most Valuable Player trophy.

There is a basketball goal with the logos of New Castle, IU, and the Olympics, as well as a big cut-out of Steve from his Indiana days, and so much more from Steve's basketball career. Stay, sleep, and dream hoops.

Steve Alford All-American Inn

Visit Hoosier Gym from the Movie Hoosiers

- **WHERE:** 355 North Washington, Knightstown, Indiana

- **COST:** Free

- **DIFFICULTY FACTOR:** Not difficult at all. Admission is free, and it's open daily from 9:00 AM to 5:00 PM. To schedule group tours, call (800) 668-1895. The facility is also available to rent out.

- **BUCKET RANK:** 🪣🪣🪣

This is probably a stretch, linking the movie *Hoosiers* to Indiana University basketball, but it's clearly an iconic movie that means something to Indiana basketball fans everywhere. The movie simply embodies the tradition of growing up in the state and the excitement that came with a single-class basketball champion.

And Hoosier Gym has become one of those places that you want to visit. Step inside, and you're immediately taken back to the 1950s and a golden age of Indiana basketball. As coach Norman Dale, played by Gene Hackman in the movie, proclaims "This is Indiana basketball."

Run on the Assembly Hall Court with the Flags at the Under-Eight-Minute Timeout

- **WHERE:** 1001 East 17th Street, Bloomington, Indiana

- **COST: $$** (Attendance at the IU game and a lot of luck)

- **DIFFICULTY FACTOR:** Being at the right place at the right time

- **BUCKET RANK:** 🪣🪣🪣🪣

Certainly this would be a lot easier if you were dressed as the gorilla in basketball shorts, or as Gumby, or some other fictional character, but the reality is that every game the IU administration is doing its best to find uniquely interesting people to participate in one of IU's treasured traditions.

If you're lucky enough to be chosen, make sure someone gets lots of pictures. Very few people get the chance to run on the court live with the flags at the under-eight-minute timeout of the first half. If you're lucky enough to be selected, make sure you can do it. It's a once-in-a-lifetime event.

Have Lunch with Angelo Pizzo

- **WHERE:** Somewhere in Bloomington

- **COST:** $$ (Depending on how much lunch costs)

- **DIFFICULTY FACTOR:** Angelo is a really good guy and he lives locally. This one may not be as difficult as you would think—you just need to figure out how to get hold of him.

- **BUCKET RANK:** 🪣🪣🪣🪣

Angelo Pizzo wrote the movie *Hoosiers* and lives locally. Our guess is, if you caught him in town and offered to buy him lunch, he'd be happy to talk about his movies. The one that is closest to the heart of Indiana basketball fans is his movie *Hoosiers*, which was directed by David Anspaugh. It tells the story of a small-town Indiana high school basketball team that defies all odds and beats the big-school team to win the state championship. It is based on the 1954 Milan High School team that won the state championship at Hinkle Fieldhouse in Indianapolis.

The movie is about Indiana high school basketball, but it's important to all Hoosiers because it speaks to the reverence and passion that the people of the state have for their basketball teams.

If you could get Angelo to sit down and talk about what inspired the movie, it might make for a most interesting afternoon.

Attend a Game in the Original Assembly Hall

• **WHERE:** An area near where the parking lot now sits, next to the Indiana Memorial Union

• **COST:** Priceless

• **DIFFICULTY FACTOR:** The building no longer exists, so the difficulty factor is high

• **BUCKET RANK:** 🗑️🗑️🗑️🗑️

This one goes under the fantasy heading. The original Assembly Hall was one of those historic buildings in which it would have been an experience to see the Hoosiers play basketball.

The original Assembly Hall had a seating capacity of 600. It cost $12,000 to build in 1895 and began hosting IU basketball games in the 1900–1901 season. It would be home to Indiana basketball until the end of the 1916–17 season, when the Hoosiers first began playing in the Men's Gymnasium.

IU's first game in the building was against Butler on February 28, 1901. The building was demolished in 1938.

About the Authors

Terry Hutchens is beginning his 20th season covering Indiana University football and basketball. For 16 seasons, he covered the Hoosiers for the *Indianapolis Star*. He is now the IU beat writer for CNHI Sports Indiana. CNHI is a newspaper group that owns more than 100 newspapers, including 13 in the state of Indiana. Terry's work is syndicated in those 13 newspapers every day.

Five times, Terry has been honored as Indiana's Sportswriter of the Year by the National Sportscasters and Sportswriters Association.

This is Terry's 11th book, including 10 on Indiana University topics. His other IU books include *Following the General* (2017), *Hoo-Hoo-Hoo Hoosiers* (2016), *So You Think You Know Indiana University Football* (2016), *So You Think You Know Indiana University Basketball* (2015), *Missing Banners* (2015), *Hoosiers Through and Through* (2014), *Rising from the Ashes* (2012), *Never Ever Quit* (2009), and *Hep Remembered* (2007). Terry has also done two revisions of the 2003 *Indiana University Basketball Encyclopedia* written by Jason Hiner. His non-IU book was titled *Let 'Er Rip*, a book about the Indianapolis Colts, which was published in 1995.

Terry and wife Susan have been married 31 years and live in Indianapolis. Their oldest son, Bryan, works at Eli Lilly and Company in Indianapolis as a financial analyst. Kevin, who graduated from Belmont University, lives in Nashville, Tennessee, where he is an accomplished keyboard player who recently came off an international tour.

Bill Murphy is a retired U.S. history teacher of 35 years who also coached basketball from grade 5 to high school for over 30 years in the Greenfield school system. He now does various speaking engagements throughout the state.

This is Bill's third book. His other books include *The Cardiac Kids: The Season To Remember* (2007) and *Branch*, the story of legendary IU coach Branch McCracken (2013).

Bill and his wife Wanda have been married for 44 years and live in Greenfield, Indiana. Their son Ryan, who had his own Bucket List moment hitting a three-point shot at the buzzer to win a sectional championship for Indian Creek High School in Trafalgar, Indiana, now lives in Huntington Beach, California, as a clothing designer. Their daughter Kate, an IU grad, lives with her husband Jeff in Orlando, Florida, where she works for Give Kids the World and is a new mom to Bill's first grandson, William Wyatt Mazelin.